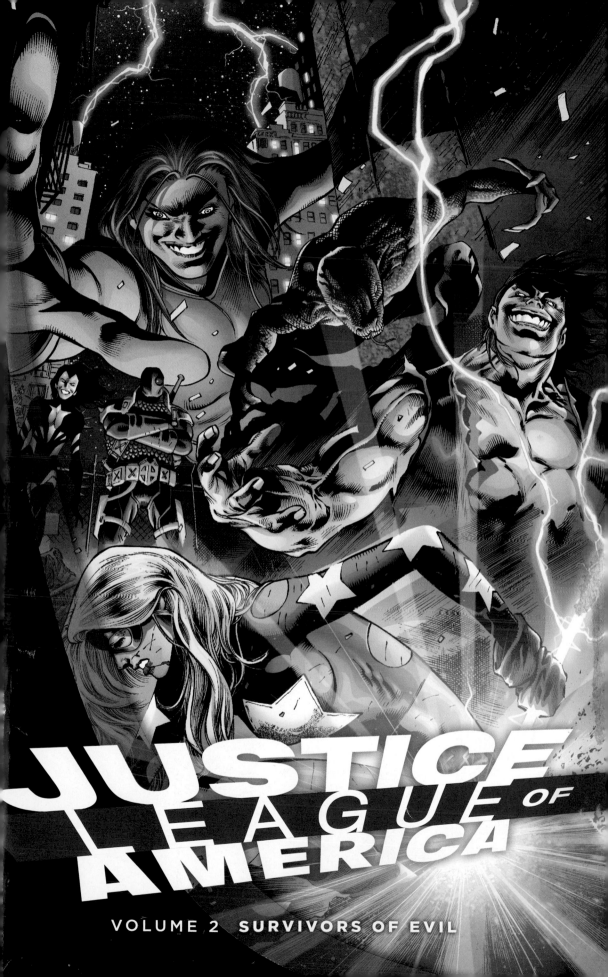

JUSTICE LEAGUE OF AMERICA

VOLUME 2 SURVIVORS OF EVIL

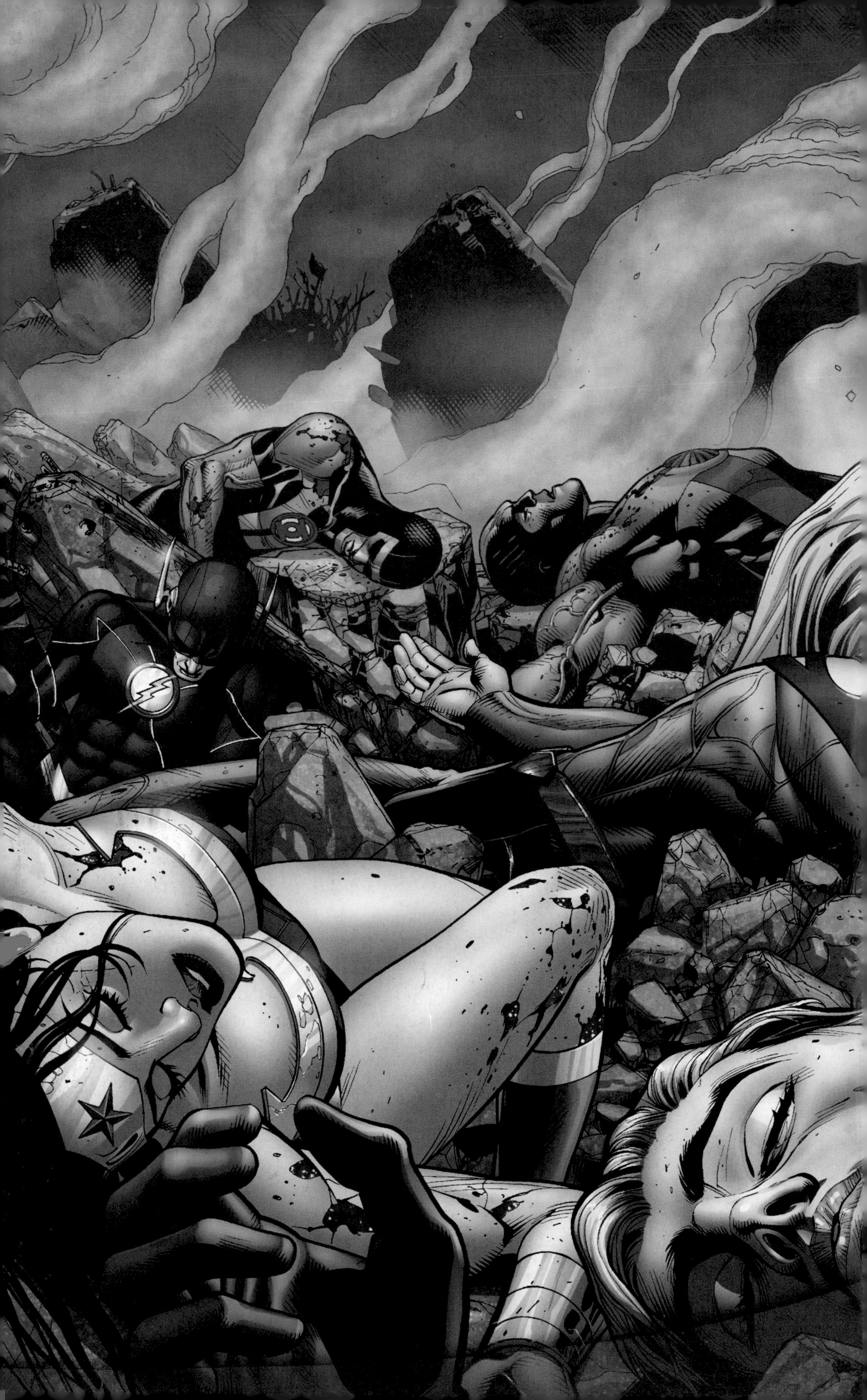

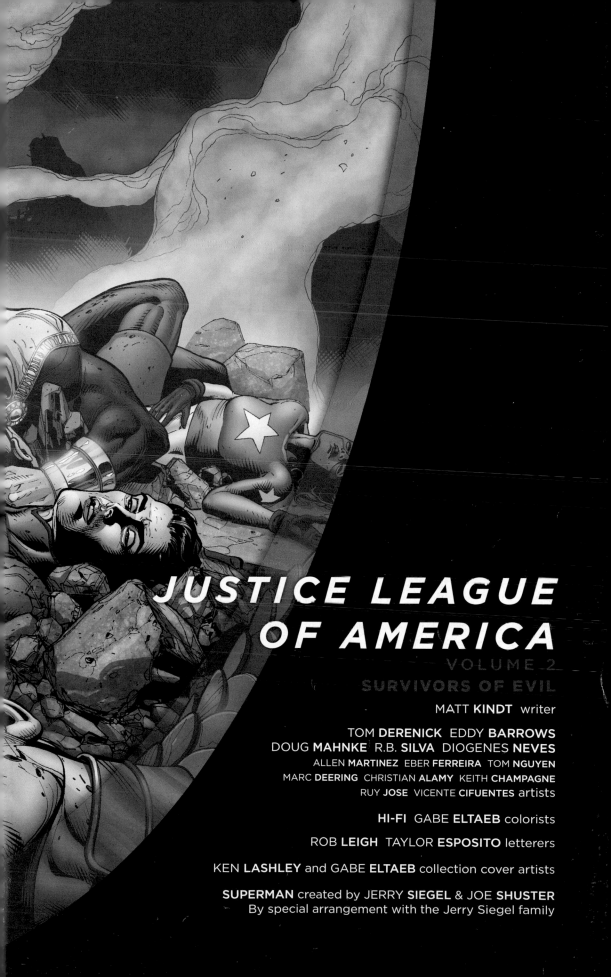

JUSTICE LEAGUE OF AMERICA
VOLUME 2
SURVIVORS OF EVIL

MATT **KINDT** writer

TOM **DERENICK**   EDDY **BARROWS**
DOUG **MAHNKE** R.B. **SILVA** DIOGENES **NEVES**
ALLEN **MARTINEZ** EBER **FERREIRA** TOM **NGUYEN**
MARC **DEERING** CHRISTIAN **ALAMY** KEITH **CHAMPAGNE**
RUY **JOSE** VICENTE **CIFUENTES** artists

HI-FI GABE **ELTAEB** colorists

ROB **LEIGH** TAYLOR **ESPOSITO** letterers

KEN **LASHLEY** and GABE **ELTAEB** collection cover artists

SUPERMAN created by JERRY **SIEGEL** & JOE **SHUSTER**
By special arrangement with the Jerry Siegel family

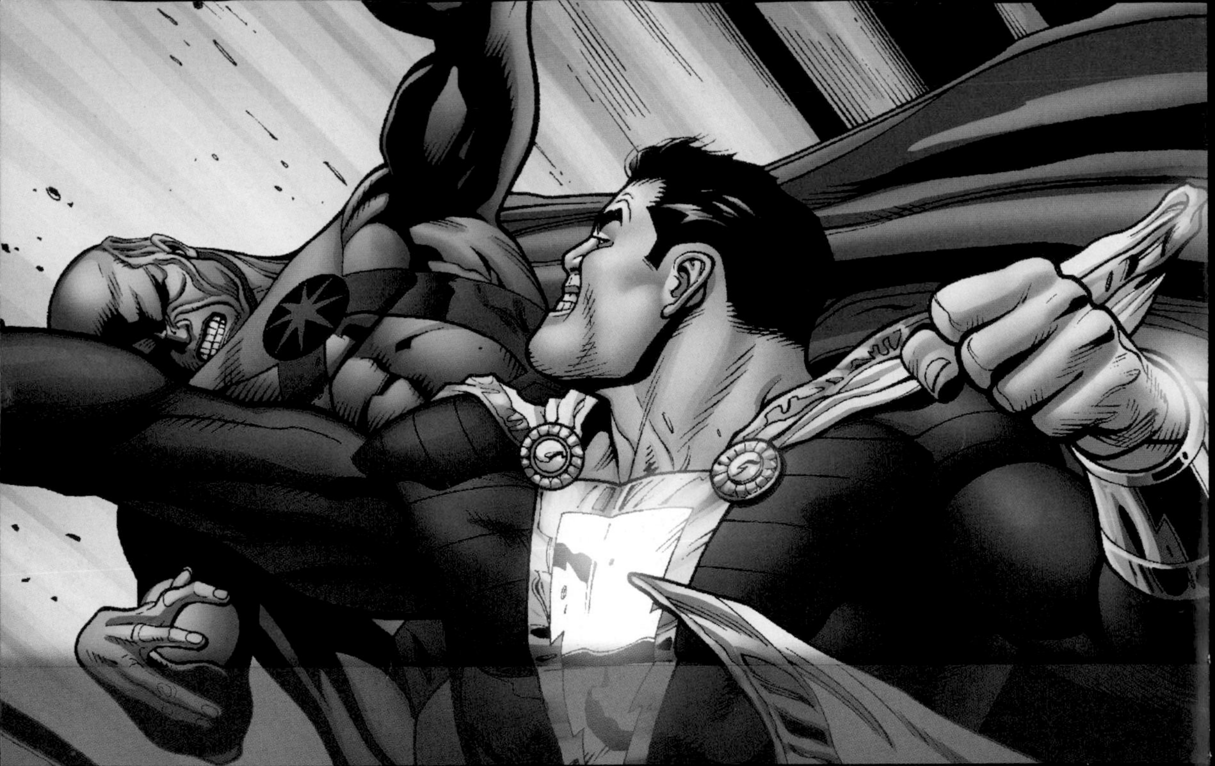

EDDIE BERGANZA Editor – Original Series RICKEY PURDIN Associate Editor – Original Series
ROBIN WILDMAN Editor ROBBIN BROSTERMAN Design Director – Books ROBBIE BIEDERMAN Publication Design

BOB HARRAS Senior VP – Editor-in-Chief, DC Comics

DIANE NELSON President DAN DIDIO and JIM LEE Co-Publishers GEOFF JOHNS Chief Creative Officer
AMIT DESAI Senior VP – Marketing and Franchise Management
AMY GENKINS Senior VP – Business and Legal Affairs NAIRI GARDINER Senior VP – Finance
JEFF BOISON VP – Publishing Planning MARK CHIARELLO VP – Art Direction and Design
JOHN CUNNINGHAM VP – Marketing TERRI CUNNINGHAM VP – Editorial Administration
LARRY GANEM VP – Talent Relations and Services ALISON GILL Senior VP – Manufacturing and Operations
HANK KANALZ Senior VP – Vertigo and Integrated Publishing JAY KOGAN VP – Business and Legal Affairs, Publishing
JACK MAHAN VP – Business Affairs, Talent NICK NAPOLITANO VP – Manufacturing Administration SUE POHJA VP – Book Sales
FRED RUIZ VP – Manufacturing Operations COURTNEY SIMMONS Senior VP – Publicity BOB WAYNE Senior VP – Sales

JUSTICE LEAGUE OF AMERICA VOLUME 2: SURVIVORS OF EVIL

DC Comics, 1700 Broadway, New York, NY 10019
A Warner Bros. Entertainment Company.
Printed by RR Donnelley, Salem, VA, USA. 8/8/14. First Printing.
HC ISBN: 978-1-4012-4726-3
SC ISBN: 978-1-4012-5047-8

Library of Congress Cataloging-in-Publication Data

Kindt, Matt, author.
Justice League of America. Volume 2, Survivors of Evil / Matt Kindt, Doug Mahnke, Christian Alamy.
pages cm
ISBN 978-1-4012-4726-3 (hardback)
1. Graphic novels. I. Mahnke, Doug, illustrator. II. Alamy, Christian, illustrator. III. Title. IV. Title: Survivors of Evil.
PN6728.J87K63 2014
741.5'973—dc23

2014011707

SUSTAINABLE FORESTRY INITIATIVE
Certified Chain of Custody
20% Certified Forest Content, 80% Certified Sourcing
www.sfiprogram.org
SFI-01042
APPLIES TO TEXT STOCK ONLY

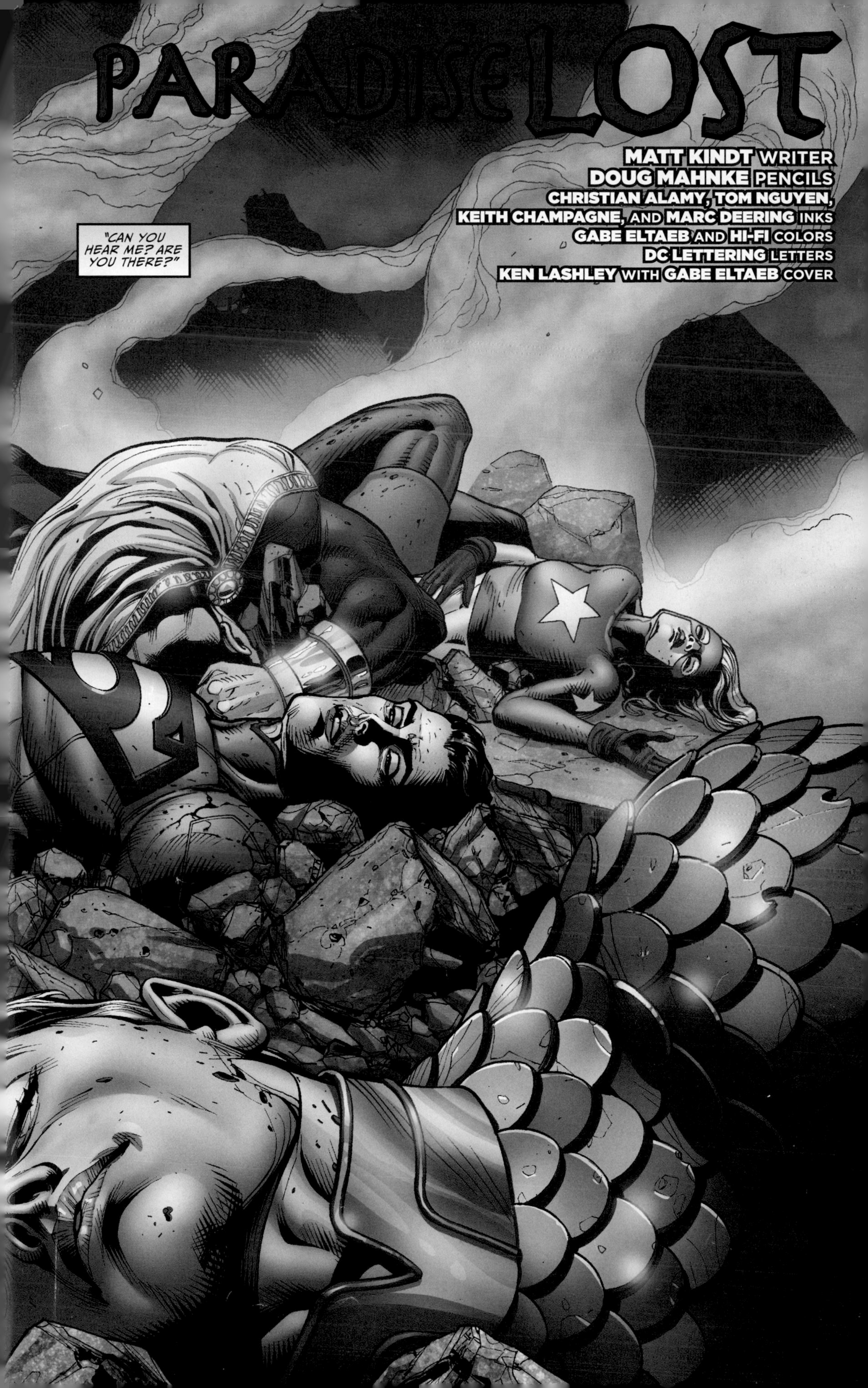
PARADISE LOST
MATT KINDT WRITER
DOUG MAHNKE PENCILS
CHRISTIAN ALAMY, TOM NGUYEN,
KEITH CHAMPAGNE, AND MARC DEERING INKS
GABE ELTAEB AND HI-FI COLORS
DC LETTERING LETTERS
KEN LASHLEY WITH GABE ELTAEB COVER
"CAN YOU HEAR ME? ARE YOU THERE?"

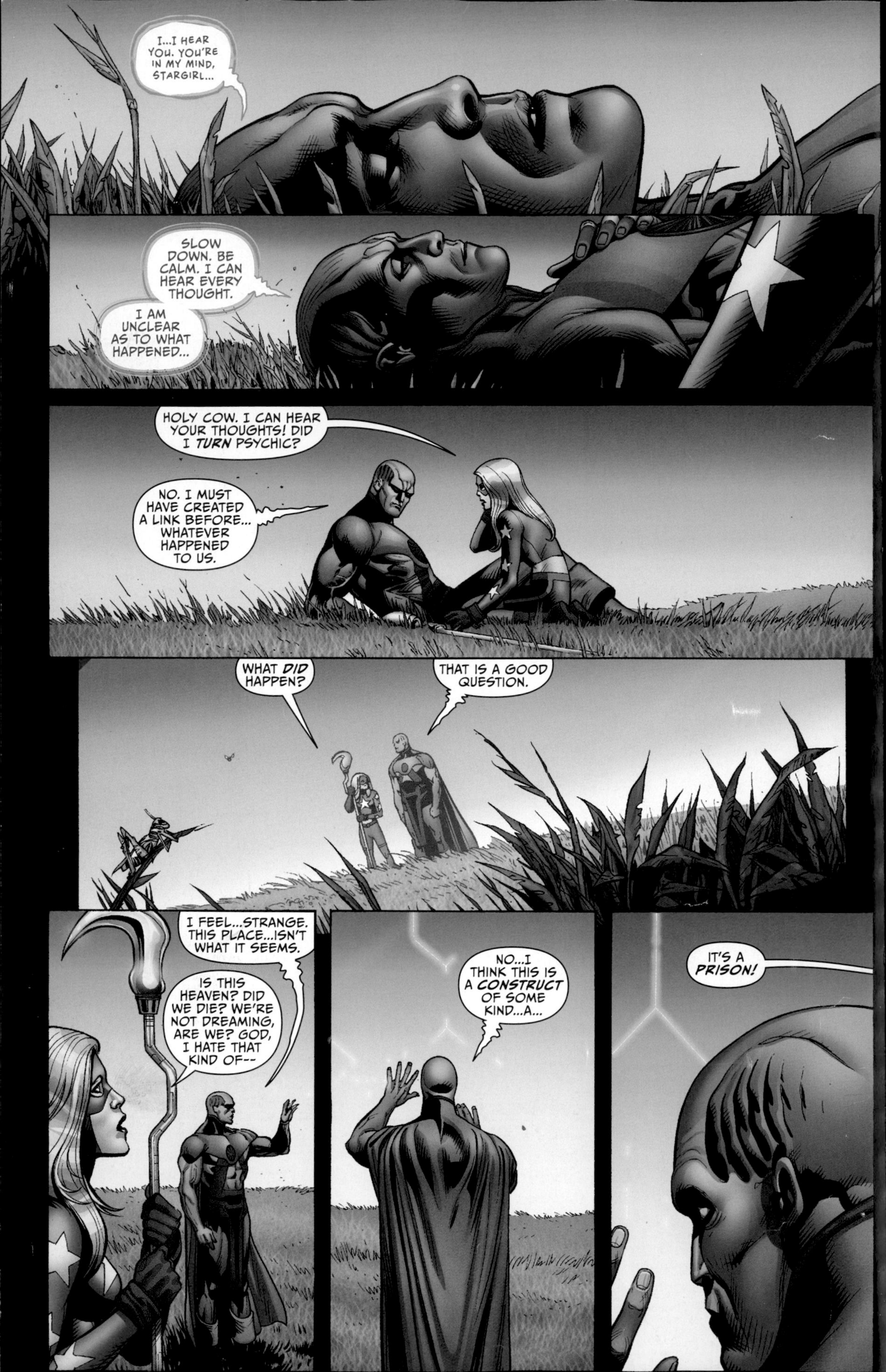
I...I HEAR YOU. YOU'RE IN MY MIND, STARGIRL...
SLOW DOWN. BE CALM. I CAN HEAR EVERY THOUGHT.
I AM UNCLEAR AS TO WHAT HAPPENED...
HOLY COW. I CAN HEAR YOUR THOUGHTS! DID I TURN PSYCHIC?
NO. I MUST HAVE CREATED A LINK BEFORE... WHATEVER HAPPENED TO US.
WHAT DID HAPPEN?
THAT IS A GOOD QUESTION.
I FEEL...STRANGE. THIS PLACE...ISN'T WHAT IT SEEMS.
IS THIS HEAVEN? DID WE DIE? WE'RE NOT DREAMING, ARE WE? GOD, I HATE THAT KIND OF--
NO...I THINK THIS IS A CONSTRUCT OF SOME KIND...A...
IT'S A PRISON!

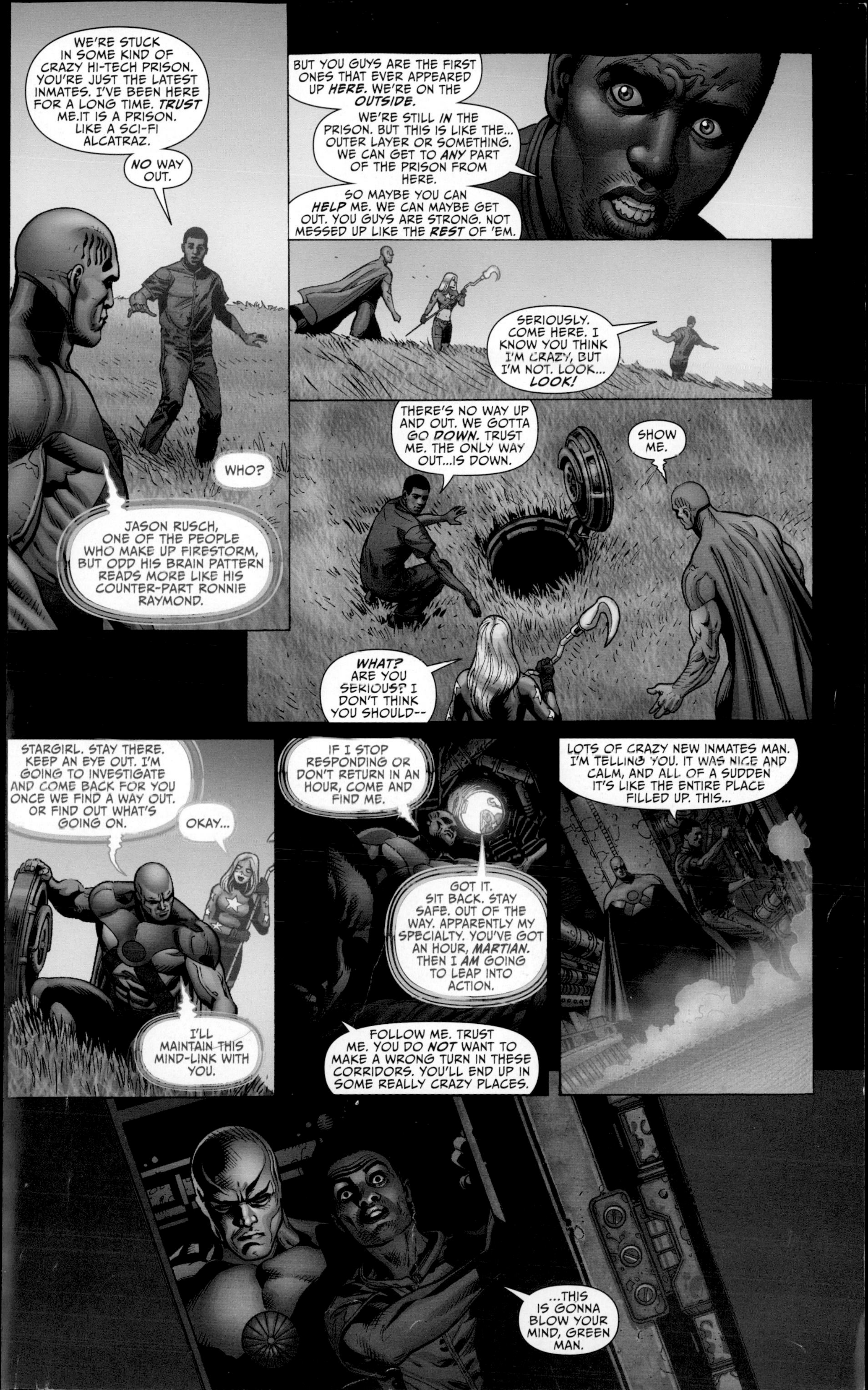
WE'RE STUCK IN SOME KIND OF CRAZY HI-TECH PRISON. YOU'RE JUST THE LATEST INMATES. I'VE BEEN HERE FOR A LONG TIME. TRUST ME.IT IS A PRISON. LIKE A SCI-FI ALCATRAZ.
NO WAY OUT.
WHO?
JASON RUSCH, ONE OF THE PEOPLE WHO MAKE UP FIRESTORM, BUT ODD HIS BRAIN PATTERN READS MORE LIKE HIS COUNTER-PART RONNIE RAYMOND.
BUT YOU GUYS ARE THE FIRST ONES THAT EVER APPEARED UP HERE. WE'RE ON THE OUTSIDE.
WE'RE STILL IN THE PRISON. BUT THIS IS LIKE THE... OUTER LAYER OR SOMETHING. WE CAN GET TO ANY PART OF THE PRISON FROM HERE.
SO MAYBE YOU CAN HELP ME. WE CAN MAYBE GET OUT. YOU GUYS ARE STRONG. NOT MESSED UP LIKE THE REST OF 'EM.
SERIOUSLY. COME HERE. I KNOW YOU THINK I'M CRAZY, BUT I'M NOT. LOOK... LOOK!
THERE'S NO WAY UP AND OUT. WE GOTTA GO DOWN. TRUST ME. THE ONLY WAY OUT...IS DOWN.
SHOW ME.
WHAT? ARE YOU SERIOUS? I DON'T THINK YOU SHOULD--
STARGIRL. STAY THERE. KEEP AN EYE OUT. I'M GOING TO INVESTIGATE AND COME BACK FOR YOU ONCE WE FIND A WAY OUT. OR FIND OUT WHAT'S GOING ON.
OKAY...
I'LL MAINTAIN THIS MIND-LINK WITH YOU.
IF I STOP RESPONDING OR DON'T RETURN IN AN HOUR, COME AND FIND ME.
GOT IT. SIT BACK. STAY SAFE. OUT OF THE WAY. APPARENTLY MY SPECIALTY. YOU'VE GOT AN HOUR, MARTIAN. THEN I AM GOING TO LEAP INTO ACTION.
FOLLOW ME. TRUST ME. YOU DO NOT WANT TO MAKE A WRONG TURN IN THESE CORRIDORS. YOU'LL END UP IN SOME REALLY CRAZY PLACES.
LOTS OF CRAZY NEW INMATES MAN. I'M TELLING YOU. IT WAS NICE AND CALM, AND ALL OF A SUDDEN IT'S LIKE THE ENTIRE PLACE FILLED UP. THIS...
...THIS IS GONNA BLOW YOUR MIND, GREEN MAN.

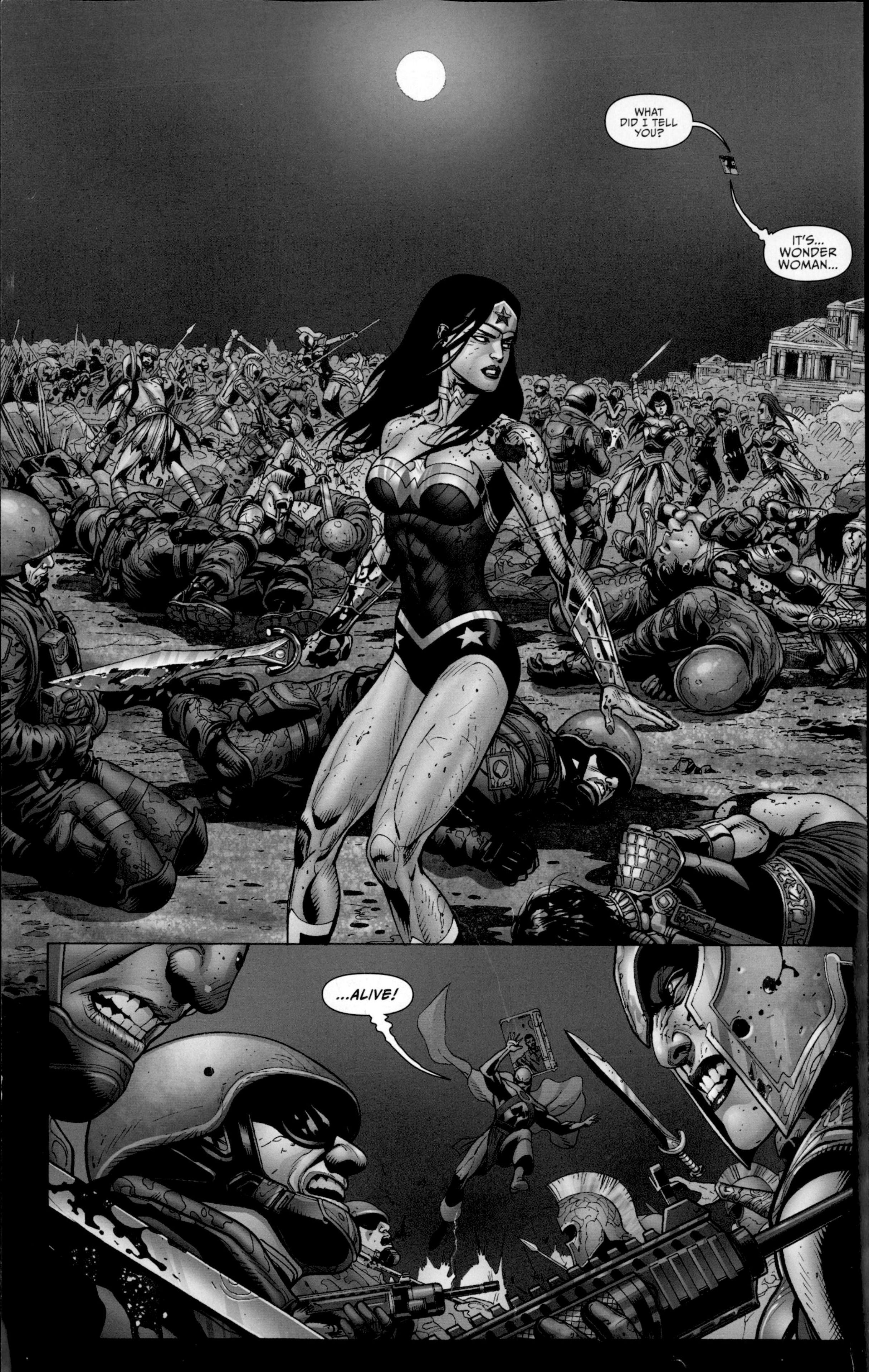
WHAT DID I TELL YOU?
IT'S... WONDER WOMAN...
...ALIVE!

UNGH!

YEAH, BE CAREFUL DOWN THERE! FORGOT TO TELL YOU. THIS PRISON HAS A WAY OF STRIPPING YOU DOWN TO YOUR WEAKEST...

BRAIN PATTERN IS AUTHENTIC. IT IS HER...BUT SHE'S... SOMETHING IS WRONG.

DIANA...

I...I DON'T KNOW WHAT TO DO.

THE AMAZONS HAVE TREVOR LOCKED UP INSIDE... READY TO KILL HIM IF I DON'T FIGHT.

THE MORTALS HAVE SUPERMAN TRAPPED SOMEWHERE...READY TO KILL HIM... LEAVING...

I AM A WARRIOR...BUT MY FEELINGS...I'M PARALYZED.

I AM DESTINED TO DIE A WARRIOR'S DEATH, NOT THIS FATE...

THIS... SIMPERING, WEAK...

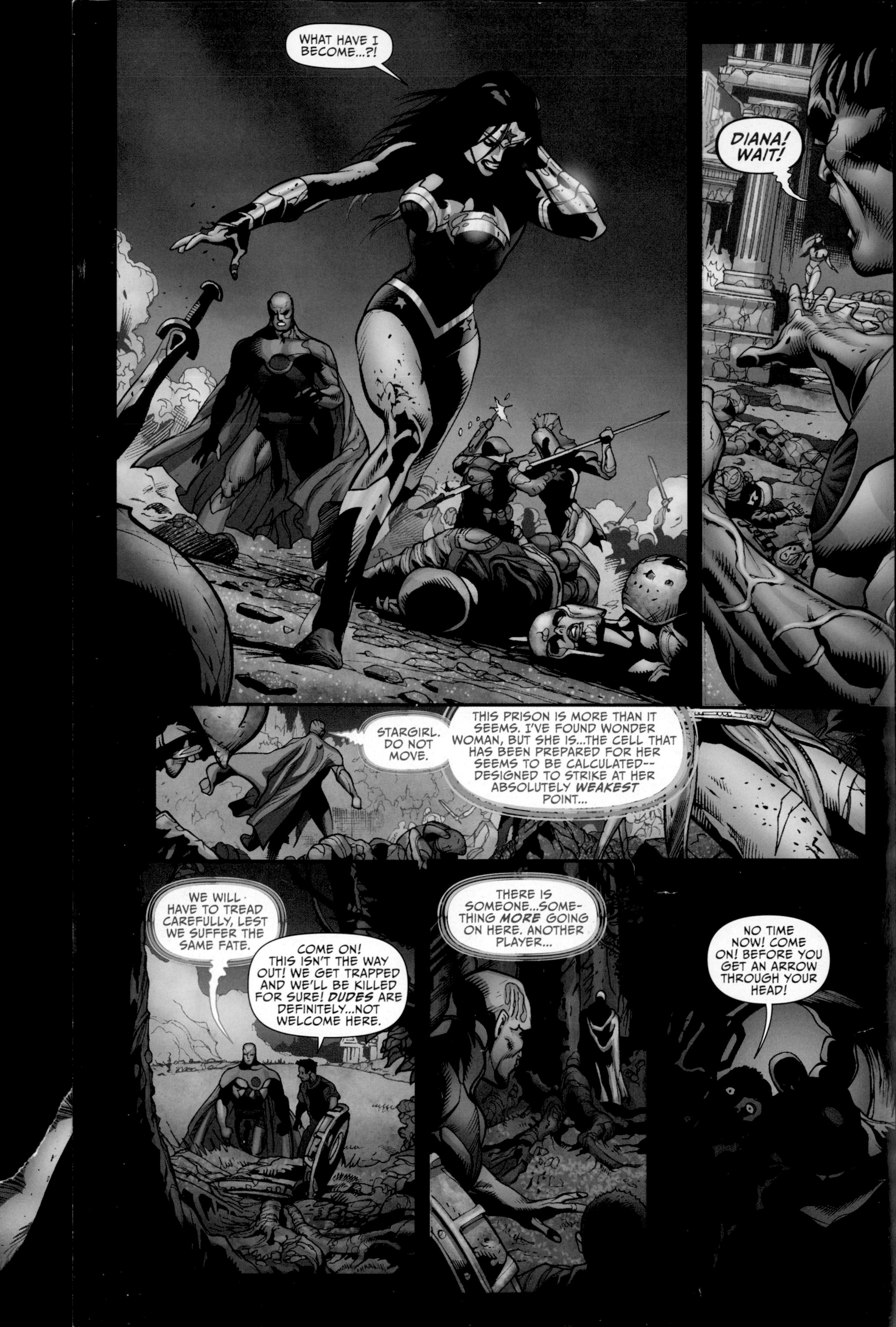

WHAT HAVE I BECOME...?!
DIANA! WAIT!
STARGIRL. DO NOT MOVE.
THIS PRISON IS MORE THAN IT SEEMS. I'VE FOUND WONDER WOMAN, BUT SHE IS...THE CELL THAT HAS BEEN PREPARED FOR HER SEEMS TO BE CALCULATED-- DESIGNED TO STRIKE AT HER ABSOLUTELY WEAKEST POINT...
WE WILL HAVE TO TREAD CAREFULLY, LEST WE SUFFER THE SAME FATE.
COME ON! THIS ISN'T THE WAY OUT! WE GET TRAPPED AND WE'LL BE KILLED FOR SURE! DUDES ARE DEFINITELY...NOT WELCOME HERE.
THERE IS SOMEONE...SOME- THING MORE GOING ON HERE. ANOTHER PLAYER...
NO TIME NOW! COME ON! BEFORE YOU GET AN ARROW THROUGH YOUR HEAD!

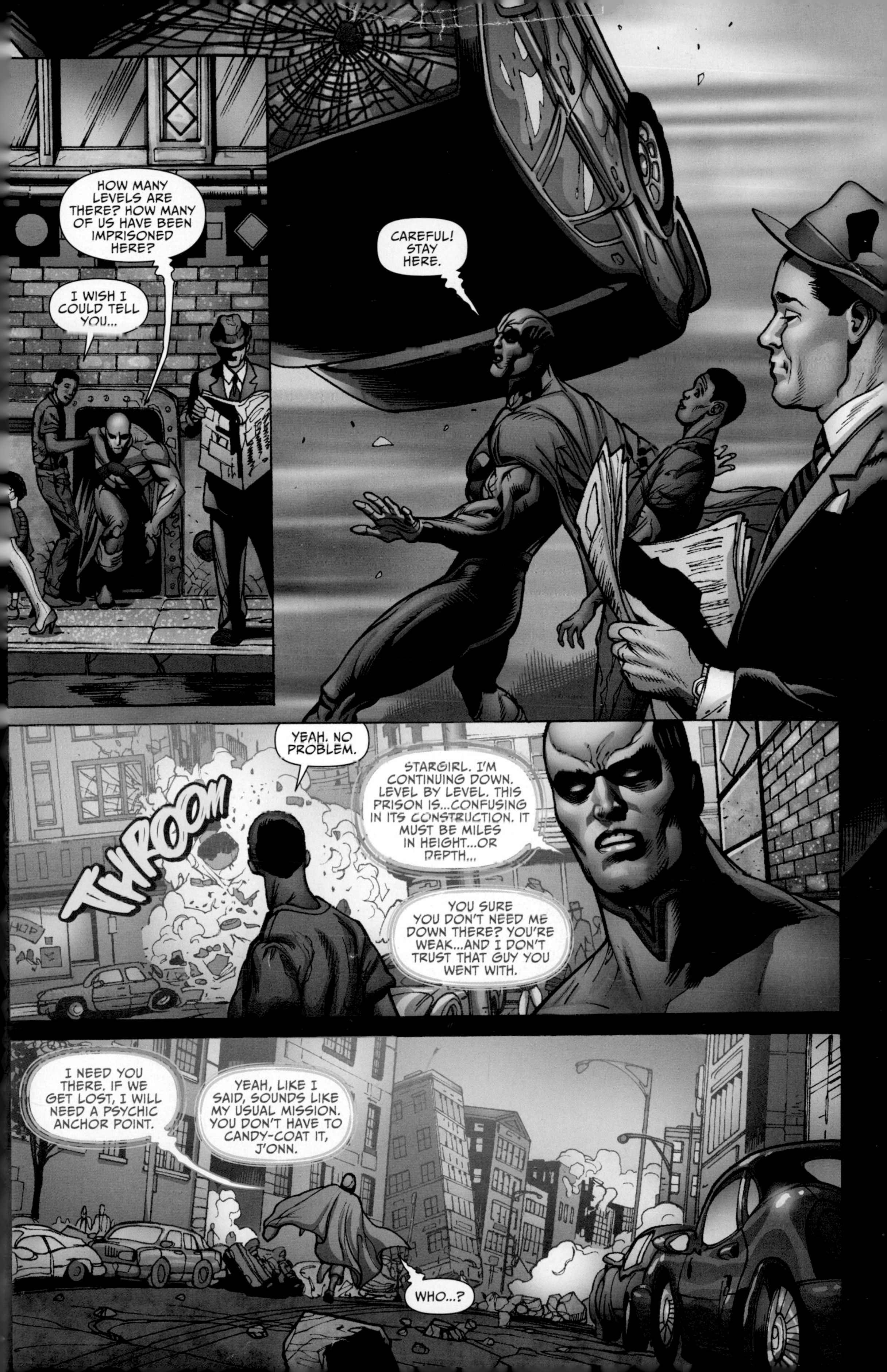
HOW MANY LEVELS ARE THERE? HOW MANY OF US HAVE BEEN IMPRISONED HERE?
I WISH I COULD TELL YOU...
CAREFUL! STAY HERE.
YEAH. NO PROBLEM.
STARGIRL. I'M CONTINUING DOWN. LEVEL BY LEVEL. THIS PRISON IS...CONFUSING IN ITS CONSTRUCTION. IT MUST BE MILES IN HEIGHT...OR DEPTH...
THROOM
YOU SURE YOU DON'T NEED ME DOWN THERE? YOU'RE WEAK...AND I DON'T TRUST THAT GUY YOU WENT WITH.
I NEED YOU THERE. IF WE GET LOST, I WILL NEED A PSYCHIC ANCHOR POINT.
YEAH, LIKE I SAID, SOUNDS LIKE MY USUAL MISSION. YOU DON'T HAVE TO CANDY-COAT IT, J'ONN.
WHO...?

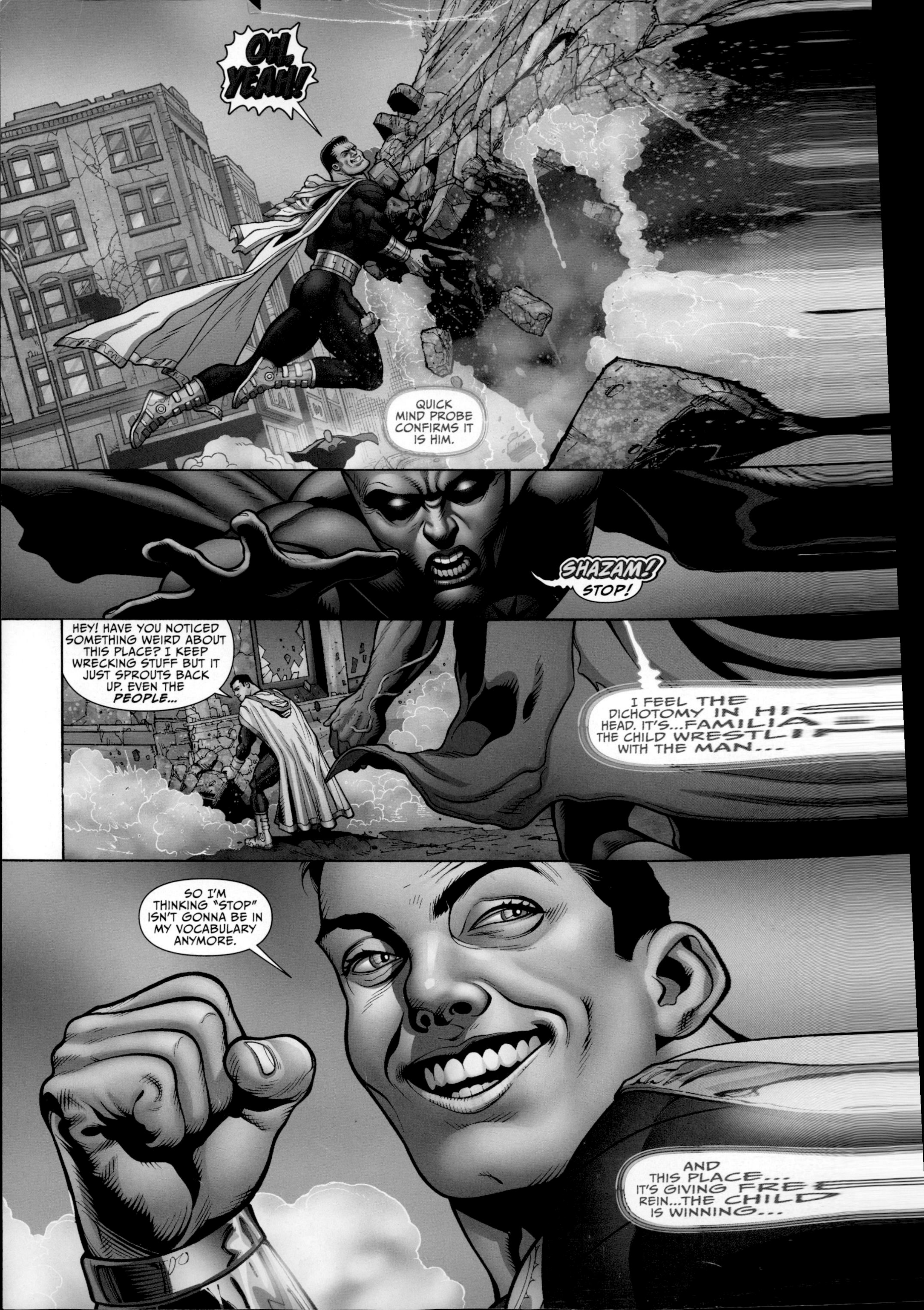

OH, YEAH!
QUICK MIND PROBE CONFIRMS IT IS HIM.
SHAZAM! STOP!
HEY! HAVE YOU NOTICED SOMETHING WEIRD ABOUT THIS PLACE? I KEEP WRECKING STUFF BUT IT JUST SPROUTS BACK UP. EVEN THE PEOPLE...
I FEEL THE DICHOTOMY IN HIS HEAD. IT'S...FAMILIAR. THE CHILD WRESTLING WITH THE MAN...
SO I'M THINKING "STOP" ISN'T GONNA BE IN MY VOCABULARY ANYMORE.
AND THIS PLACE... IT'S GIVING FREE REIN...THE CHILD IS WINNING...

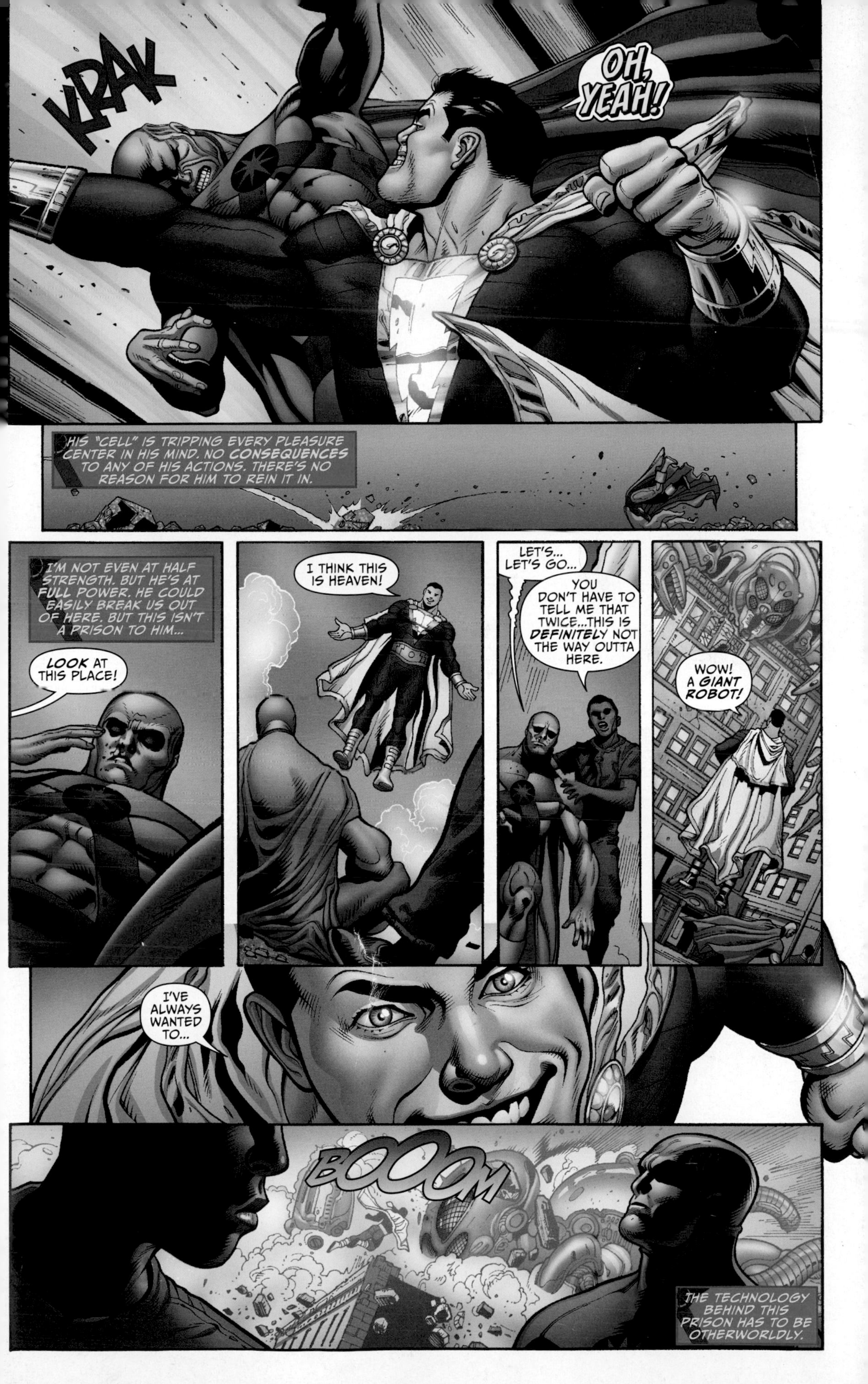
KRAK
OH, YEAH!
HIS "CELL" IS TRIPPING EVERY PLEASURE CENTER IN HIS MIND. NO CONSEQUENCES TO ANY OF HIS ACTIONS. THERE'S NO REASON FOR HIM TO REIN IT IN.
I'M NOT EVEN AT HALF STRENGTH. BUT HE'S AT FULL POWER. HE COULD EASILY BREAK US OUT OF HERE. BUT THIS ISN'T A PRISON TO HIM...
LOOK AT THIS PLACE!
I THINK THIS IS HEAVEN!
LET'S... LET'S GO...
YOU DON'T HAVE TO TELL ME THAT TWICE...THIS IS DEFINITELY NOT THE WAY OUTTA HERE.
WOW! A GIANT ROBOT!
I'VE ALWAYS WANTED TO...
BOOOOM
THE TECHNOLOGY BEHIND THIS PRISON HAS TO BE OTHERWORLDLY.

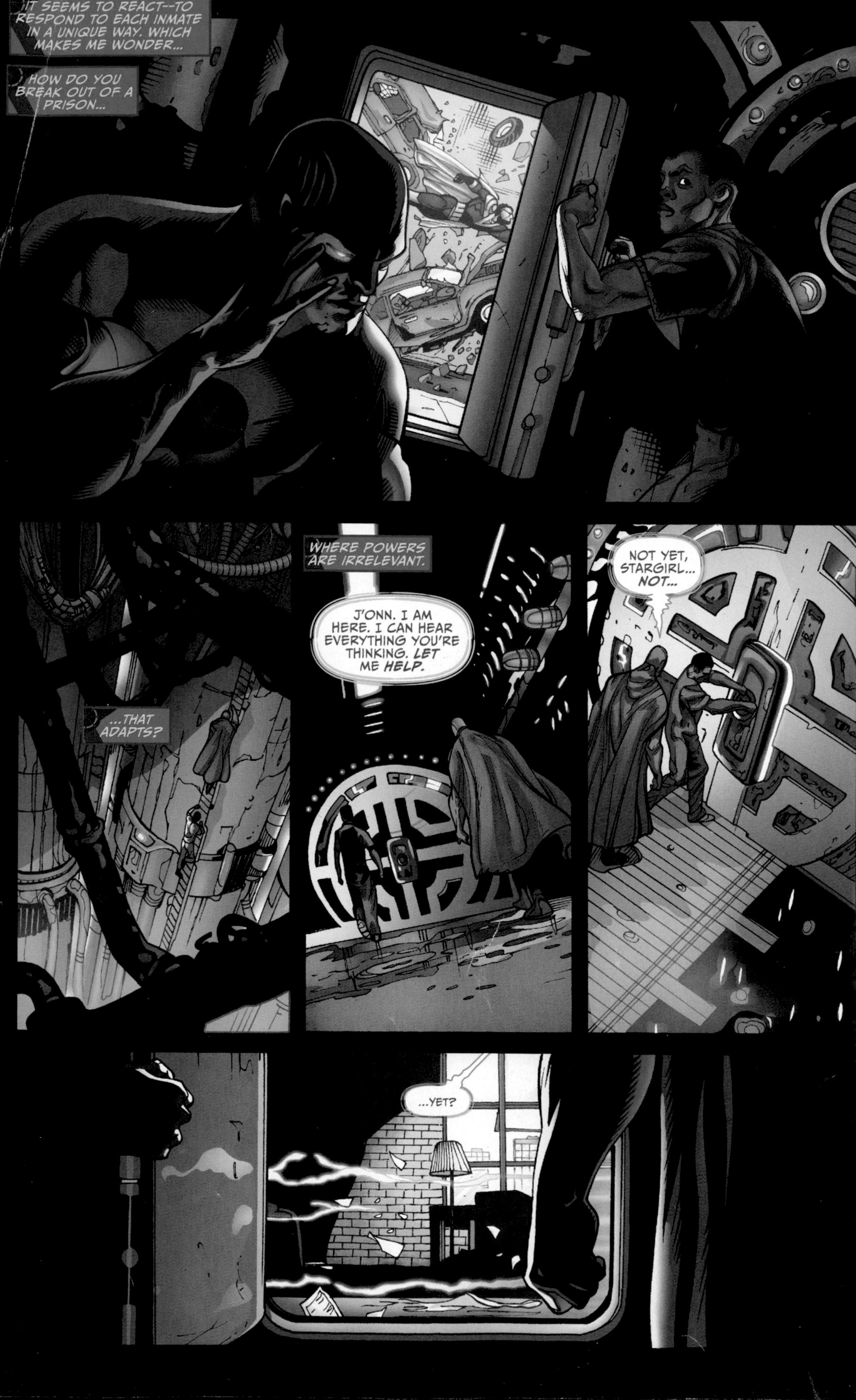
IT SEEMS TO REACT--TO RESPOND TO EACH INMATE IN A UNIQUE WAY. WHICH MAKES ME WONDER...
HOW DO YOU BREAK OUT OF A PRISON...
...THAT ADAPTS?
WHERE POWERS ARE IRRELEVANT.
J'ONN. I AM HERE. I CAN HEAR EVERYTHING YOU'RE THINKING. LET ME HELP.
NOT YET, STARGIRL... NOT...
...YET?

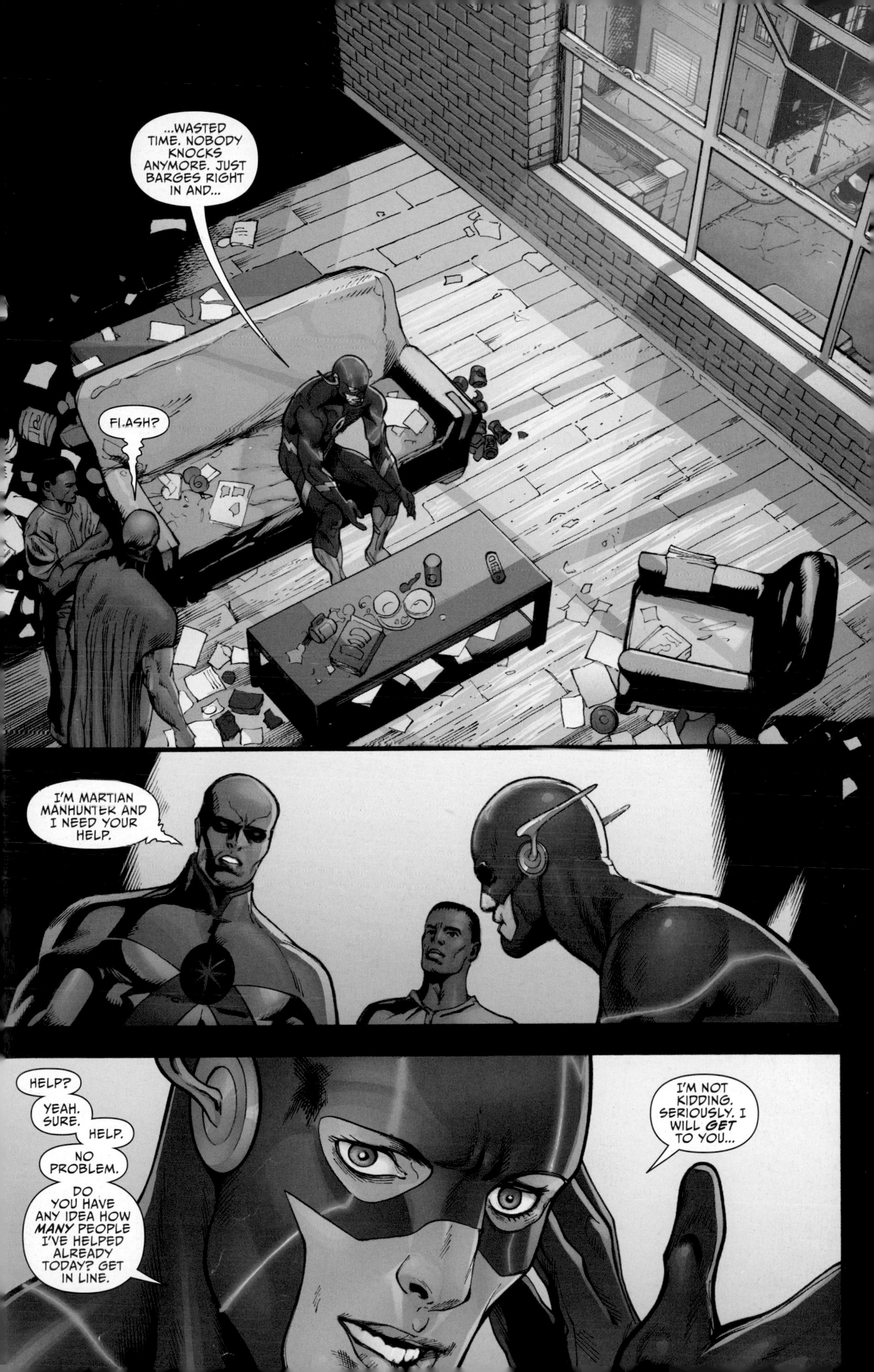
...WASTED TIME. NOBODY KNOCKS ANYMORE. JUST BARGES RIGHT IN AND...
FLASH?
I'M MARTIAN MANHUNTER AND I NEED YOUR HELP.
HELP?
YEAH. SURE.
HELP.
NO PROBLEM.
DO YOU HAVE ANY IDEA HOW *MANY* PEOPLE I'VE HELPED ALREADY TODAY? GET IN LINE.
I'M NOT KIDDING. SERIOUSLY. I WILL *GET* TO YOU...

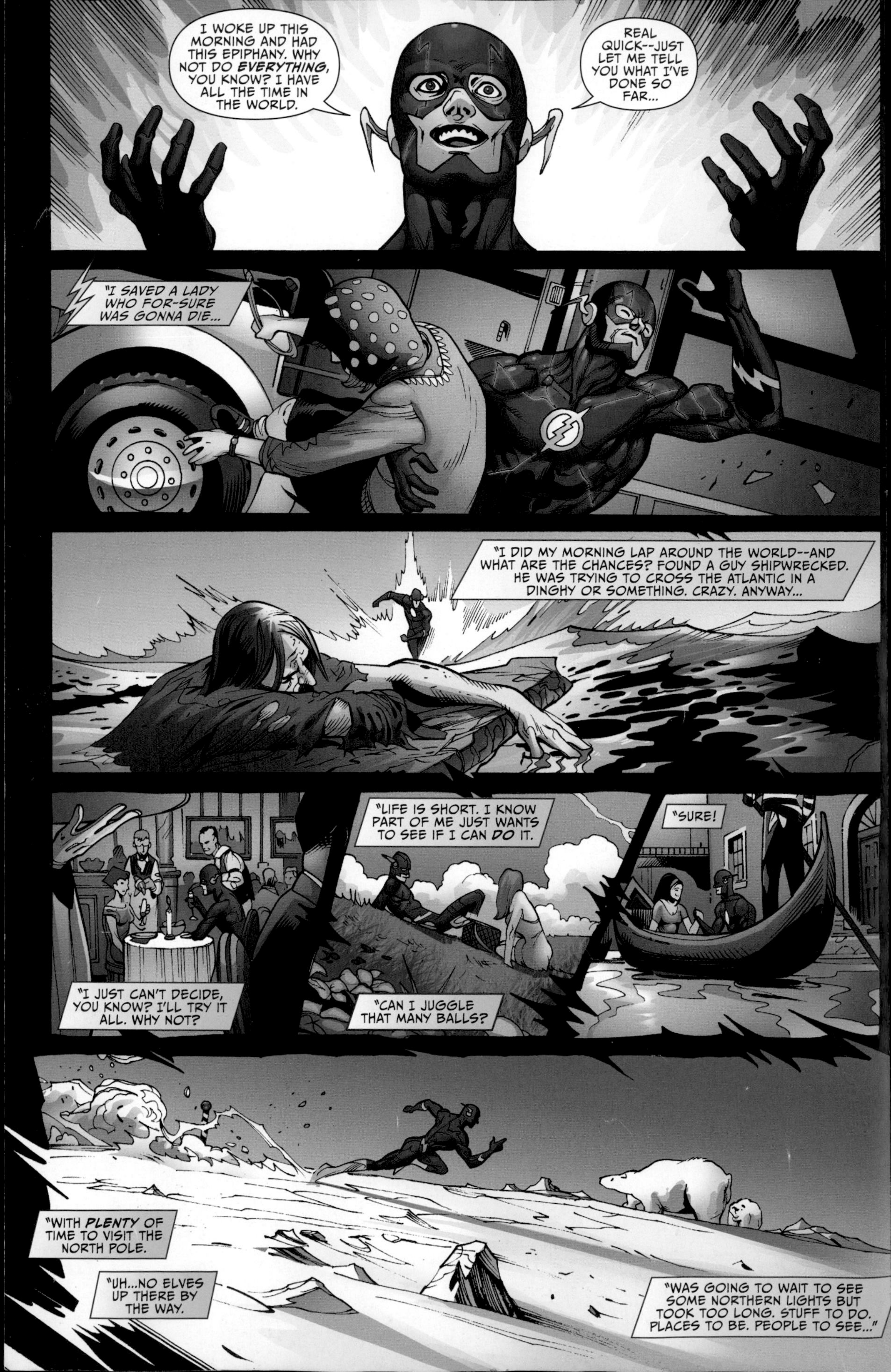
I WOKE UP THIS MORNING AND HAD THIS EPIPHANY. WHY NOT DO EVERYTHING, YOU KNOW? I HAVE ALL THE TIME IN THE WORLD.
REAL QUICK--JUST LET ME TELL YOU WHAT I'VE DONE SO FAR...
"I SAVED A LADY WHO FOR-SURE WAS GONNA DIE...
"I DID MY MORNING LAP AROUND THE WORLD--AND WHAT ARE THE CHANCES? FOUND A GUY SHIPWRECKED. HE WAS TRYING TO CROSS THE ATLANTIC IN A DINGHY OR SOMETHING. CRAZY. ANYWAY...
"I JUST CAN'T DECIDE, YOU KNOW? I'LL TRY IT ALL. WHY NOT?
"LIFE IS SHORT. I KNOW PART OF ME JUST WANTS TO SEE IF I CAN DO IT.
"CAN I JUGGLE THAT MANY BALLS?
"SURE!
"WITH PLENTY OF TIME TO VISIT THE NORTH POLE.
"UH...NO ELVES UP THERE BY THE WAY.
"WAS GOING TO WAIT TO SEE SOME NORTHERN LIGHTS BUT TOOK TOO LONG. STUFF TO DO. PLACES TO BE. PEOPLE TO SEE..."

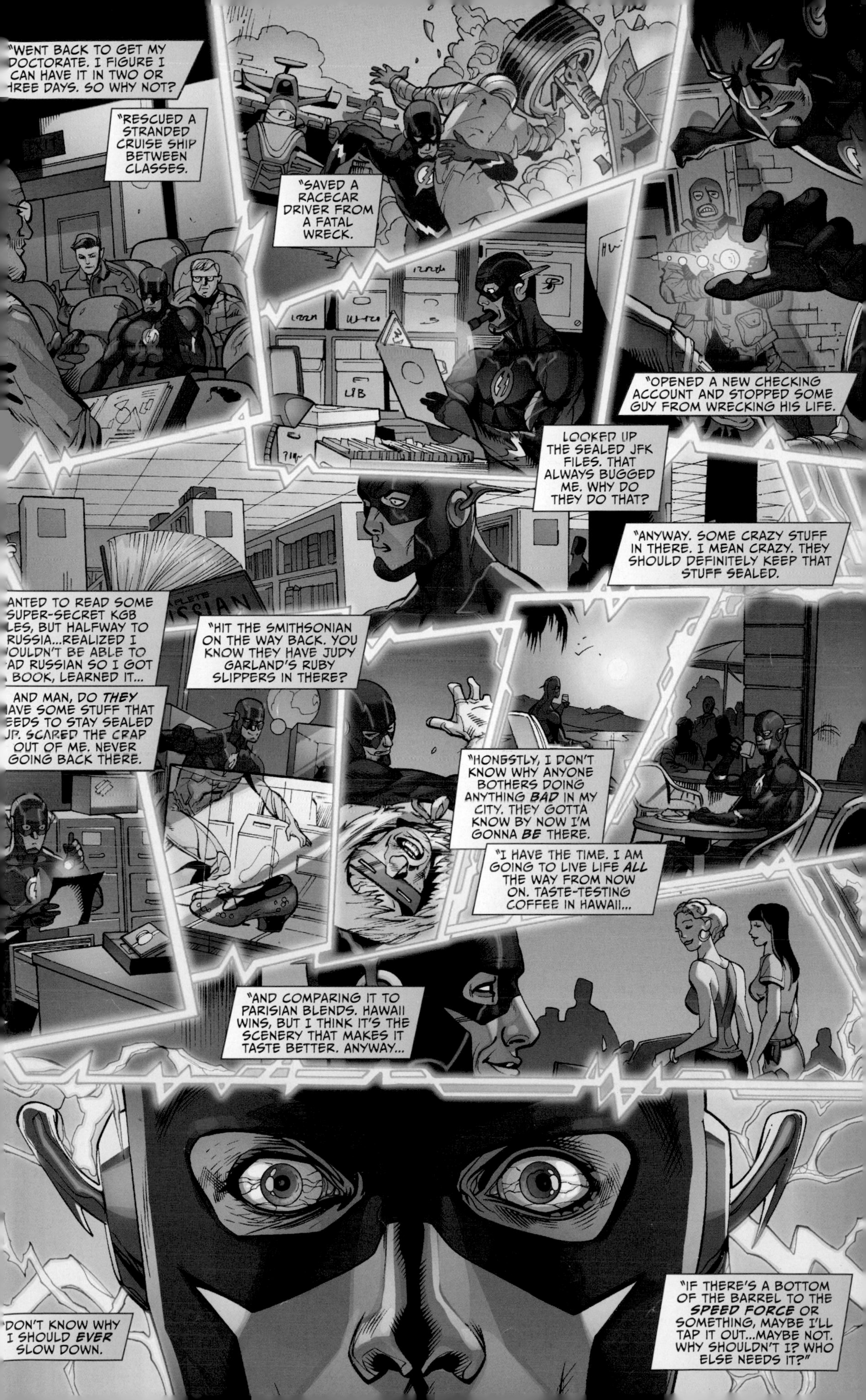
"WENT BACK TO GET MY
DOCTORATE. I FIGURE I
CAN HAVE IT IN TWO OR
HREE DAYS. SO WHY NOT?
"RESCUED A STRANDED CRUISE SHIP BETWEEN CLASSES.
"SAVED A RACECAR DRIVER FROM A FATAL WRECK.
"OPENED A NEW CHECKING ACCOUNT AND STOPPED SOME GUY FROM WRECKING HIS LIFE.
LOOKED UP THE SEALED JFK FILES. THAT ALWAYS BUGGED ME. WHY DO THEY DO THAT?
"ANYWAY. SOME CRAZY STUFF IN THERE. I MEAN CRAZY. THEY SHOULD DEFINITELY KEEP THAT STUFF SEALED.
ANTED TO READ SOME SUPER-SECRET KGB LES, BUT HALFWAY TO RUSSIA...REALIZED I OULDN'T BE ABLE TO AD RUSSIAN SO I GOT BOOK, LEARNED IT...
AND MAN, DO *THEY* AVE SOME STUFF THAT EEDS TO STAY SEALED JP. SCARED THE CRAP OUT OF ME. NEVER GOING BACK THERE.
"HIT THE SMITHSONIAN ON THE WAY BACK. YOU KNOW THEY HAVE JUDY GARLAND'S RUBY SLIPPERS IN THERE?
"HONESTLY, I DON'T KNOW WHY ANYONE BOTHERS DOING ANYTHING *BAD* IN MY CITY. THEY GOTTA KNOW BY NOW I'M GONNA *BE* THERE.
"I HAVE THE TIME. I AM GOING TO LIVE LIFE *ALL* THE WAY FROM NOW ON. TASTE-TESTING COFFEE IN HAWAII...
"AND COMPARING IT TO PARISIAN BLENDS. HAWAII WINS, BUT I THINK IT'S THE SCENERY THAT MAKES IT TASTE BETTER. ANYWAY...
DON'T KNOW WHY I SHOULD *EVER* SLOW DOWN.
"IF THERE'S A BOTTOM OF THE BARREL TO THE *SPEED FORCE* OR SOMETHING, MAYBE I'LL TAP IT OUT...MAYBE NOT. WHY SHOULDN'T I? WHO ELSE NEEDS IT?"

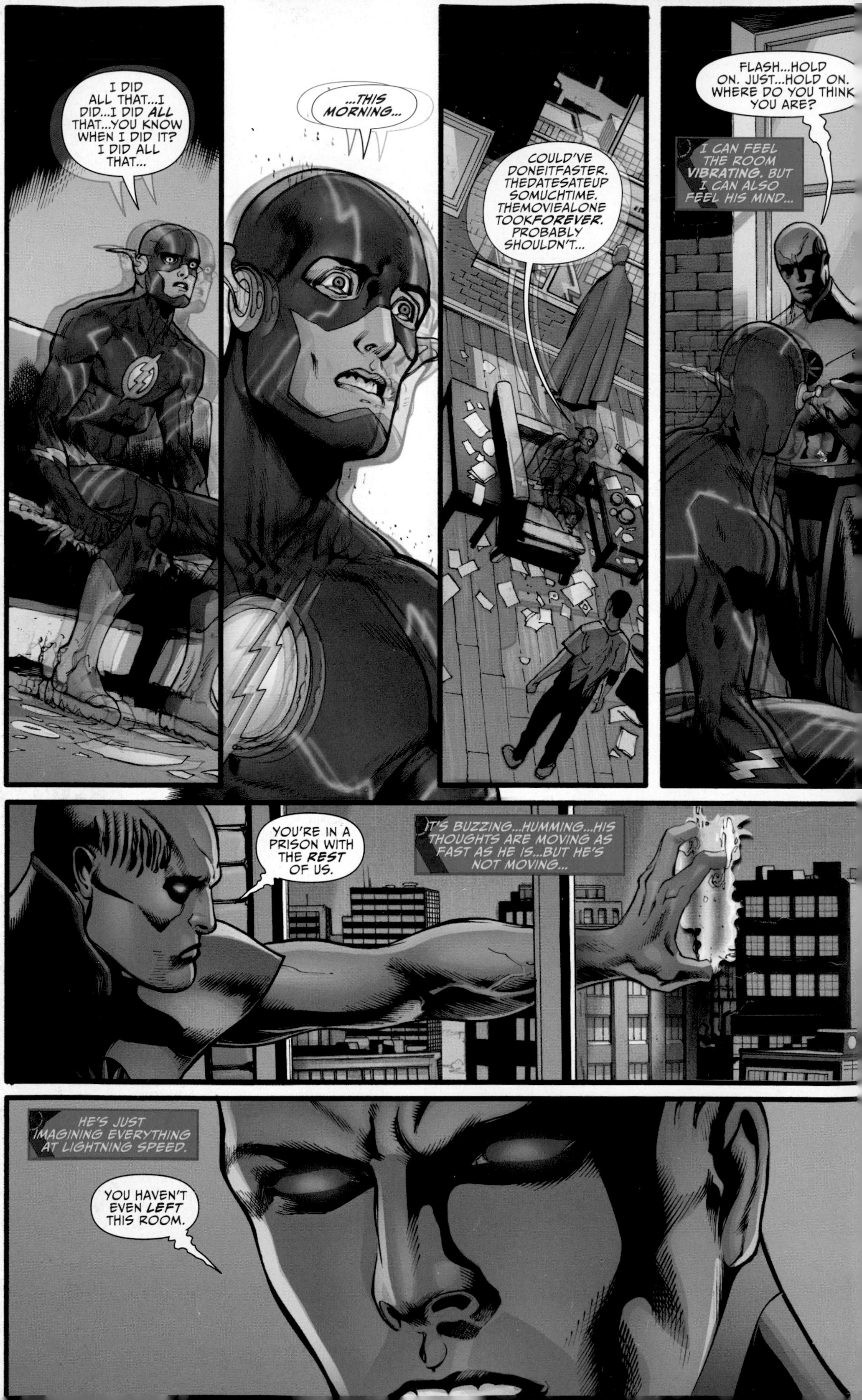
I DID ALL THAT...I DID...I DID ALL THAT...YOU KNOW WHEN I DID IT? I DID ALL THAT...
...THIS MORNING...
COULD'VE DONEITFASTER. THEDATESATEUP SOMUCHTIME. THEMOVIEALONE TOOKFOREVER. PROBABLY SHOULDN'T...
FLASH...HOLD ON. JUST...HOLD ON. WHERE DO YOU THINK YOU ARE?
I CAN FEEL THE ROOM VIBRATING. BUT I CAN ALSO FEEL HIS MIND...
YOU'RE IN A PRISON WITH THE REST OF US.
IT'S BUZZING...HUMMING...HIS THOUGHTS ARE MOVING AS FAST AS HE IS...BUT HE'S NOT MOVING...
HE'S JUST IMAGINING EVERYTHING AT LIGHTNING SPEED.
YOU HAVEN'T EVEN LEFT THIS ROOM.

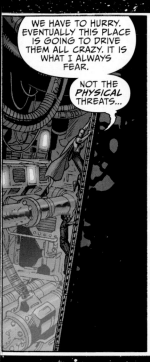

WE HAVE TO HURRY. EVENTUALLY THIS PLACE IS GOING TO DRIVE THEM ALL CRAZY. IT IS WHAT I ALWAYS FEAR.

NOT THE *PHYSICAL* THREATS...

BUT THE *MENTAL* ONES.

THIS WAY, BOSS...I, UH...I THINK I'M GONNA *WAIT* HERE FOR YOU.

I *KNOW* WHO THIS IS.

HIS MIND IS STRONG. ONE OF THE STRONGEST I'VE EVER ENCOUNTERED...

NEVER FELT SUCH A DEEP SENSE OF TRUTH. OF GOOD.

OF JUSTICE...

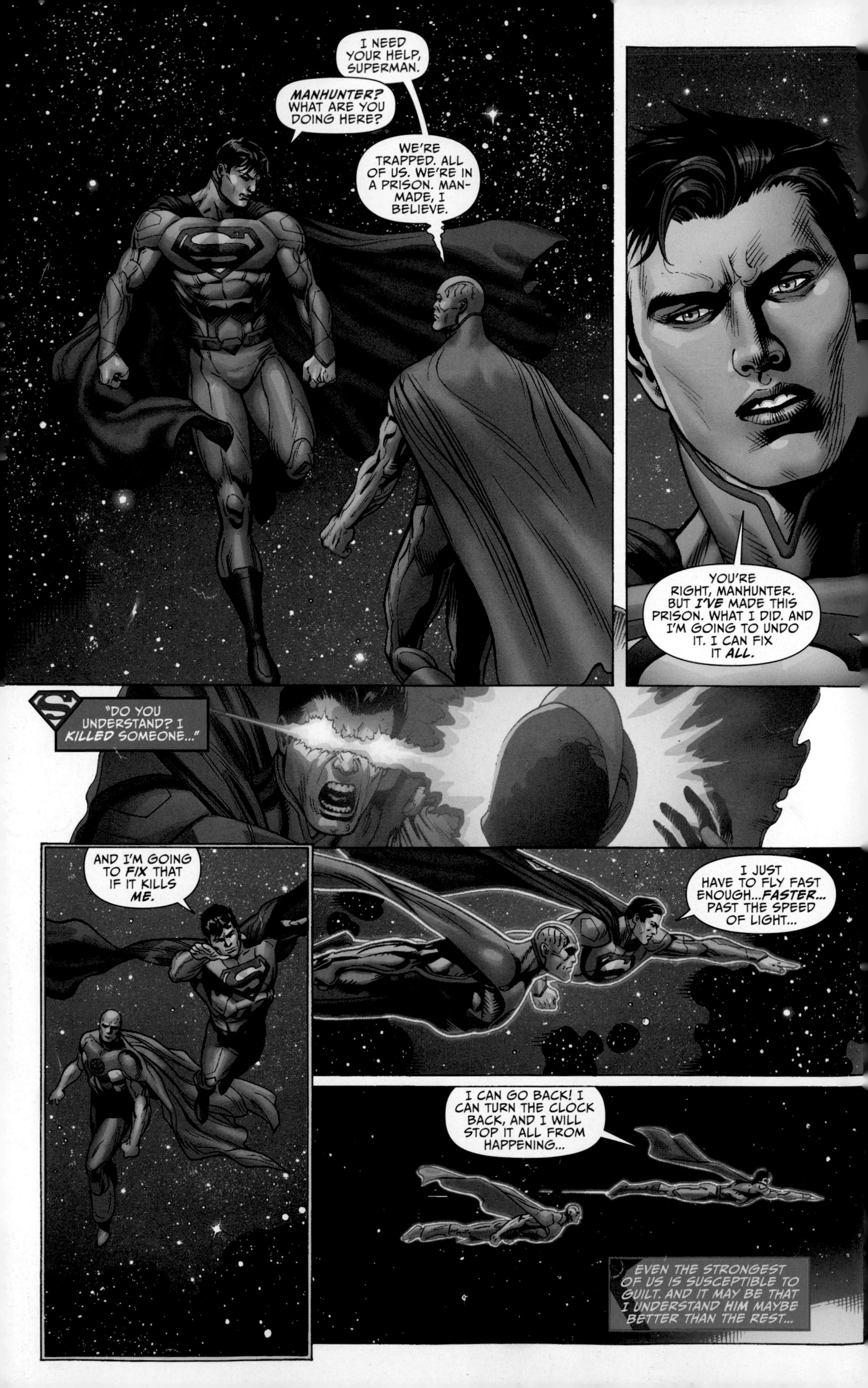
I NEED YOUR HELP, SUPERMAN.
MANHUNTER? WHAT ARE YOU DOING HERE?
WE'RE TRAPPED. ALL OF US. WE'RE IN A PRISON. MAN-MADE, I BELIEVE.
YOU'RE RIGHT, MANHUNTER. BUT I'VE MADE THIS PRISON. WHAT I DID. AND I'M GOING TO UNDO IT. I CAN FIX IT ALL.
"DO YOU UNDERSTAND? I KILLED SOMEONE..."
AND I'M GOING TO FIX THAT IF IT KILLS ME.
I JUST HAVE TO FLY FAST ENOUGH...FASTER... PAST THE SPEED OF LIGHT...
I CAN GO BACK! I CAN TURN THE CLOCK BACK, AND I WILL STOP IT ALL FROM HAPPENING...
EVEN THE STRONGEST OF US IS SUSCEPTIBLE TO GUILT. AND IT MAY BE THAT I UNDERSTAND HIM MAYBE BETTER THAN THE REST...

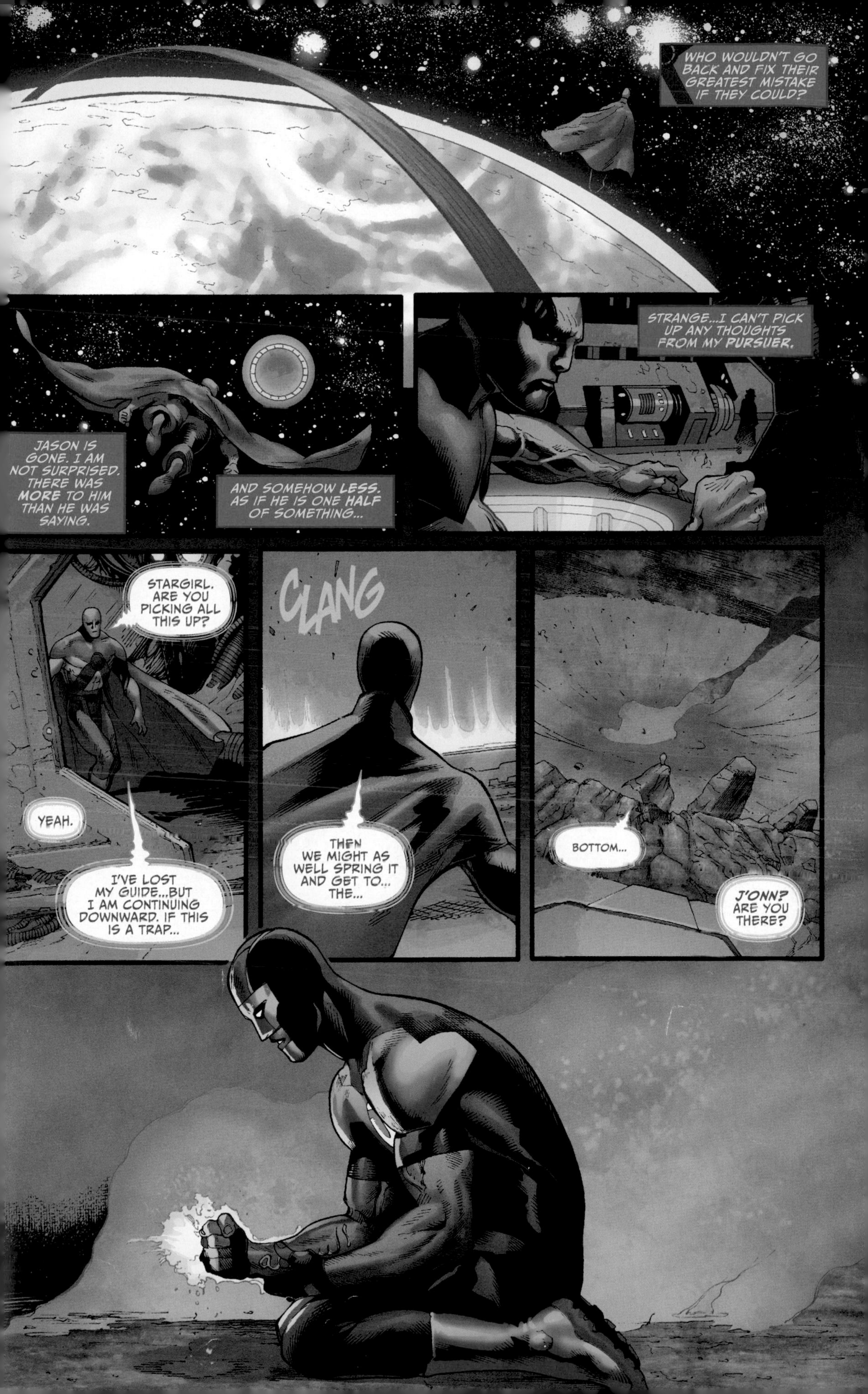
WHO WOULDN'T GO BACK AND FIX THEIR GREATEST MISTAKE IF THEY COULD?
JASON IS GONE. I AM NOT SURPRISED. THERE WAS MORE TO HIM THAN HE WAS SAYING.
AND SOMEHOW LESS. AS IF HE IS ONE HALF OF SOMETHING...
STRANGE...I CAN'T PICK UP ANY THOUGHTS FROM MY PURSUER.
STARGIRL. ARE YOU PICKING ALL THIS UP?
YEAH.
I'VE LOST MY GUIDE...BUT I AM CONTINUING DOWNWARD. IF THIS IS A TRAP...
CLANG
THEN WE MIGHT AS WELL SPRING IT AND GET TO... THE...
BOTTOM...
J'ONN? ARE YOU THERE?

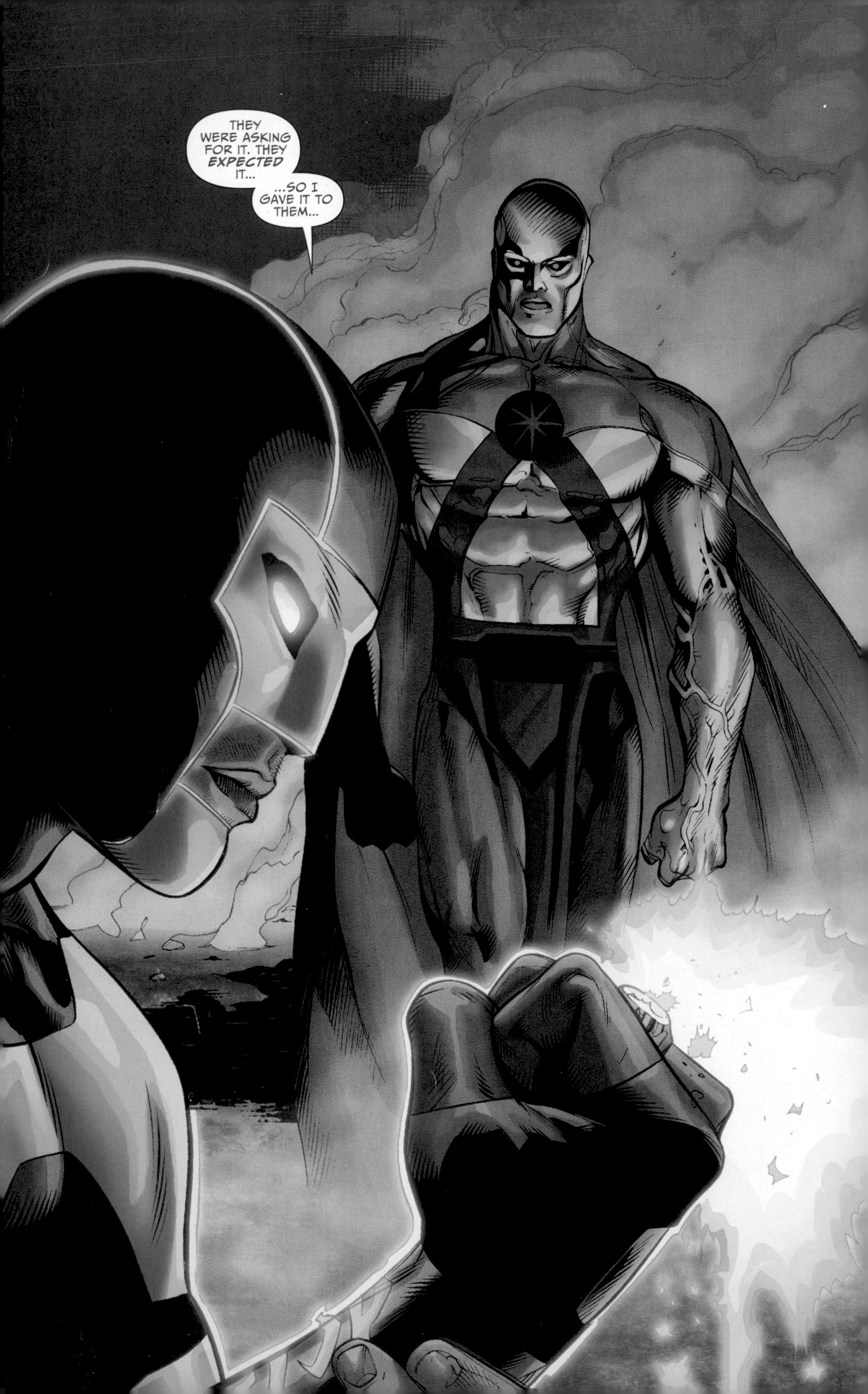
THEY WERE ASKING FOR IT. THEY *EXPECTED* IT...
...SO I GAVE IT TO THEM...

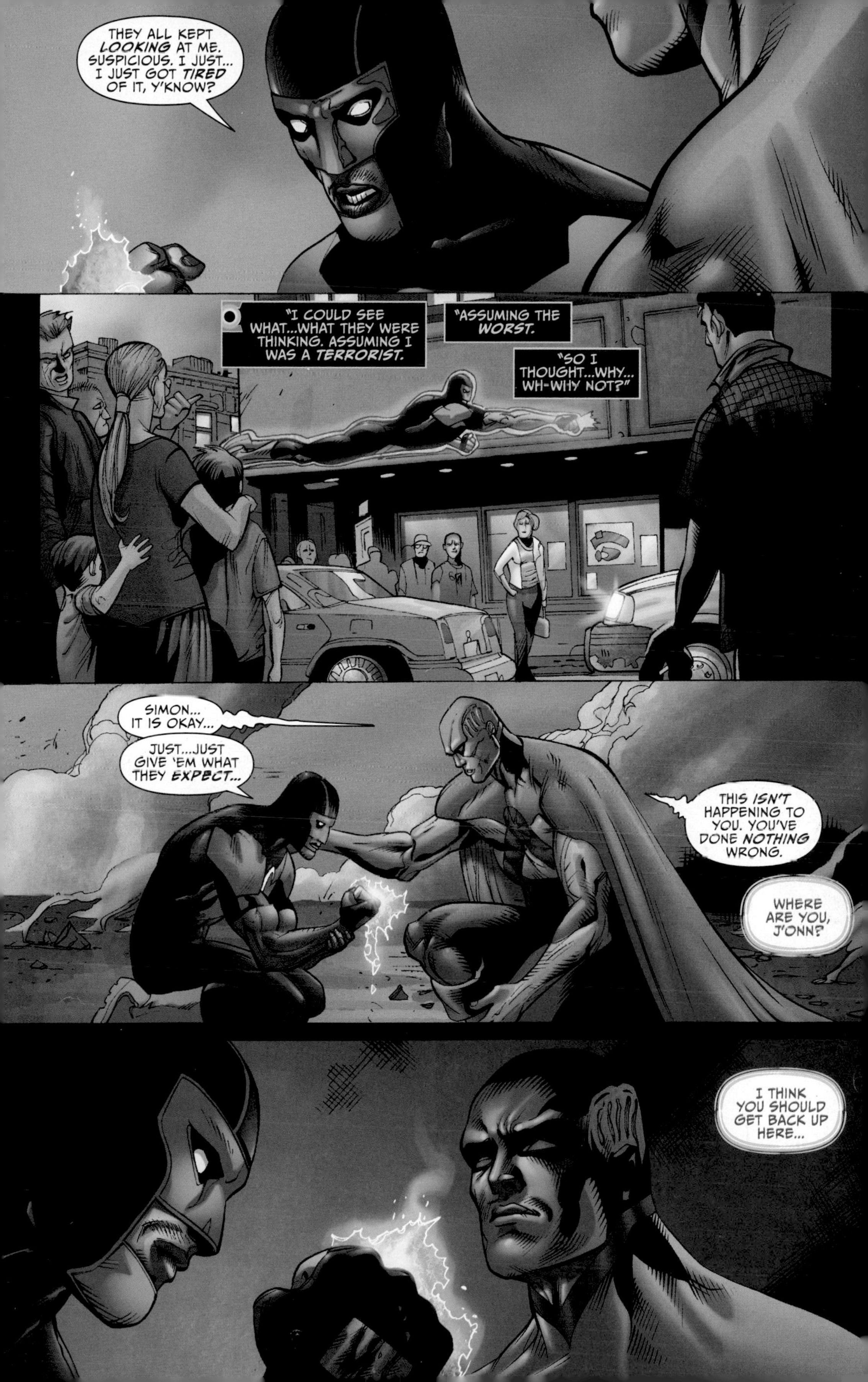
THEY ALL KEPT LOOKING AT ME. SUSPICIOUS. I JUST... I JUST GOT TIRED OF IT, Y'KNOW?
"I COULD SEE WHAT...WHAT THEY WERE THINKING. ASSUMING I WAS A TERRORIST.
"ASSUMING THE WORST.
"SO I THOUGHT...WHY... WH-WHY NOT?"
SIMON... IT IS OKAY...
JUST...JUST GIVE 'EM WHAT THEY EXPECT...
THIS ISN'T HAPPENING TO YOU. YOU'VE DONE NOTHING WRONG.
WHERE ARE YOU, J'ONN?
I THINK YOU SHOULD GET BACK UP HERE...

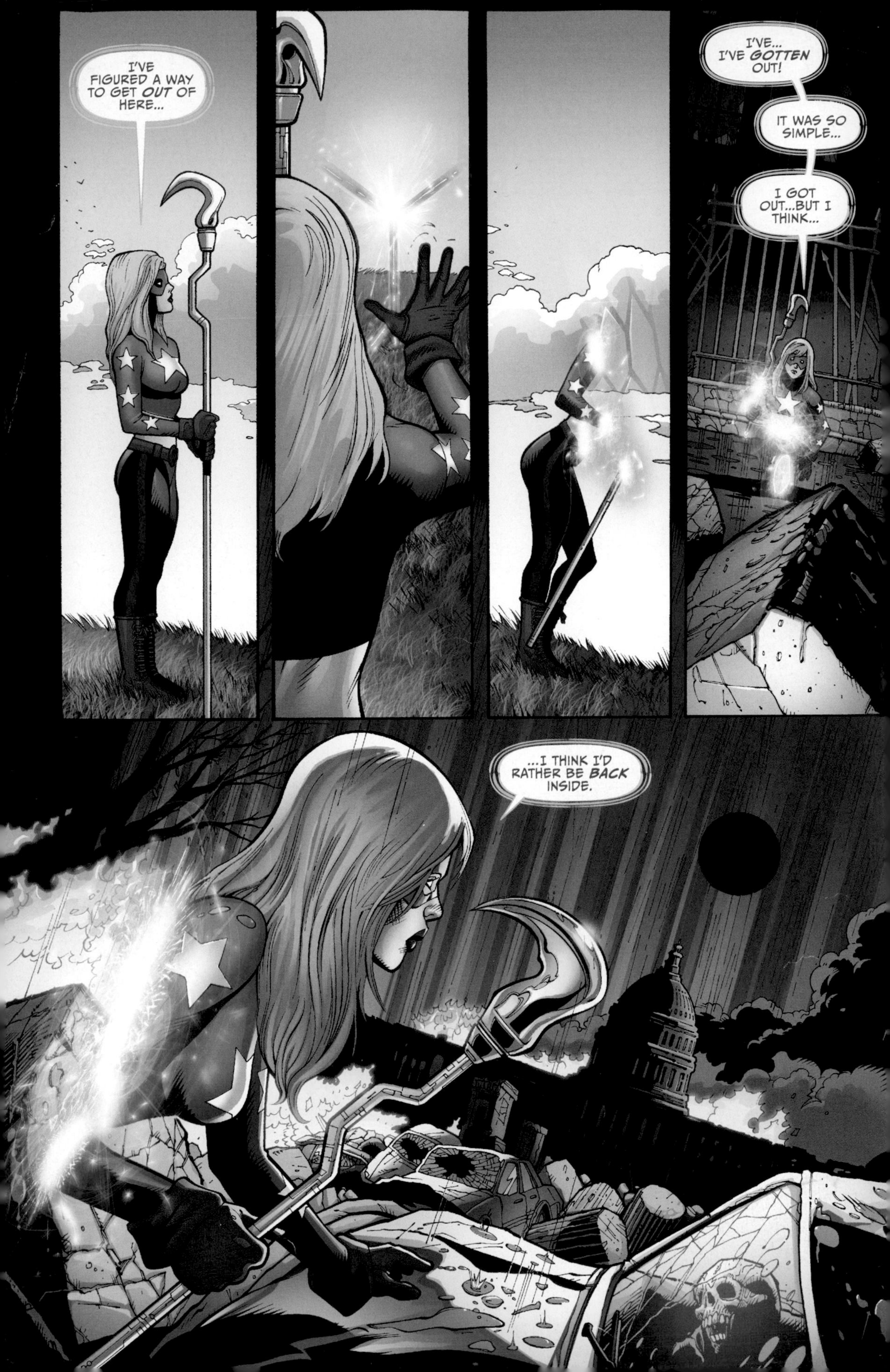
I'VE FIGURED A WAY TO GET OUT OF HERE...
I'VE... I'VE GOTTEN OUT!
IT WAS SO SIMPLE...
I GOT OUT...BUT I THINK...
...I THINK I'D RATHER BE BACK INSIDE.

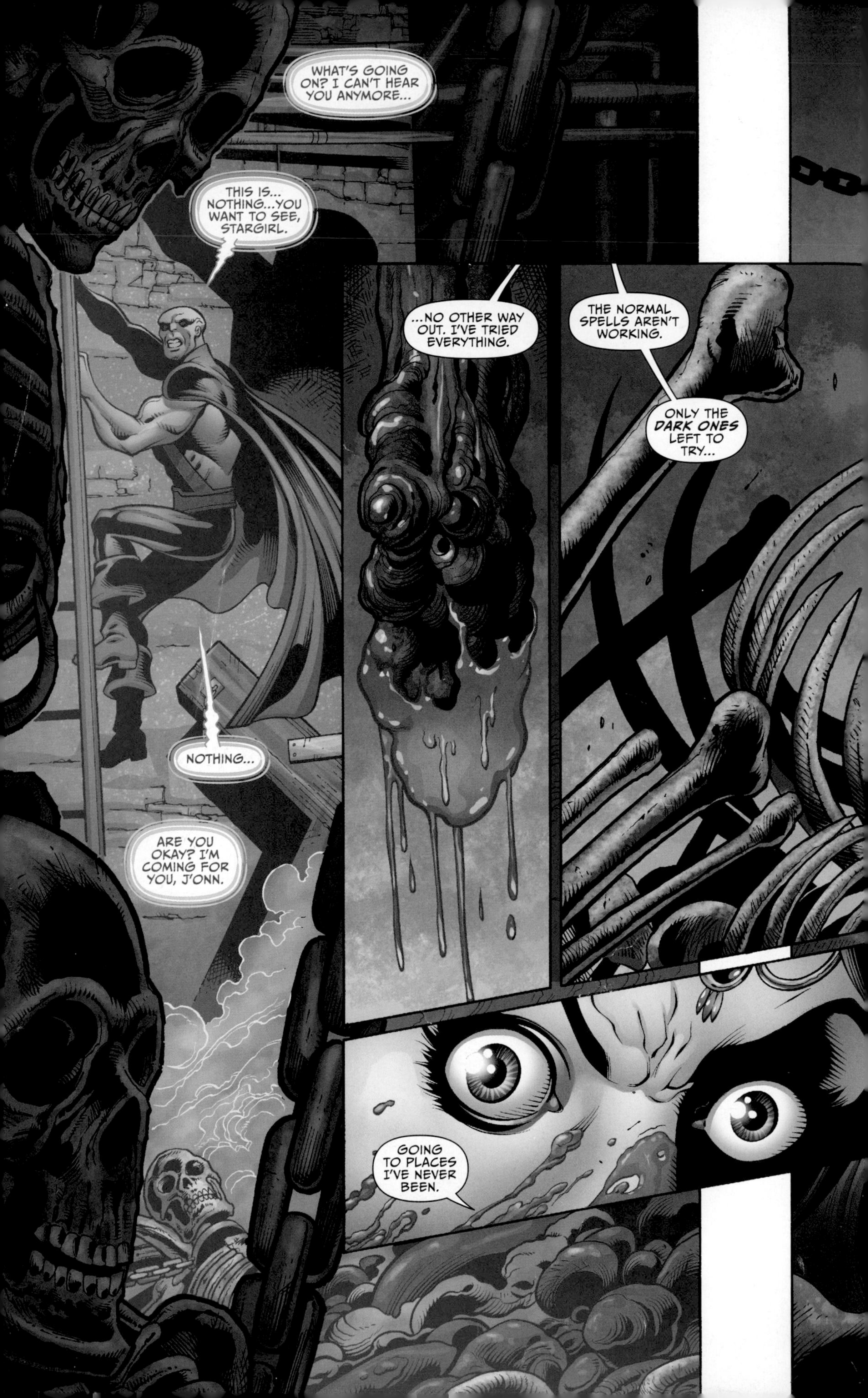
WHAT'S GOING ON? I CAN'T HEAR YOU ANYMORE...
THIS IS... NOTHING...YOU WANT TO SEE, STARGIRL.
NOTHING...
ARE YOU OKAY? I'M COMING FOR YOU, J'ONN.
...NO OTHER WAY OUT. I'VE TRIED EVERYTHING.
THE NORMAL SPELLS AREN'T WORKING.
ONLY THE DARK ONES LEFT TO TRY...
GOING TO PLACES I'VE NEVER BEEN.

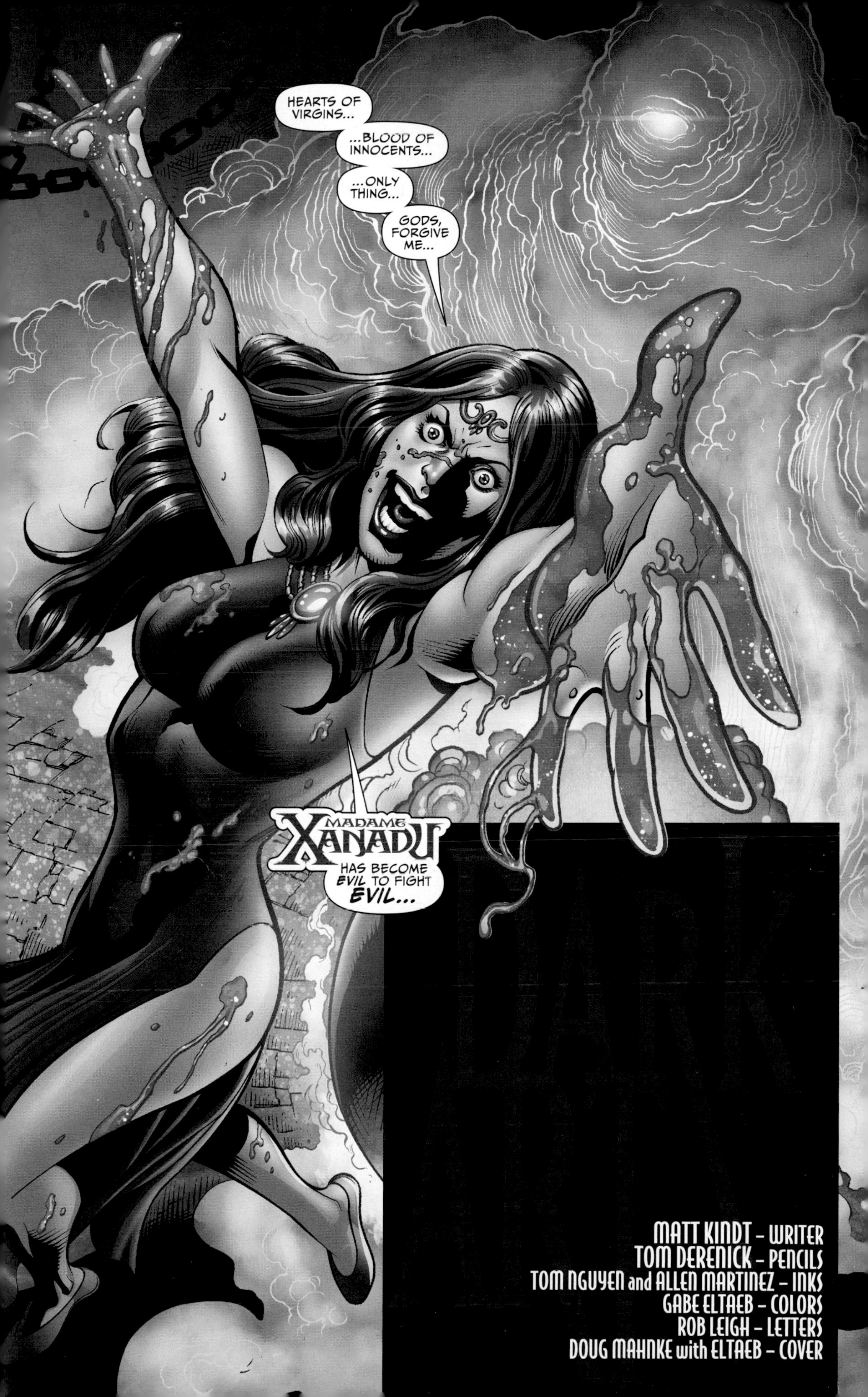
HEARTS OF VIRGINS...
...BLOOD OF INNOCENTS...
...ONLY THING...
GODS, FORGIVE ME...
MADAME XANADU HAS BECOME EVIL TO FIGHT EVIL...
MATT KINDT – WRITER
TOM DERENICK – PENCILS
TOM NGUYEN and ALLEN MARTINEZ – INKS
GABE ELTAEB – COLORS
ROB LEIGH – LETTERS
DOUG MAHNKE with ELTAEB – COVER

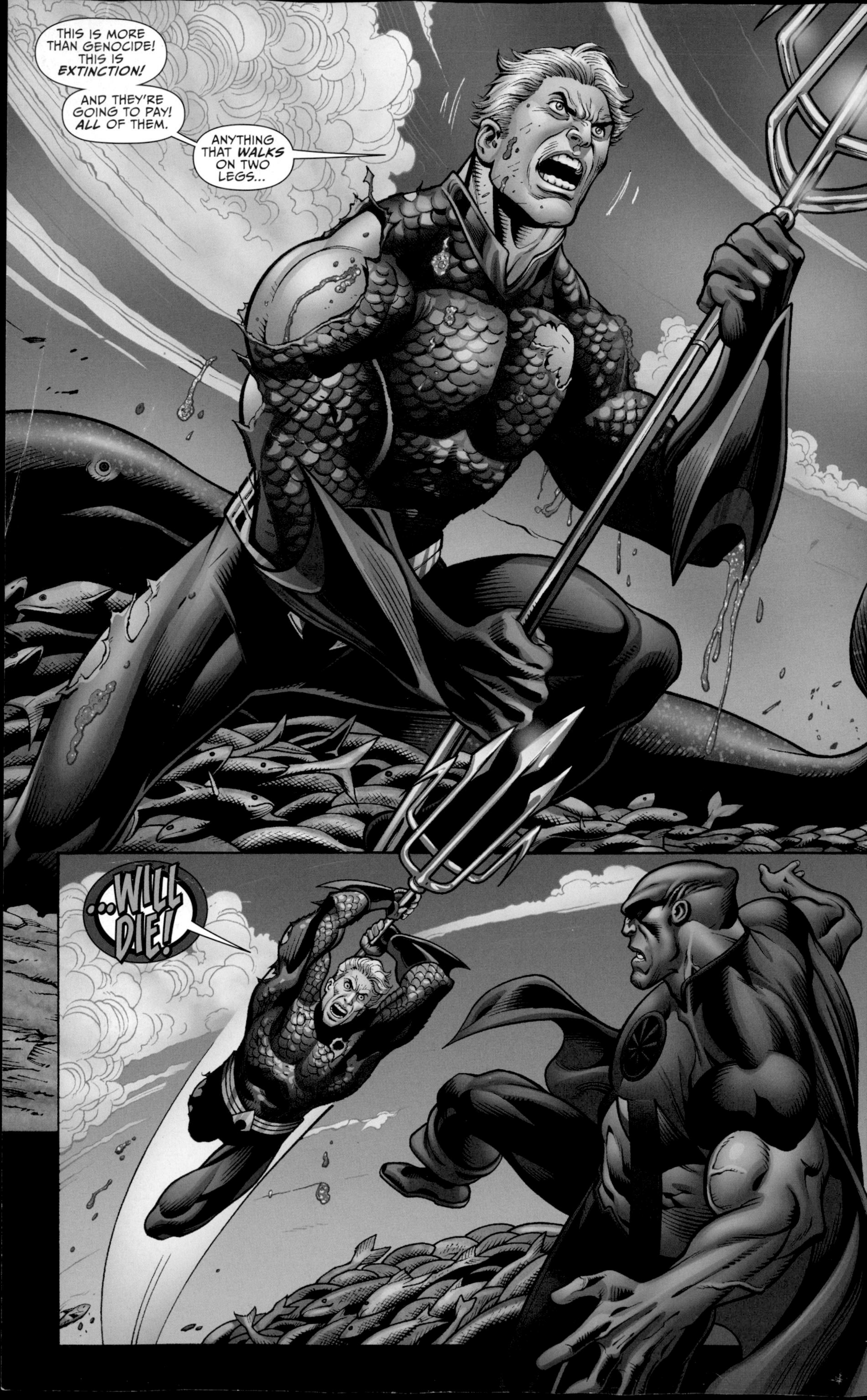
THIS IS MORE THAN GENOCIDE! THIS IS EXTINCTION!
AND THEY'RE GOING TO PAY! ALL OF THEM.
ANYTHING THAT WALKS ON TWO LEGS...
...WILL DIE!

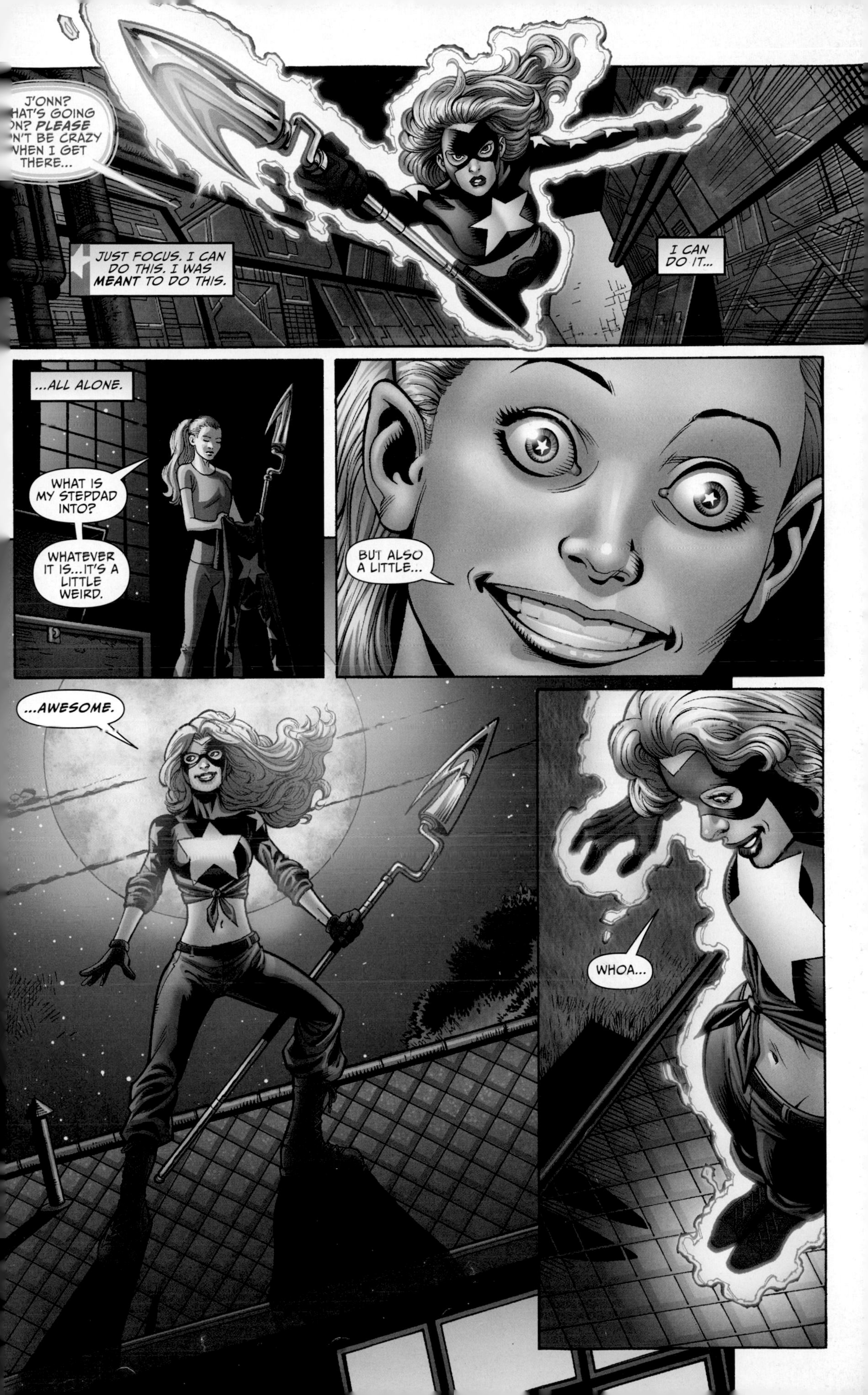
J'ONN? HAT'S GOING ON? PLEASE N'T BE CRAZY WHEN I GET THERE...
JUST FOCUS. I CAN DO THIS. I WAS MEANT TO DO THIS.
I CAN DO IT...
...ALL ALONE.
WHAT IS MY STEPDAD INTO?
WHATEVER IT IS...IT'S A LITTLE WEIRD.
BUT ALSO A LITTLE...
...AWESOME.
WHOA...

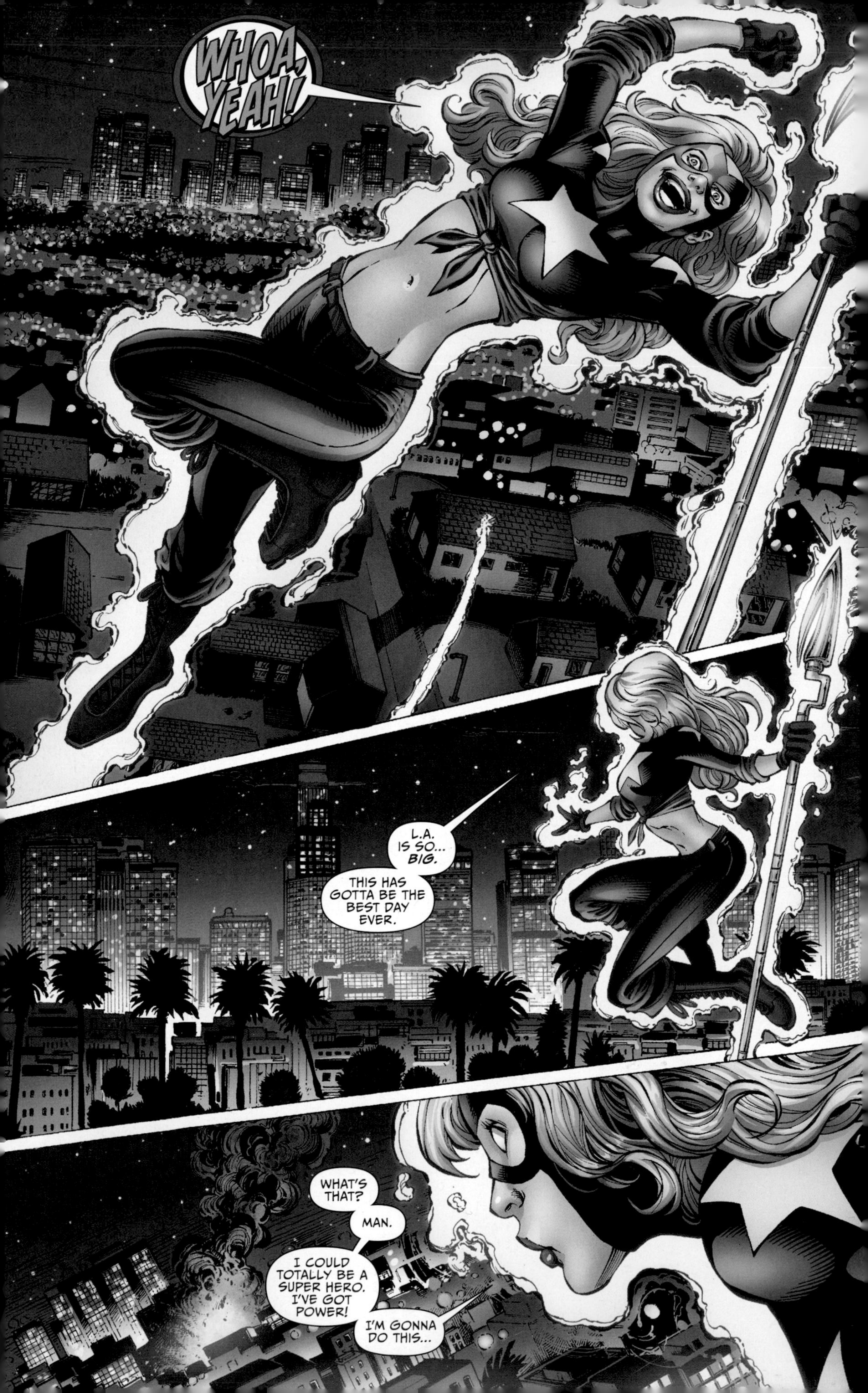
WHOA, YEAH!
L.A. IS SO... BIG.
THIS HAS GOTTA BE THE BEST DAY EVER.
WHAT'S THAT?
MAN.
I COULD TOTALLY BE A SUPER HERO. I'VE GOT POWER!
I'M GONNA DO THIS...

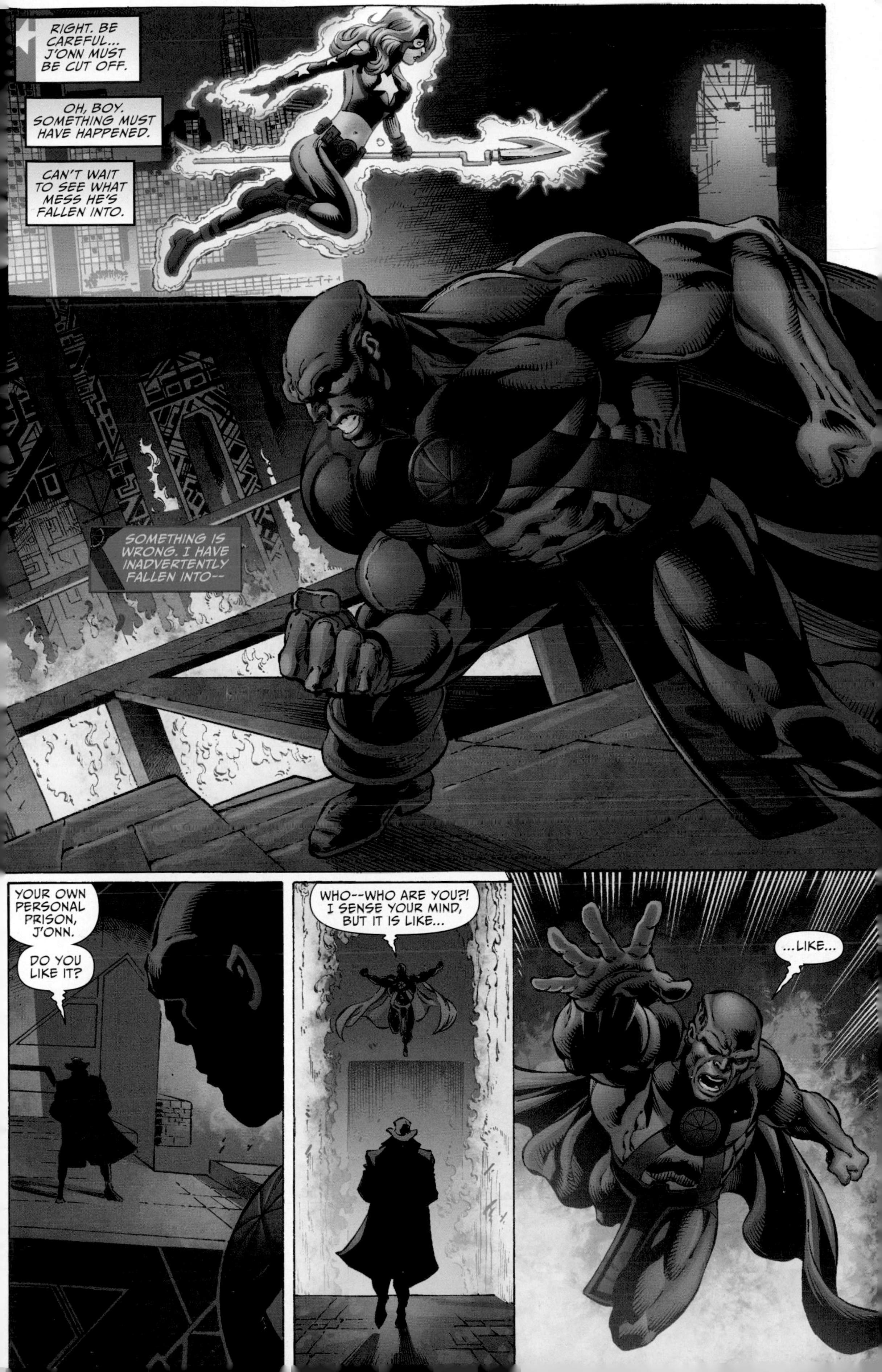
RIGHT. BE CAREFUL... J'ONN MUST BE CUT OFF.
OH, BOY. SOMETHING MUST HAVE HAPPENED.
CAN'T WAIT TO SEE WHAT MESS HE'S FALLEN INTO.
SOMETHING IS WRONG. I HAVE INADVERTENTLY FALLEN INTO--
YOUR OWN PERSONAL PRISON, J'ONN.
DO YOU LIKE IT?
WHO--WHO ARE YOU?! I SENSE YOUR MIND, BUT IT IS LIKE...
...LIKE...

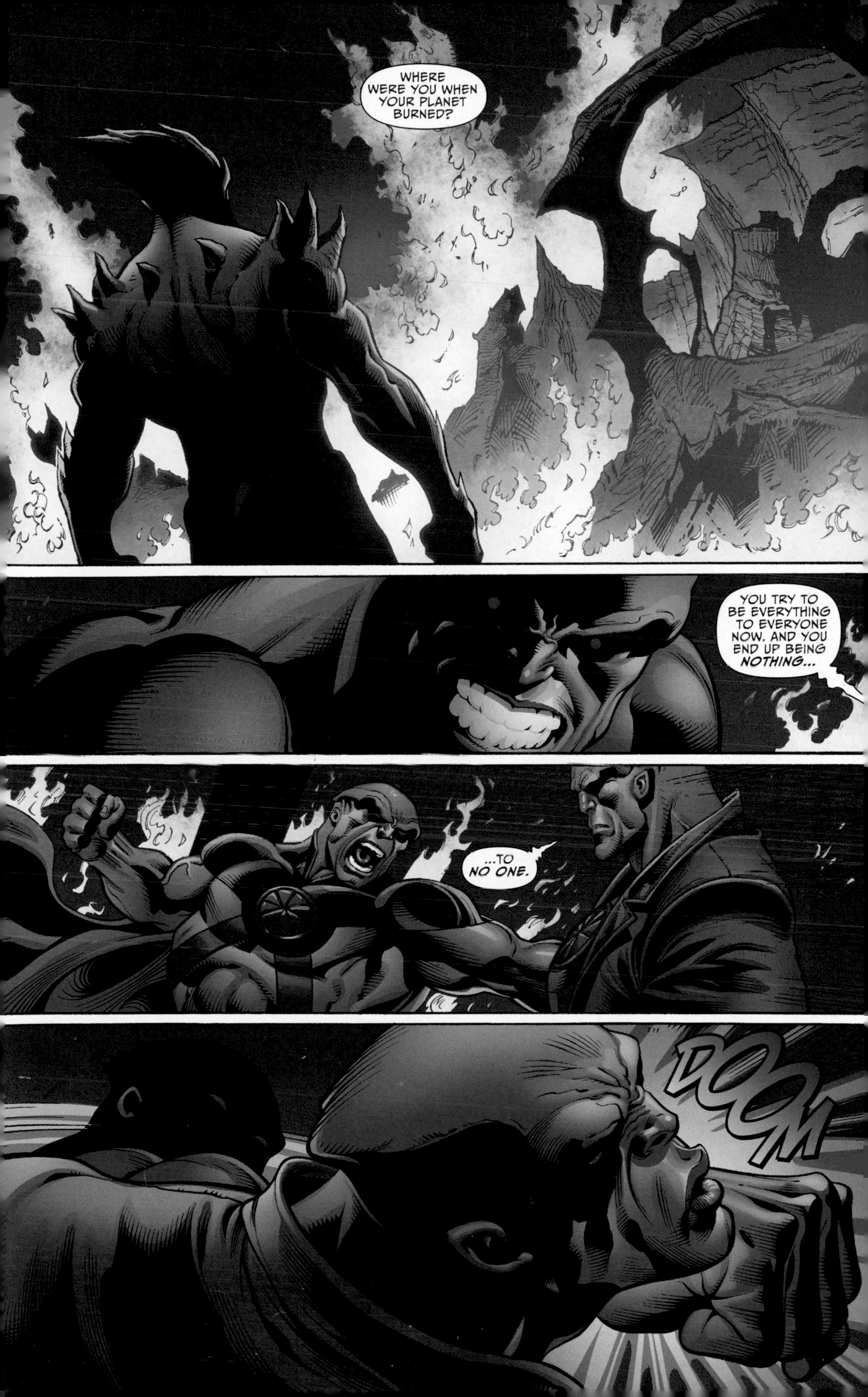
WHERE WERE YOU WHEN YOUR PLANET BURNED?
YOU TRY TO BE EVERYTHING TO EVERYONE NOW. AND YOU END UP BEING *NOTHING*...
...TO *NO ONE*.
DOOM

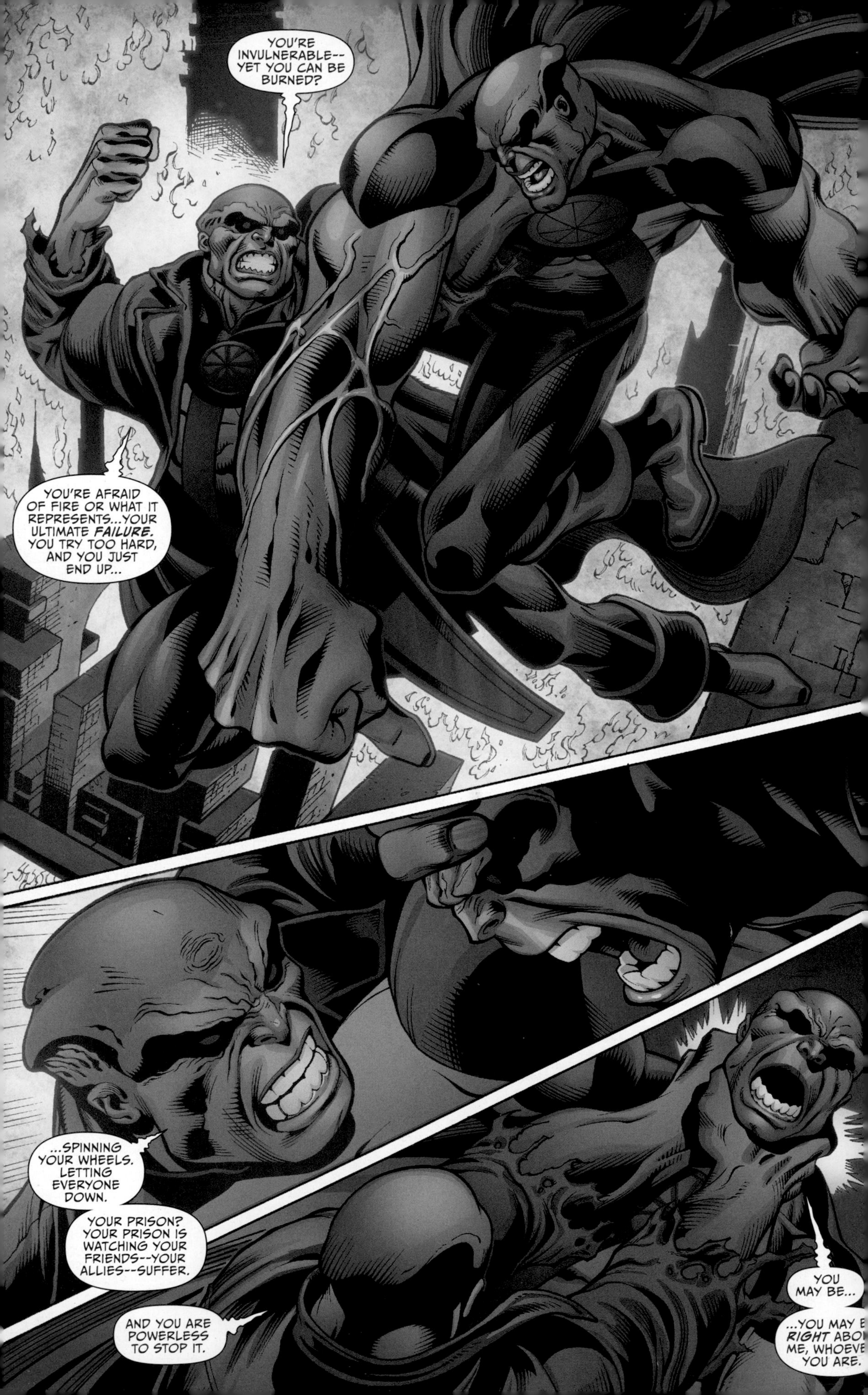
YOU'RE INVULNERABLE-- YET YOU CAN BE BURNED?
YOU'RE AFRAID OF FIRE OR WHAT IT REPRESENTS...YOUR ULTIMATE *FAILURE.* YOU TRY TOO HARD, AND YOU JUST END UP...
...SPINNING YOUR WHEELS. LETTING EVERYONE DOWN.
YOUR PRISON? YOUR PRISON IS WATCHING YOUR FRIENDS--YOUR ALLIES--SUFFER.
AND YOU ARE POWERLESS TO STOP IT.
YOU MAY BE...
...YOU MAY BE *RIGHT* ABOUT ME, WHOEVER YOU ARE.

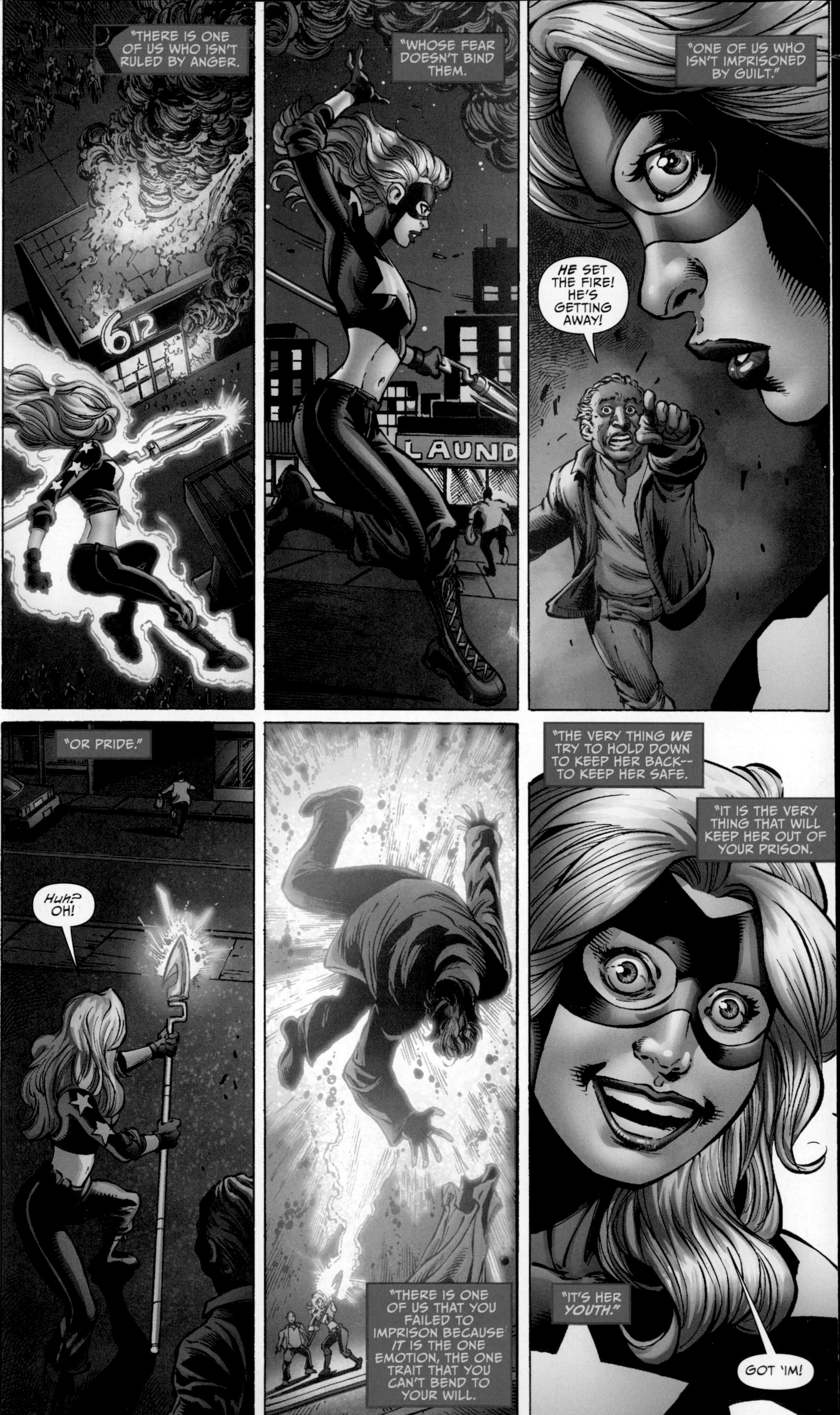
"THERE IS ONE OF US WHO ISN'T RULED BY ANGER.
"WHOSE FEAR DOESN'T BIND THEM.
LAUND
"ONE OF US WHO ISN'T IMPRISONED BY GUILT."
HE SET THE FIRE! HE'S GETTING AWAY!
"OR PRIDE."
Huh? OH!
"THERE IS ONE OF US THAT YOU FAILED TO IMPRISON BECAUSE IT IS THE ONE EMOTION, THE ONE TRAIT THAT YOU CAN'T BEND TO YOUR WILL.
"THE VERY THING WE TRY TO HOLD DOWN TO KEEP HER BACK-- TO KEEP HER SAFE.
"IT IS THE VERY THING THAT WILL KEEP HER OUT OF YOUR PRISON.
"IT'S HER YOUTH."
GOT 'IM!

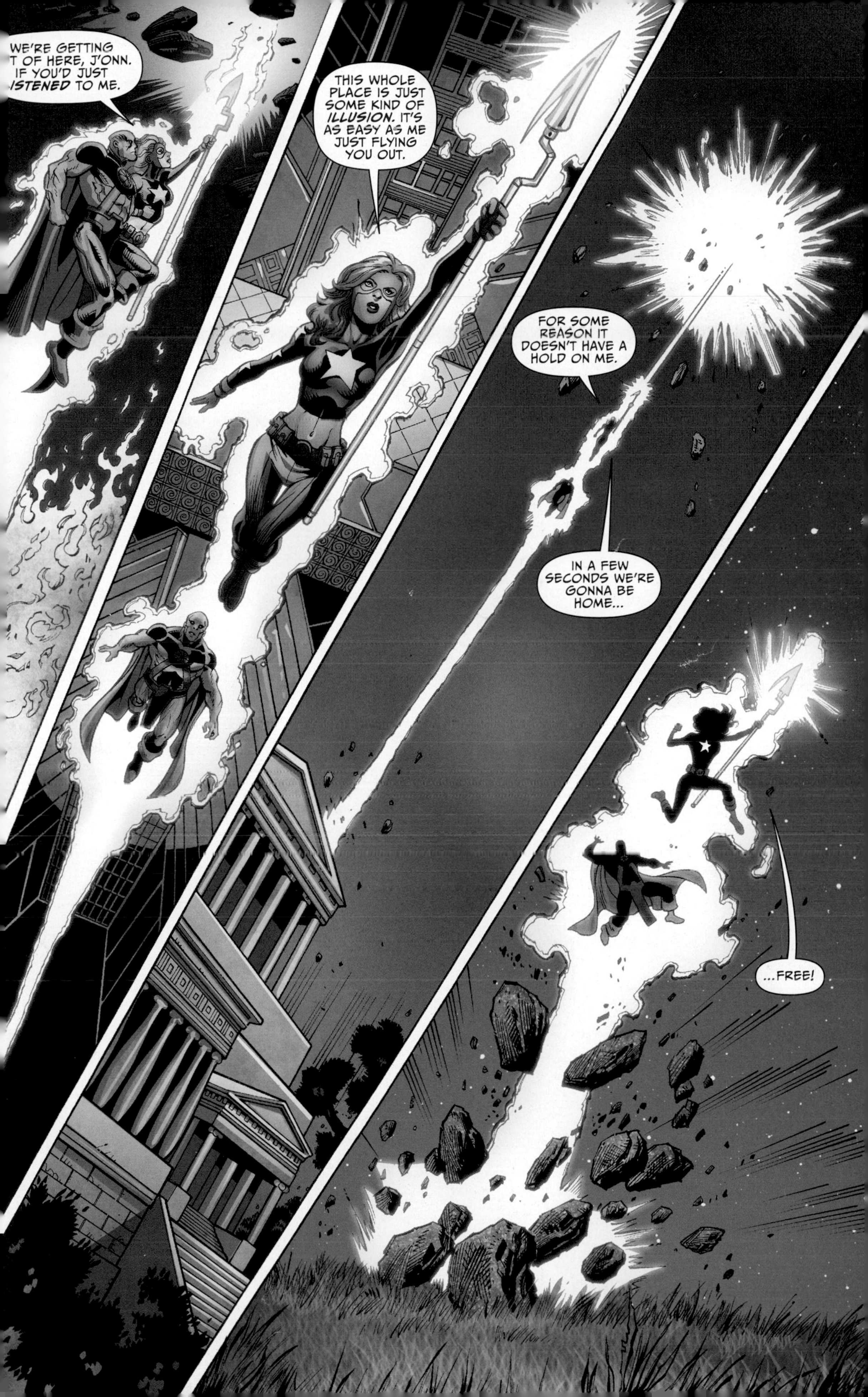
WE'RE GETTING
T OF HERE, J'ONN.
IF YOU'D JUST
ISTENED TO ME.
THIS WHOLE PLACE IS JUST SOME KIND OF *ILLUSION*. IT'S AS EASY AS ME JUST FLYING YOU OUT.
FOR SOME REASON IT DOESN'T HAVE A HOLD ON ME.
IN A FEW SECONDS WE'RE GONNA BE HOME...
...FREE!

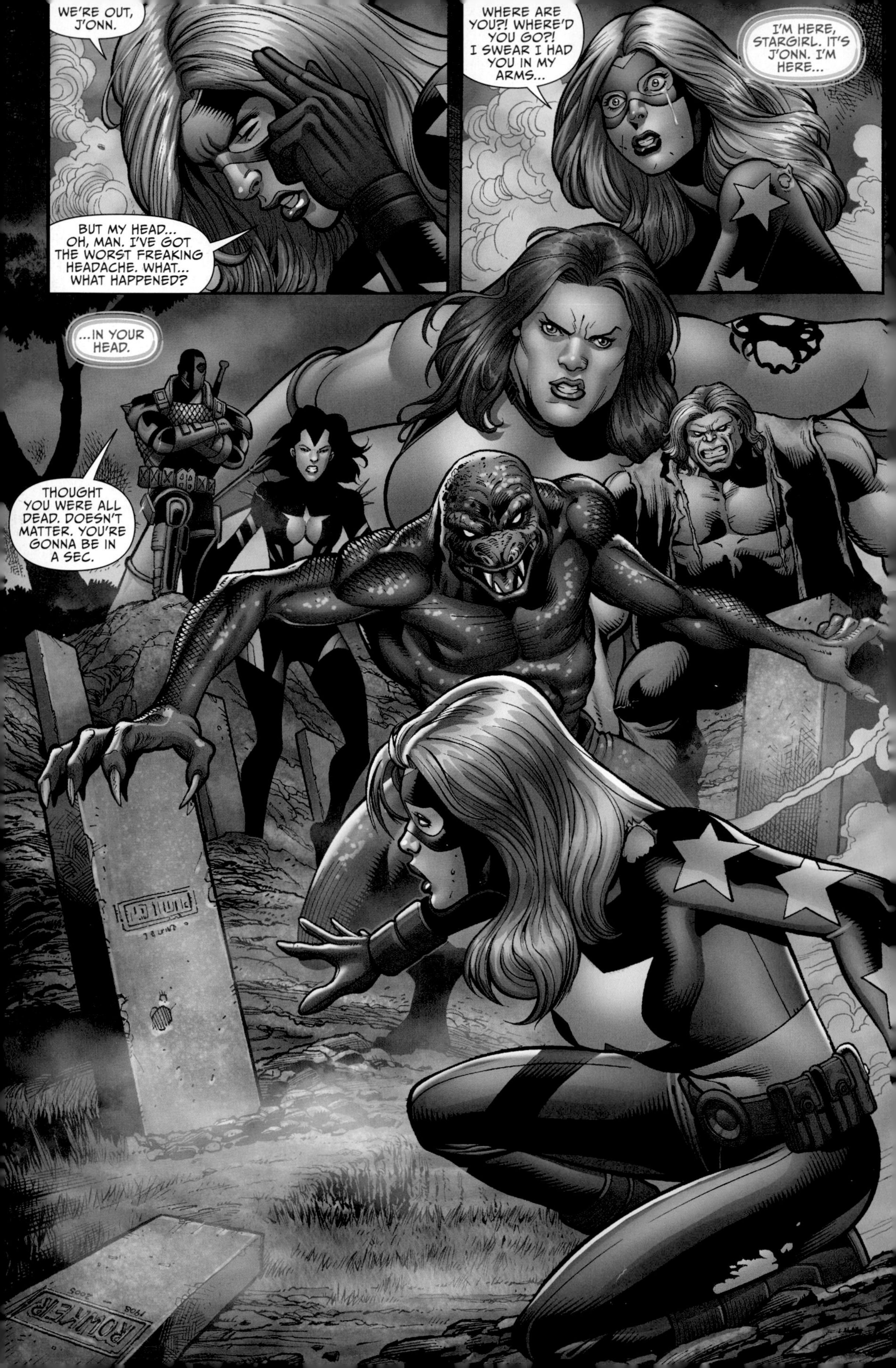
WE'RE OUT, J'ONN.
BUT MY HEAD... OH, MAN. I'VE GOT THE WORST FREAKING HEADACHE. WHAT... WHAT HAPPENED?
WHERE ARE YOU?! WHERE'D YOU GO?! I SWEAR I HAD YOU IN MY ARMS...
I'M HERE, STARGIRL. IT'S J'ONN. I'M HERE...
...IN YOUR HEAD.
THOUGHT YOU WERE ALL DEAD. DOESN'T MATTER. YOU'RE GONNA BE IN A SEC.

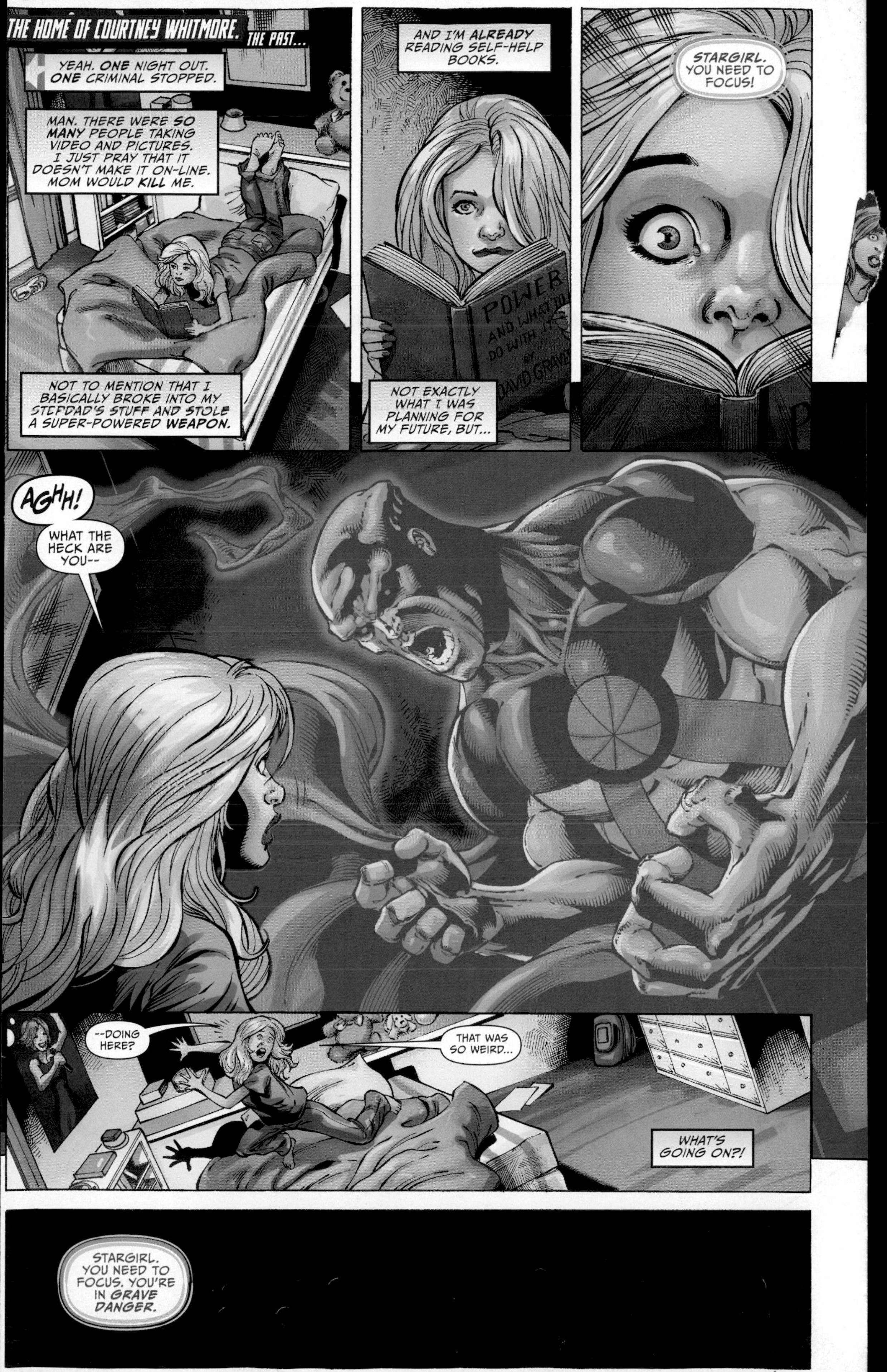
THE HOME OF COURTNEY WHITMORE.
THE PAST...
YEAH. ONE NIGHT OUT. ONE CRIMINAL STOPPED.
MAN. THERE WERE SO MANY PEOPLE TAKING VIDEO AND PICTURES. I JUST PRAY THAT IT DOESN'T MAKE IT ON-LINE. MOM WOULD KILL ME.
NOT TO MENTION THAT I BASICALLY BROKE INTO MY STEPDAD'S STUFF AND STOLE A SUPER-POWERED WEAPON.
AND I'M ALREADY READING SELF-HELP BOOKS.
POWER AND WHAT TO DO WITH IT BY DAVID GRAVE
NOT EXACTLY WHAT I WAS PLANNING FOR MY FUTURE, BUT...
STARGIRL. YOU NEED TO FOCUS!
AGHH!
WHAT THE HECK ARE YOU--
--DOING HERE?
THAT WAS SO WEIRD...
WHAT'S GOING ON?!
STARGIRL. YOU NEED TO FOCUS. YOU'RE IN GRAVE DANGER.

LATER...

...YOU NEED A *WAY* BETTER COSTUME. THAT VIDEO WAS GOOD BUT YOUR OUTFIT WAS...KIND OF *EMBARRASSING*, COURTNEY.

I KNOW. IT'S THE BEST I COULD DO, *TUAN*. HOW DID I KNOW THE FREAKING *WORLD* WOULD END UP SEEING ME?

WELL... *THAT* PLACE WAS GROSS.

TRUST ME. YOU'RE GOING TO LOOK GREAT. RED, WHITE, AND BLUE, GIRL. PEOPLE WON'T BE ABLE TO *HELP* BUT LOVE YOU.

I DON'T KNOW. HONESTLY, I WAS JUST SCREWING AROUND AND ACCIDENTALLY DID SOMETHING *GOOD*. I KEEP THINKING IF I JUST STOP NOW I CAN GO BACK TO NORMAL.

THIS IS YOUR *CHANCE*. YOU'RE HONESTLY THE MOST GENUINE, PUREST GIRL I KNOW, COURTNEY. THIS IS YOUR *CALLING*.

ALL COSTUMES

OKAY! SHOW 'EM WHAT YOU GOT!

• REC ▭

I KNOW IT SEEMED LIKE I WAS TRYING TO DO IT. TO GET ATTENTION. TO GET FAMOUS LIKE EVERYONE ELSE WITH A CAMERA AND A LAPTOP.

BUT THAT WASN'T IT. I REALLY JUST LOVED FLYING.

AND I LOVED THE IDEA OF A *NORMAL* KID DOING SOMETHING *DIFFERENT*.

NEW BLONDE SUPERHERO

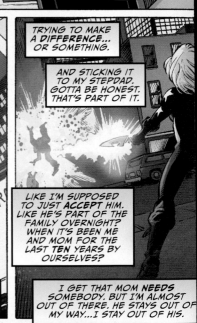

TRYING TO MAKE A *DIFFERENCE*... OR SOMETHING.

AND STICKING IT TO MY STEPDAD. GOTTA BE HONEST. THAT'S PART OF IT.

LIKE I'M SUPPOSED TO JUST *ACCEPT* HIM. LIKE HE'S PART OF THE FAMILY OVERNIGHT? WHEN IT'S BEEN ME AND MOM FOR THE LAST *TEN* YEARS BY OURSELVES?

I GET THAT MOM *NEEDS* SOMEBODY. BUT I'M ALMOST OUT OF THERE. HE STAYS OUT OF MY WAY...I STAY OUT OF HIS.

OH CRAP. I MIGHT BE IN TROUBLE. T... MILLION VIEWS?

STAR TEEN

LAUNDR...

RELAX...

OH MAN!

...OTHING KE FLYING N A SUNNY DAY.

I KNOW PAT WANTS ME TO TAKE IT SLOW, BUT THE MORE I USE THE ROD AND THE FLYING BELT, THE BETTER I'M GOING TO BE. HE'S SO CAUTIOUS ALL THE TIME. *SCARED*, MORE LIKE IT.

BY THE TIME HE GETS AROUND TO GIVING ME FLYING LESSONS, I'LL BE AN *EXPERT*.

STARGIRL...

HEY, GUYS!

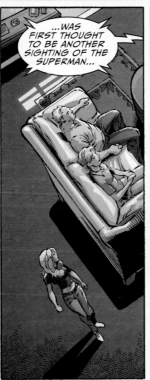

...WAS FIRST THOUGHT TO BE ANOTHER SIGHTING OF THE SUPERMAN...

...BUT FROM THE LONG BLONDE HAIR, IT WAS OBVIOUSLY NOT...

WHAT?

3WX

...UNIDENTIFIED FEMALE FLYING OVER THE CITY OF *LOS ANGELES* TODAY. KIDS IN THE NEIGHBORHOOD HAVE ALREADY NICKNAMED HER... "STARGIRL..."

...hm...

STARGIRL!

YOU'VE GOT TO STOP RETREATING INTO YOUR PAST. I NEED YOU. *WE* NEED YOU IN THE HERE AND...

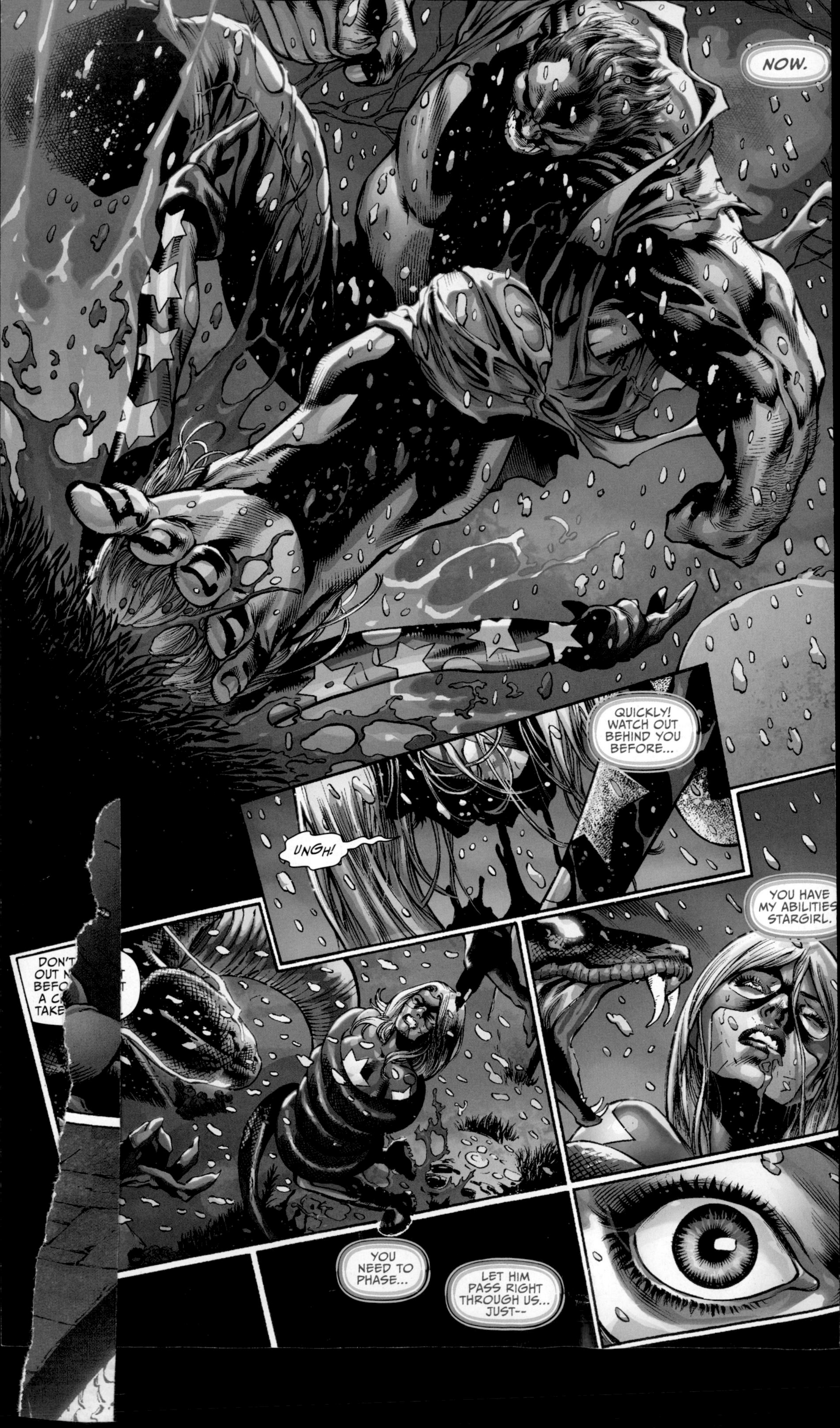
NOW.
QUICKLY! WATCH OUT BEHIND YOU BEFORE...
UNGH!
YOU HAVE MY ABILITIES STARGIRL.
DON'T
YOU NEED TO PHASE...
LET HIM PASS RIGHT THROUGH US... JUST--

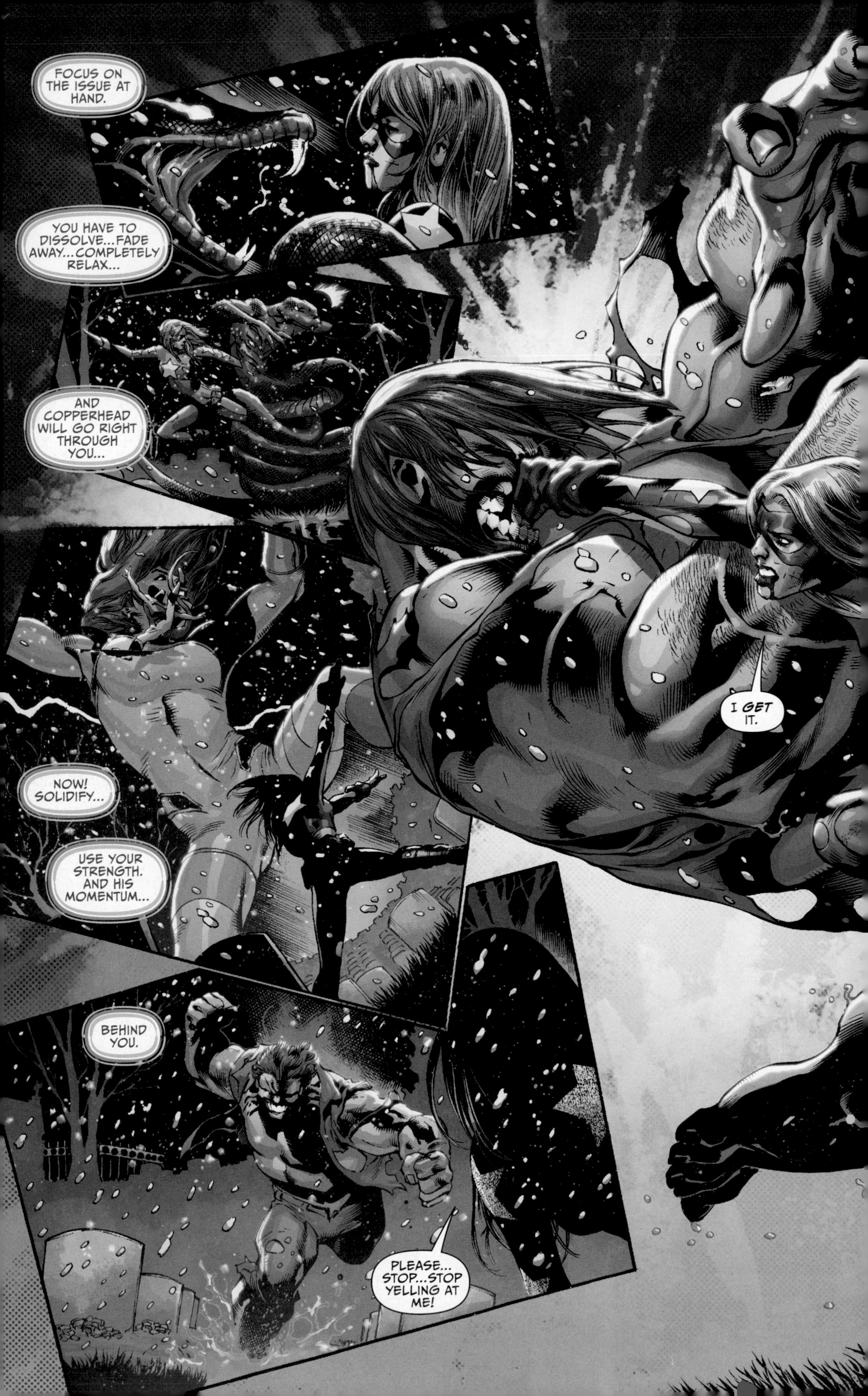
FOCUS ON THE ISSUE AT HAND.
YOU HAVE TO DISSOLVE...FADE AWAY...COMPLETELY RELAX...
AND COPPERHEAD WILL GO RIGHT THROUGH YOU...
I GET IT.
NOW! SOLIDIFY...
USE YOUR STRENGTH. AND HIS MOMENTUM...
BEHIND YOU.
PLEASE... STOP...STOP YELLING AT ME!

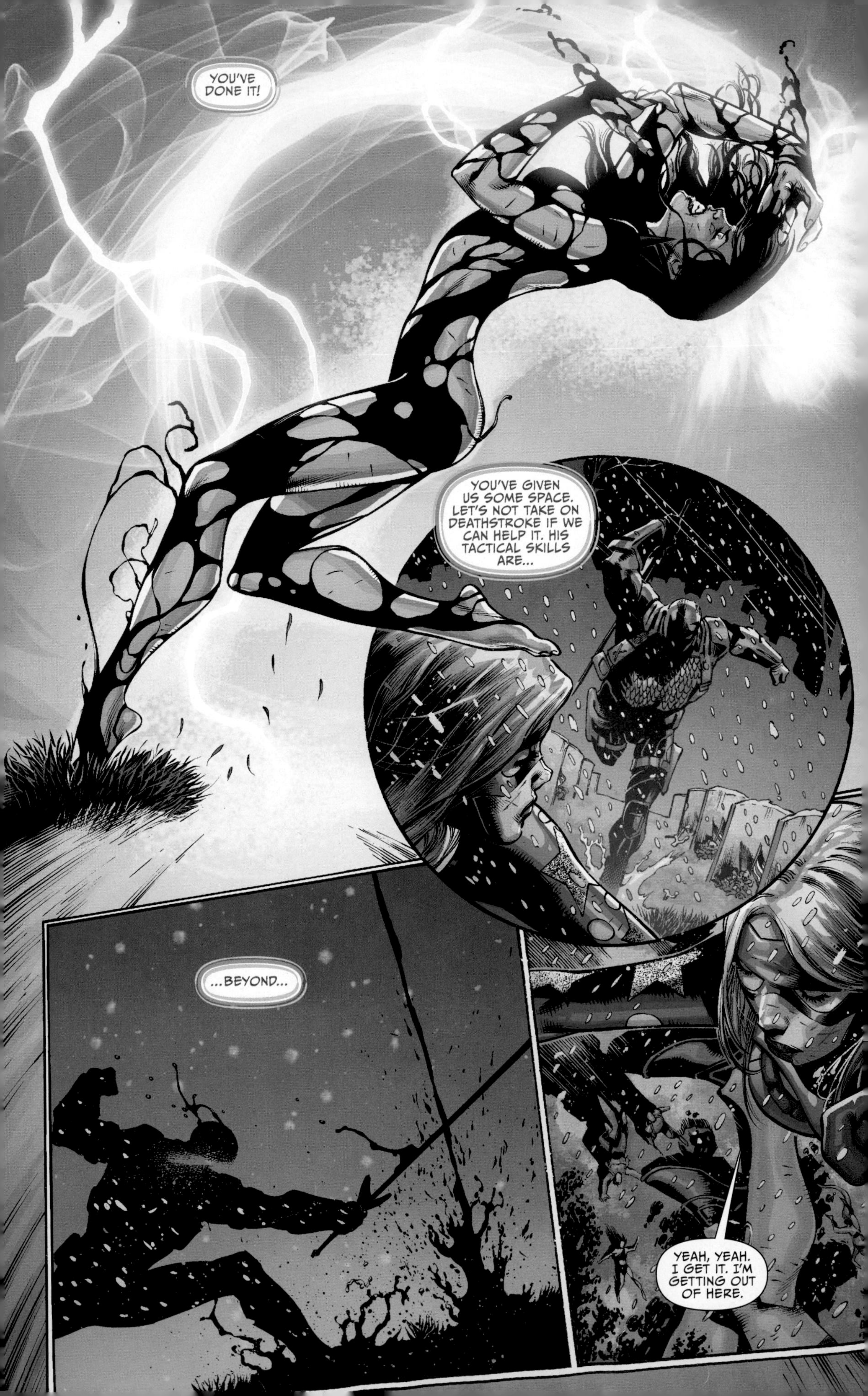
YOU'VE DONE IT!
YOU'VE GIVEN US SOME SPACE. LET'S NOT TAKE ON DEATHSTROKE IF WE CAN HELP IT. HIS TACTICAL SKILLS ARE...
...BEYOND...
YEAH, YEAH. I GET IT. I'M GETTING OUT OF HERE.

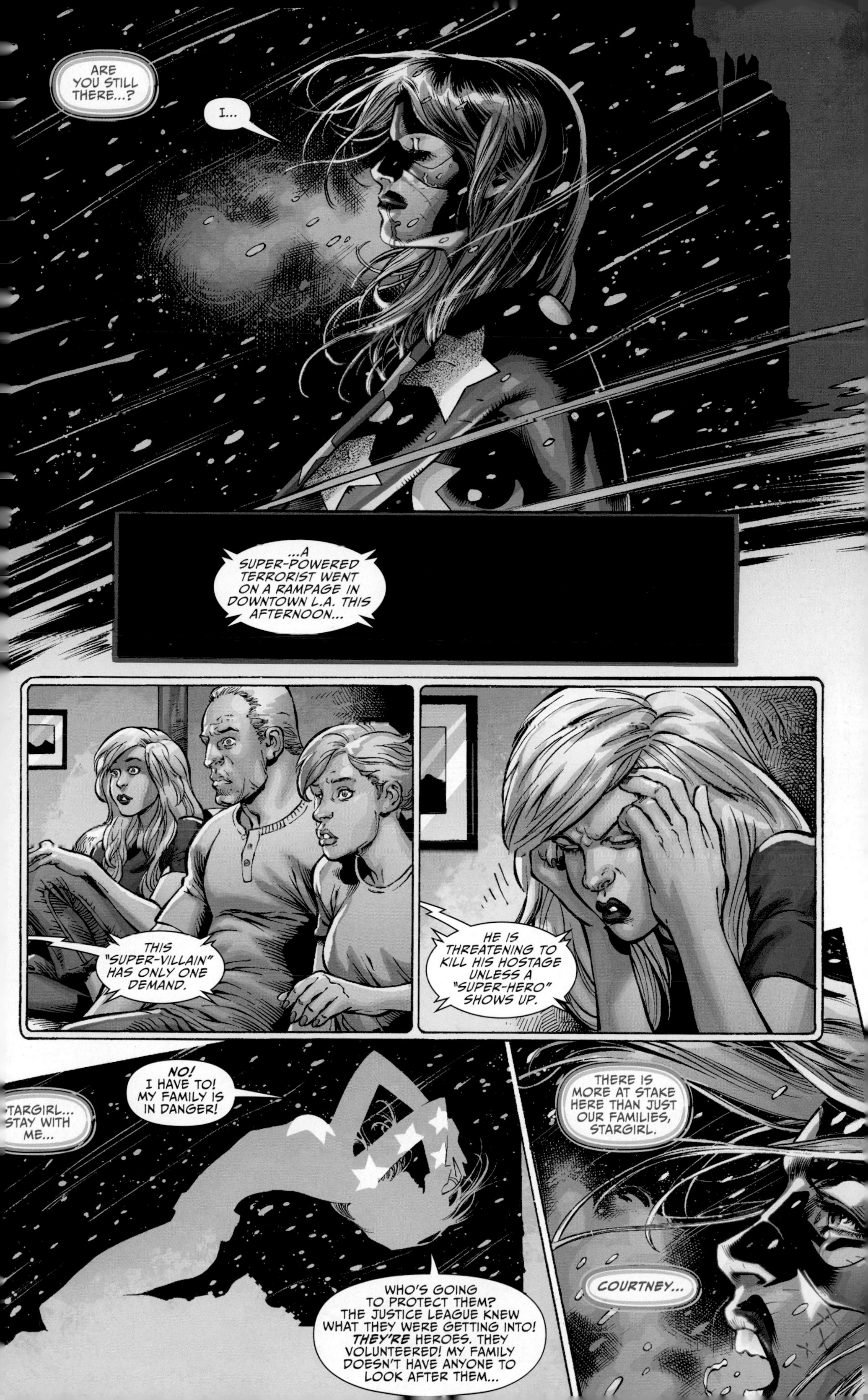

ARE YOU STILL THERE...?
I...
...A SUPER-POWERED TERRORIST WENT ON A RAMPAGE IN DOWNTOWN L.A. THIS AFTERNOON...
THIS "SUPER-VILLAIN" HAS ONLY ONE DEMAND.
HE IS THREATENING TO KILL HIS HOSTAGE UNLESS A "SUPER-HERO" SHOWS UP.
STARGIRL... STAY WITH ME...
NO! I HAVE TO! MY FAMILY IS IN DANGER!
THERE IS MORE AT STAKE HERE THAN JUST OUR FAMILIES, STARGIRL.
WHO'S GOING TO PROTECT THEM? THE JUSTICE LEAGUE KNEW WHAT THEY WERE GETTING INTO! THEY'RE HEROES. THEY VOLUNTEERED! MY FAMILY DOESN'T HAVE ANYONE TO LOOK AFTER THEM...
COURTNEY...

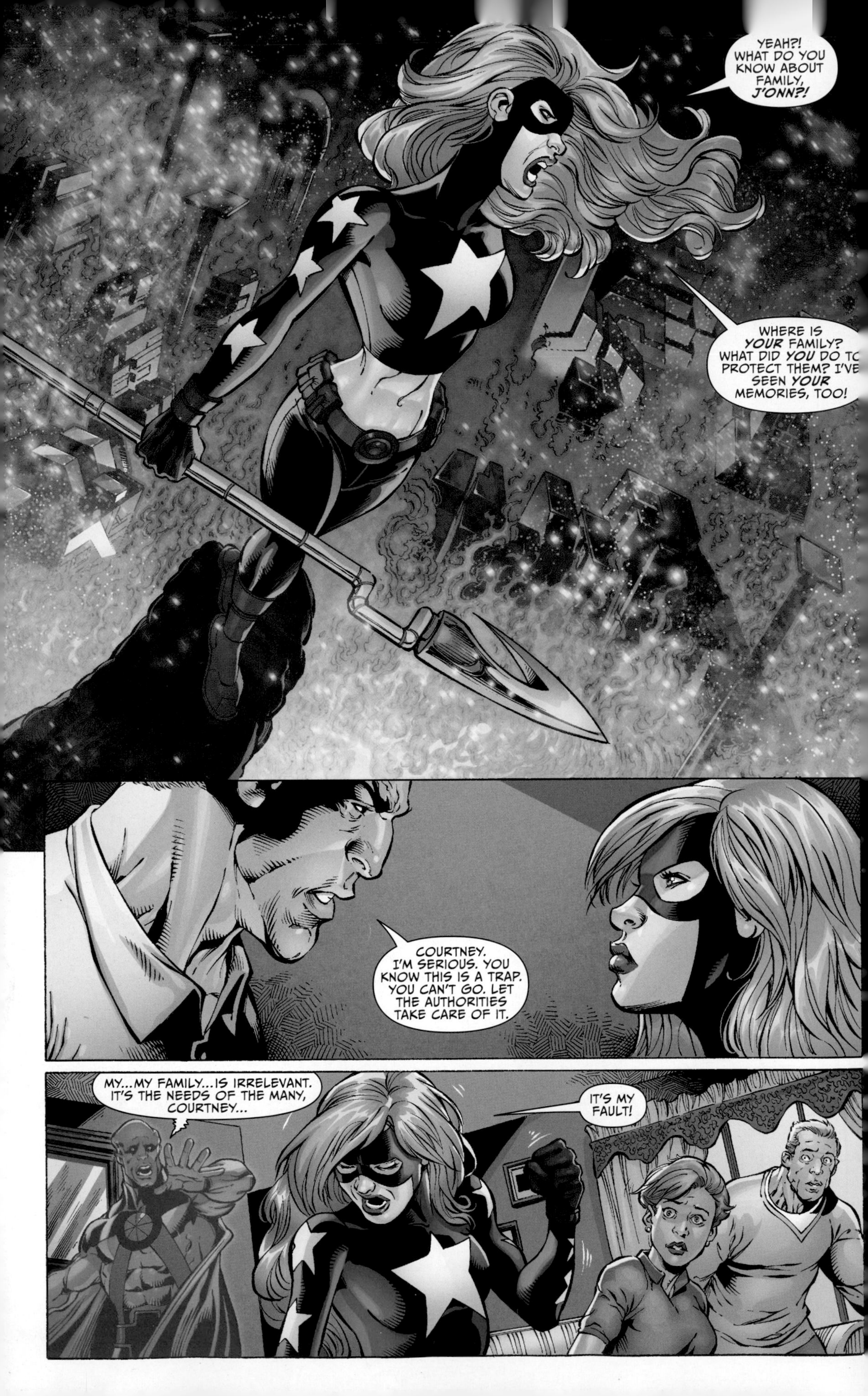
YEAH?! WHAT DO YOU KNOW ABOUT FAMILY, J'ONN?!
WHERE IS YOUR FAMILY? WHAT DID YOU DO TO PROTECT THEM? I'VE SEEN YOUR MEMORIES, TOO!
COURTNEY. I'M SERIOUS. YOU KNOW THIS IS A TRAP. YOU CAN'T GO. LET THE AUTHORITIES TAKE CARE OF IT.
MY...MY FAMILY...IS IRRELEVANT. IT'S THE NEEDS OF THE MANY, COURTNEY...
IT'S MY FAULT!

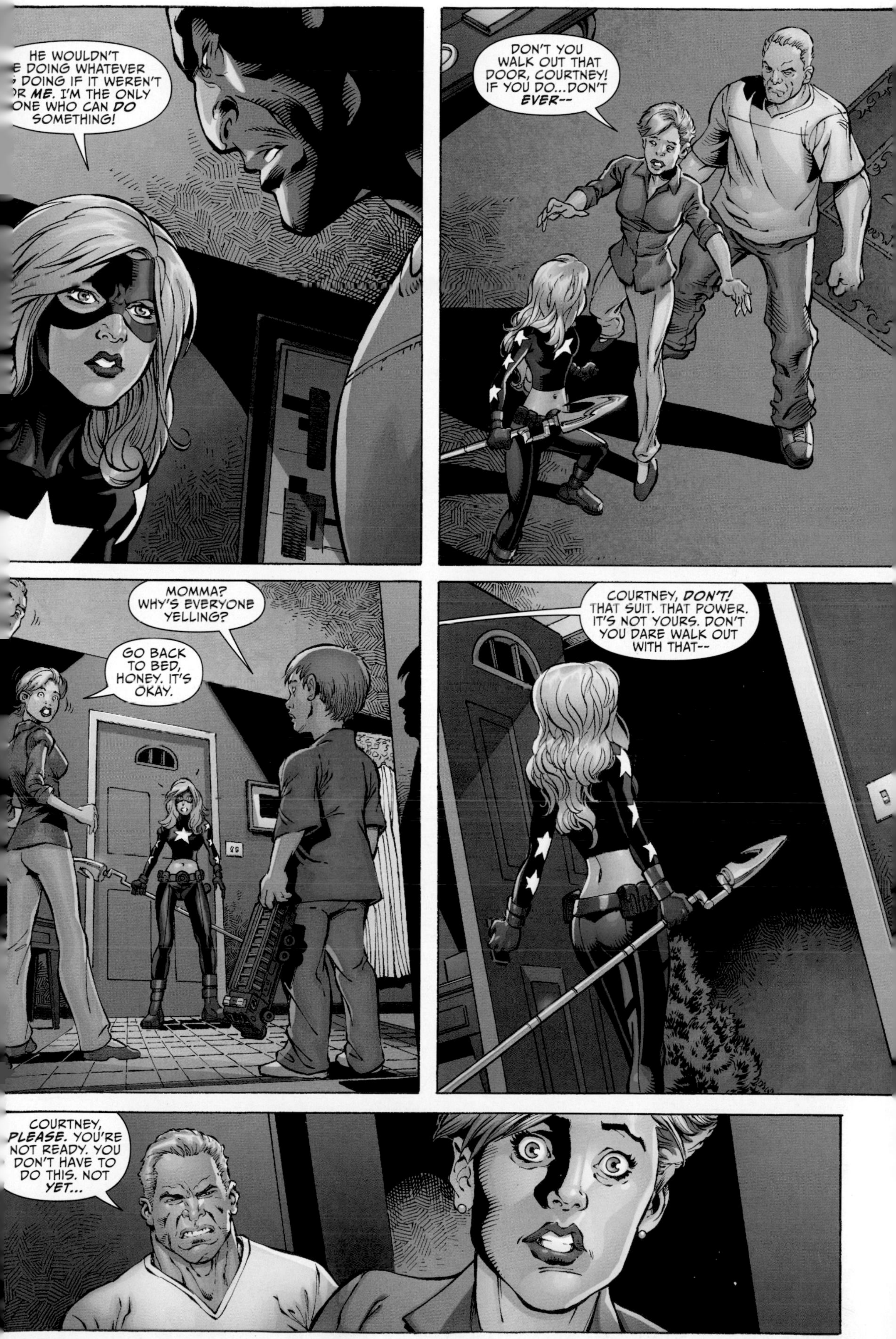
HE WOULDN'T
E DOING WHATEVER
G DOING IF IT WEREN'T
OR ME. I'M THE ONLY
ONE WHO CAN DO
SOMETHING!
DON'T YOU WALK OUT THAT DOOR, COURTNEY! IF YOU DO...DON'T EVER--
MOMMA? WHY'S EVERYONE YELLING?
GO BACK TO BED, HONEY. IT'S OKAY.
COURTNEY, DON'T! THAT SUIT. THAT POWER. IT'S NOT YOURS. DON'T YOU DARE WALK OUT WITH THAT--
COURTNEY, PLEASE. YOU'RE NOT READY. YOU DON'T HAVE TO DO THIS. NOT YET...

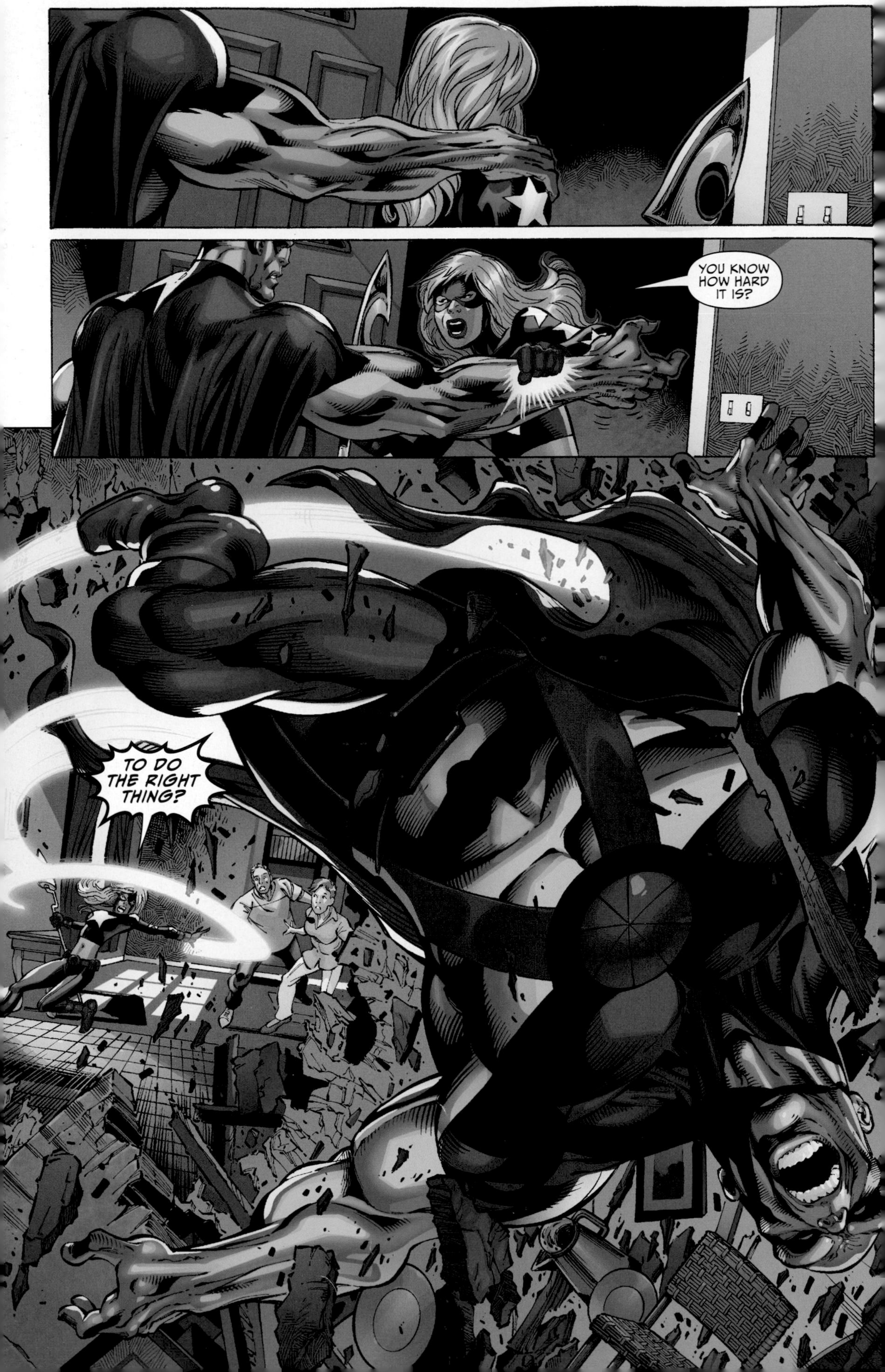
YOU KNOW HOW HARD IT IS?
TO DO THE RIGHT THING?

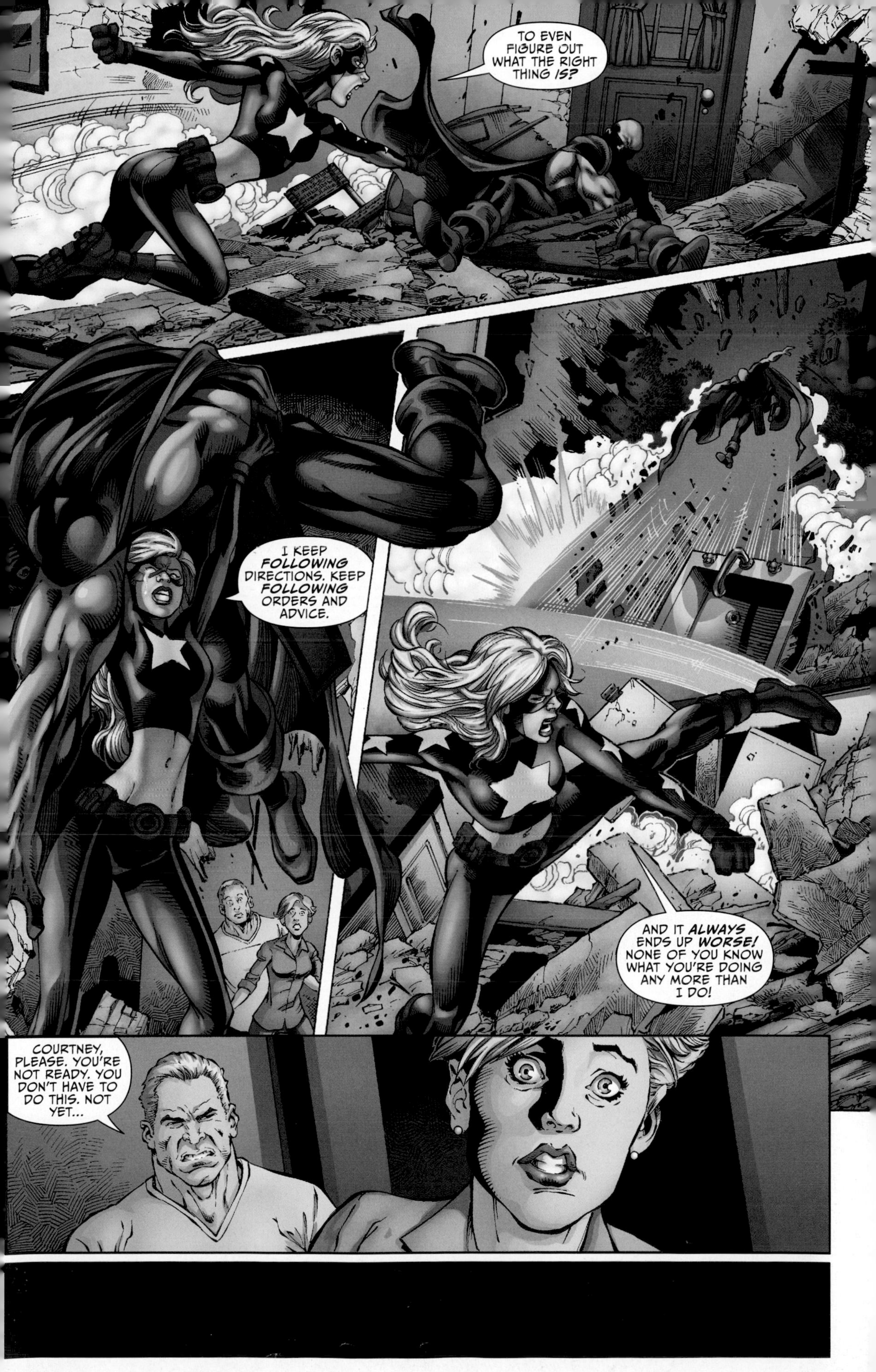
TO EVEN FIGURE OUT WHAT THE RIGHT THING *IS?*
I KEEP **FOLLOWING** DIRECTIONS. KEEP **FOLLOWING** ORDERS AND ADVICE.
AND IT ***ALWAYS*** ENDS UP ***WORSE!*** NONE OF YOU KNOW WHAT YOU'RE DOING ANY MORE THAN I DO!
COURTNEY, PLEASE. YOU'RE NOT READY. YOU DON'T HAVE TO DO THIS. NOT YET...

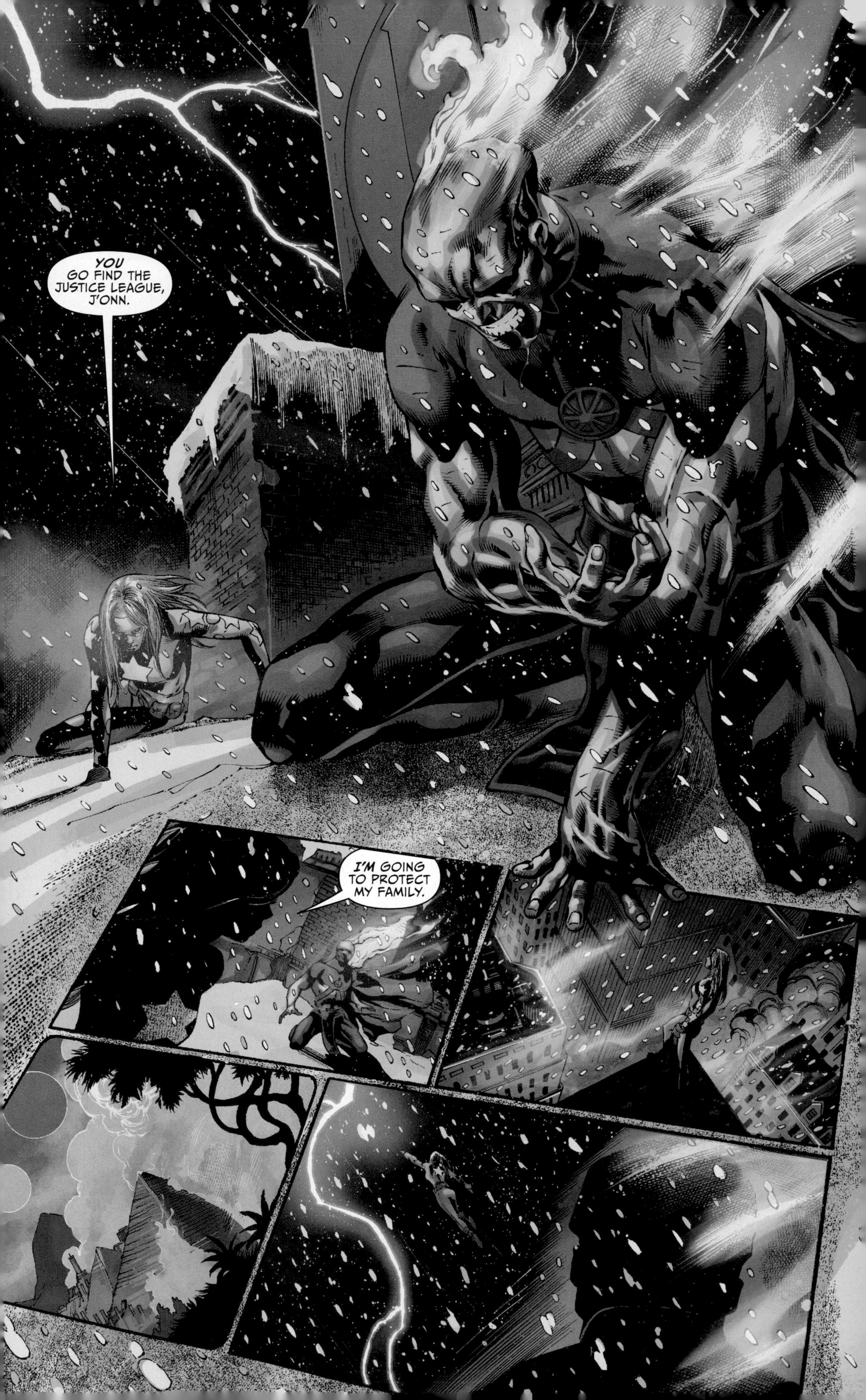
YOU GO FIND THE JUSTICE LEAGUE, J'ONN.
I'M GOING TO PROTECT MY FAMILY.

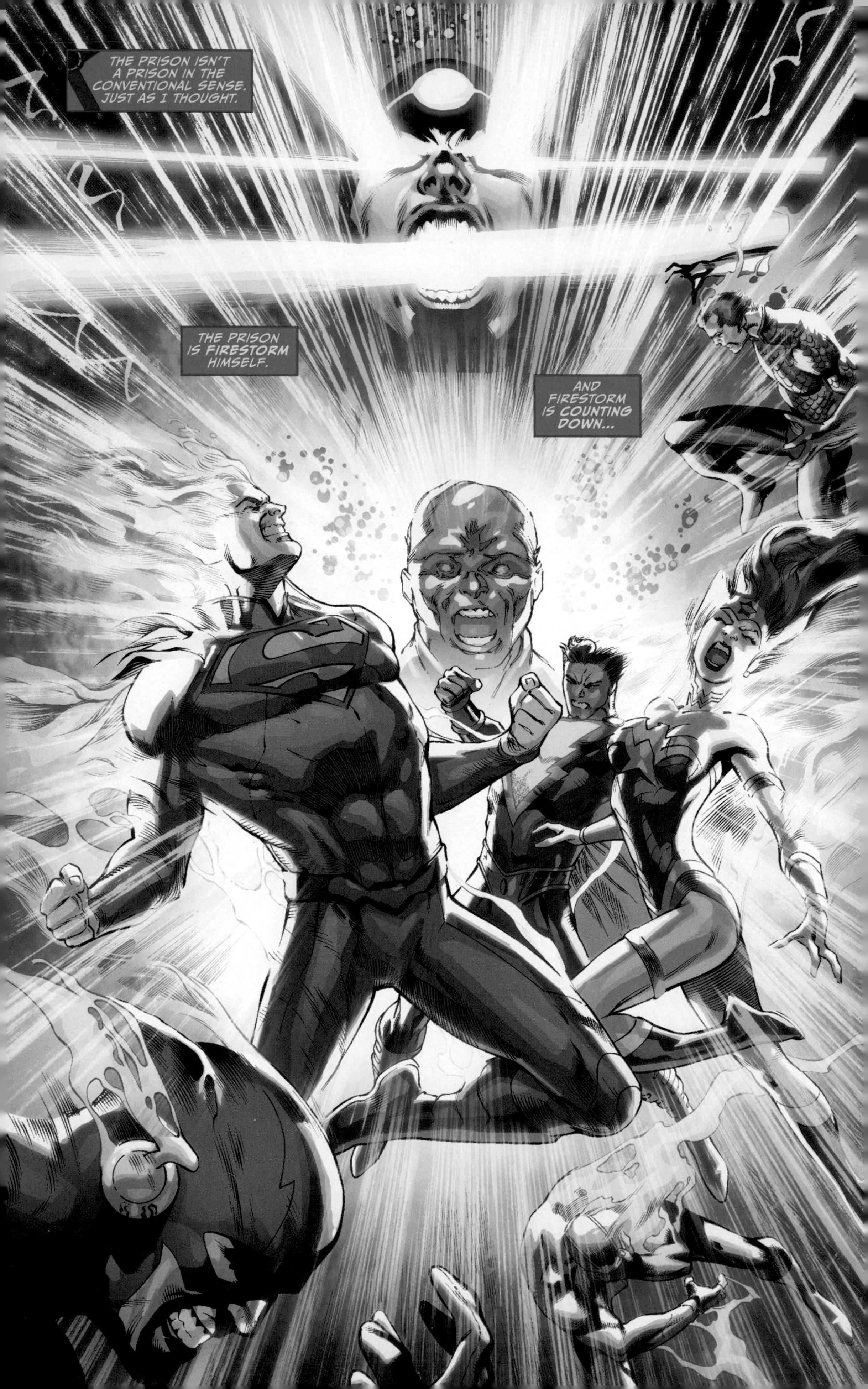
THE PRISON ISN'T A PRISON IN THE CONVENTIONAL SENSE. JUST AS I THOUGHT.
THE PRISON IS FIRESTORM HIMSELF.
AND FIRESTORM IS COUNTING DOWN...

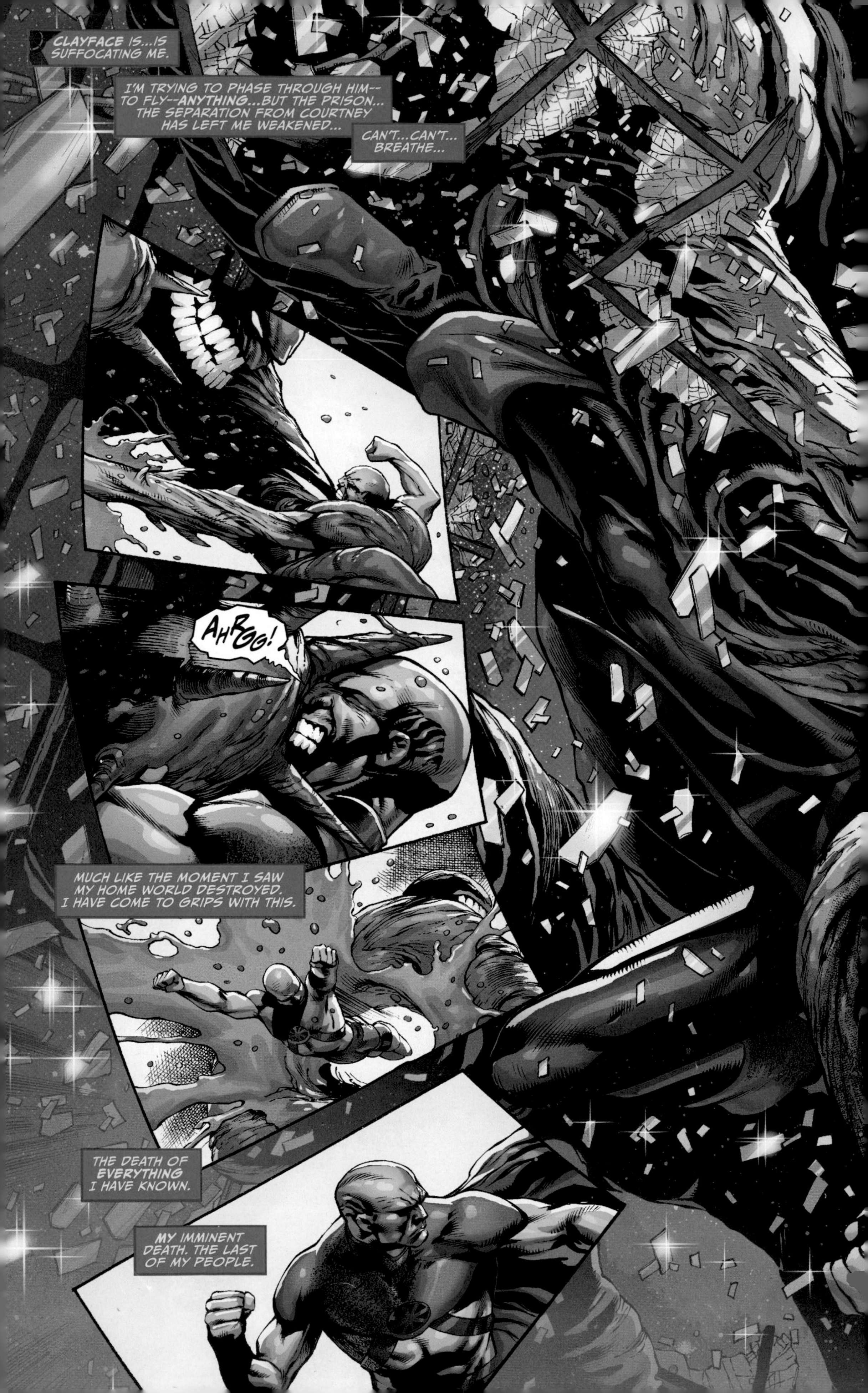
CLAYFACE IS...IS SUFFOCATING ME.
I'M TRYING TO PHASE THROUGH HIM--TO FLY--ANYTHING...BUT THE PRISON... THE SEPARATION FROM COURTNEY HAS LEFT ME WEAKENED...
CAN'T...CAN'T... BREATHE...
AHRGG!
MUCH LIKE THE MOMENT I SAW MY HOME WORLD DESTROYED. I HAVE COME TO GRIPS WITH THIS.
THE DEATH OF EVERYTHING I HAVE KNOWN.
MY IMMINENT DEATH. THE LAST OF MY PEOPLE.

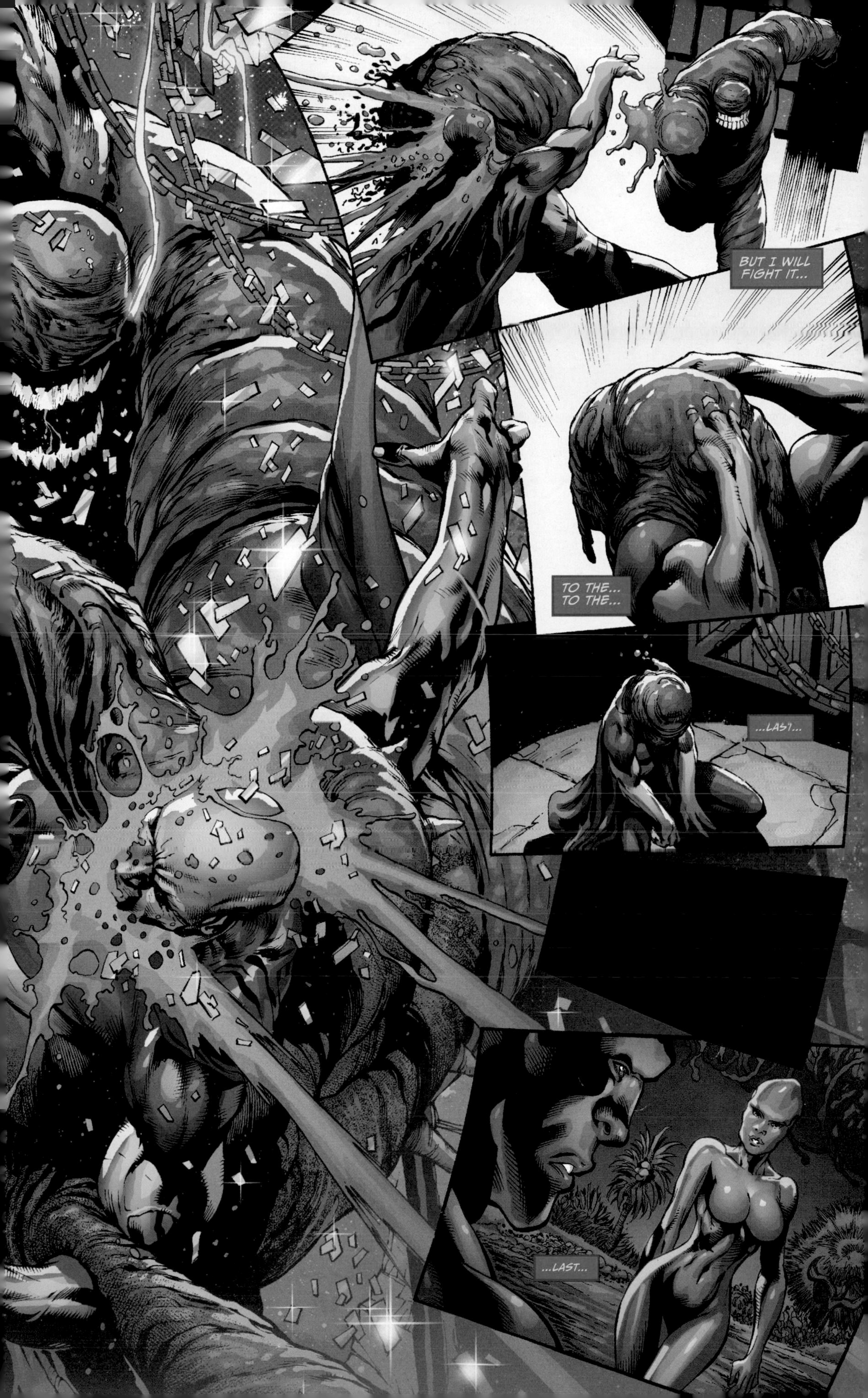
BUT I WILL
FIGHT IT...
TO THE...
TO THE...
...LAST...
...LAST...

MATT KINDT *writer*
TOM DERENICK and EDDY BARROWS *pencils*
DERENICK, EBER FERREIRA,
RUY JOSE & ALLEN MARTINEZ *inks*
HI-FI *colors*
ROB LEIGH *letters*
BARROWS & FERREIRA with MARCELO MAIOLO *cover*

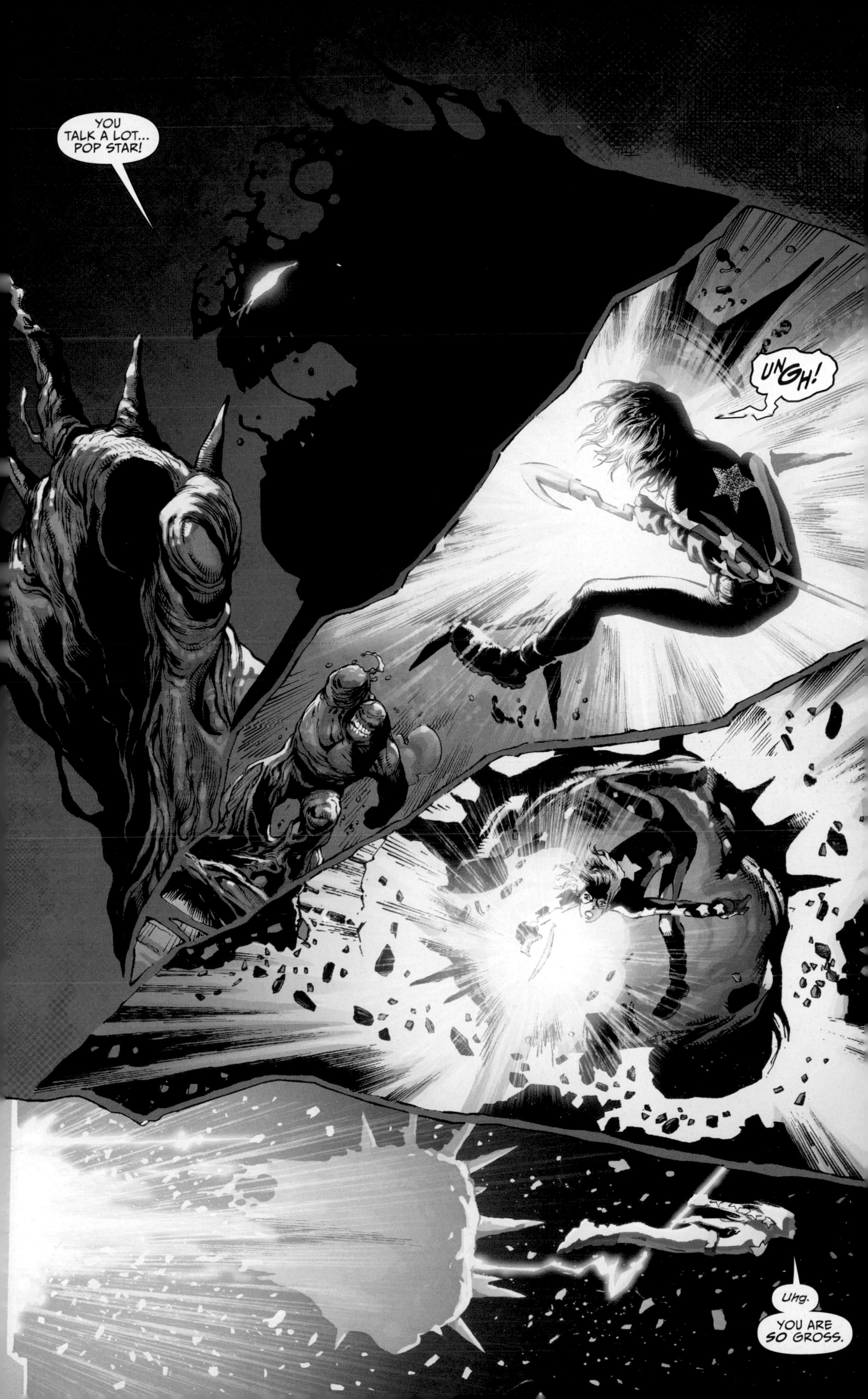
YOU TALK A LOT... POP STAR!
UNGH!
Uhg.
YOU ARE SO GROSS.

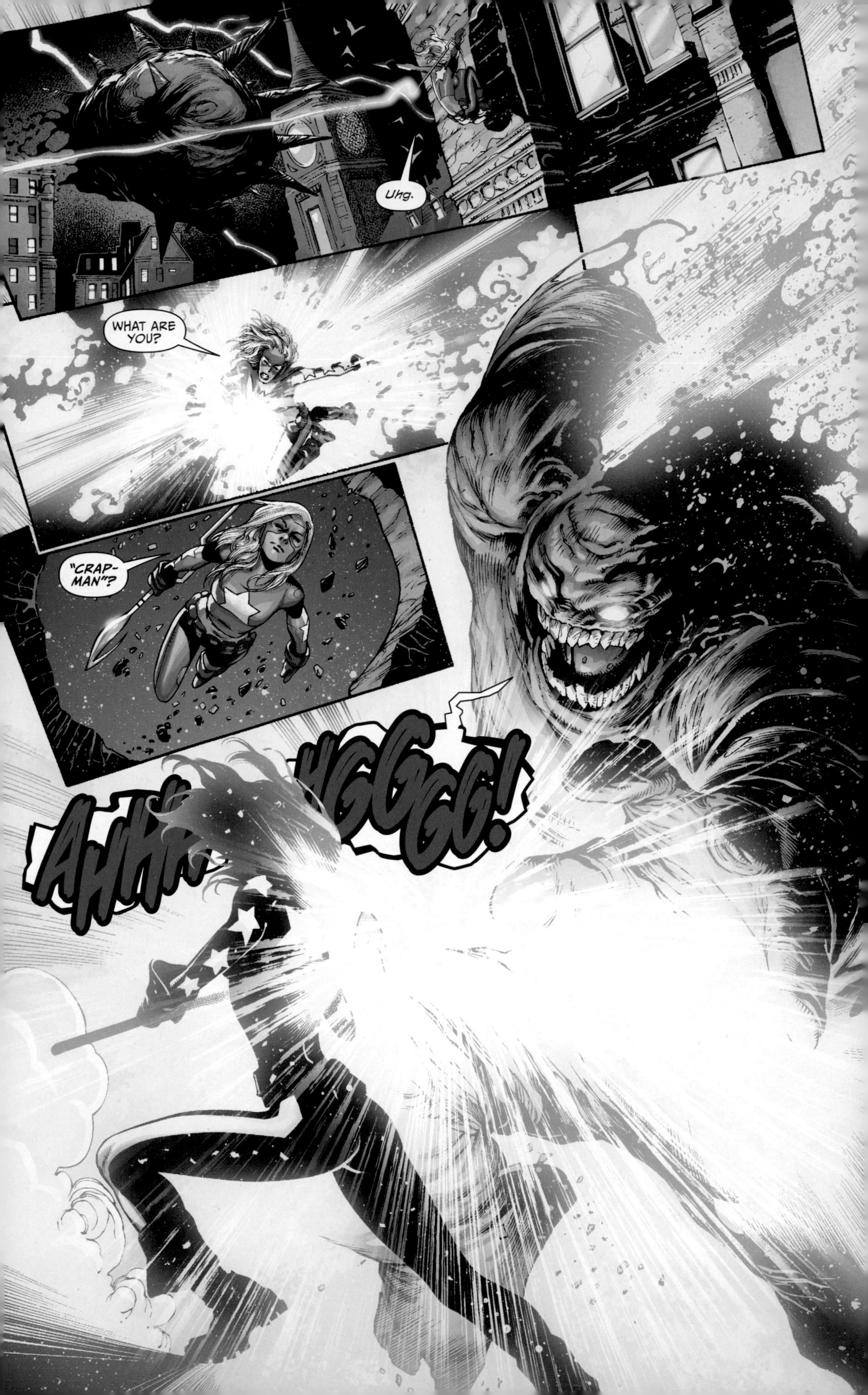
Uhg.
WHAT ARE YOU?
"CRAP-MAN"?
HGGGG!

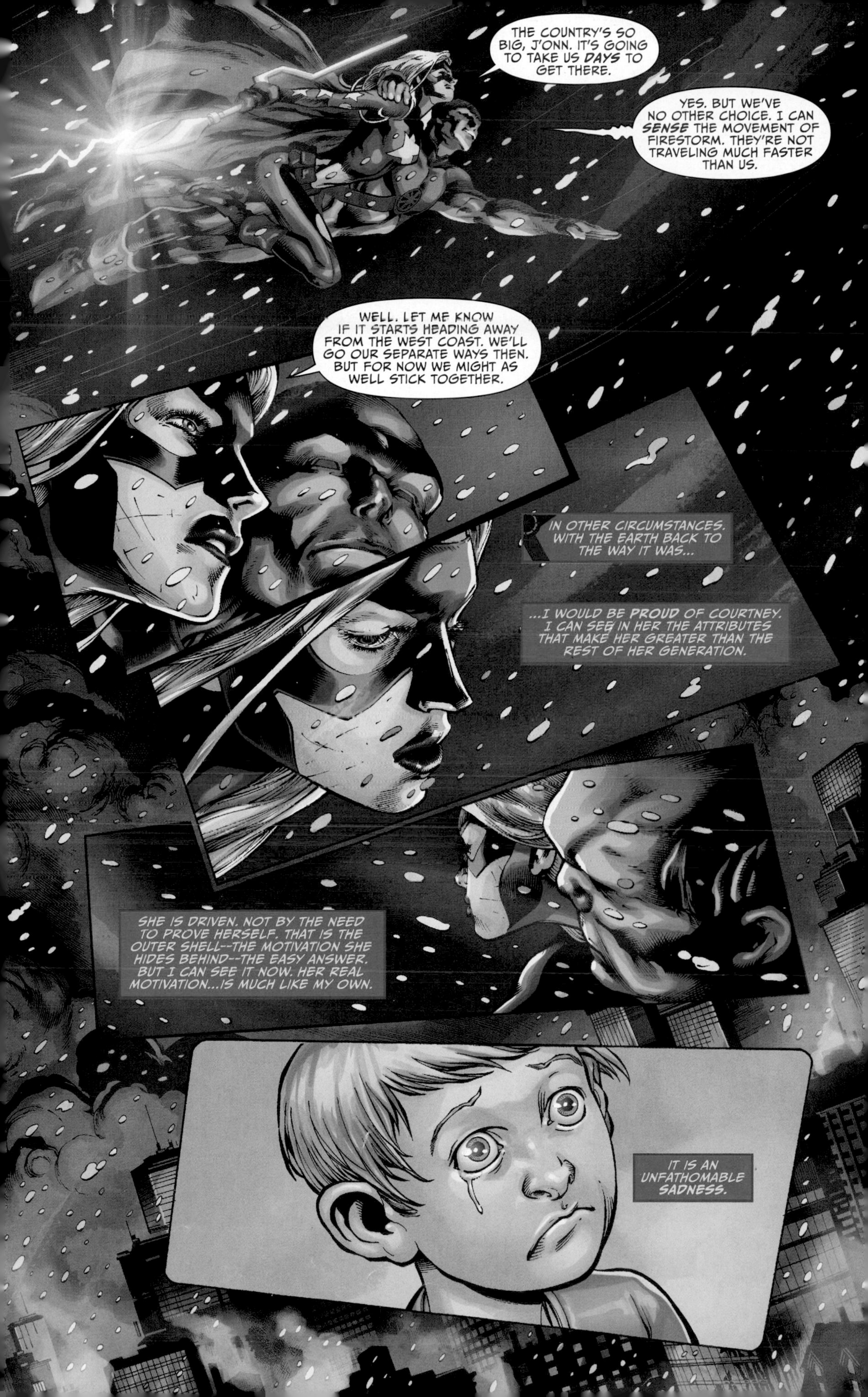
THE COUNTRY'S SO BIG, J'ONN. IT'S GOING TO TAKE US DAYS TO GET THERE.
YES. BUT WE'VE NO OTHER CHOICE. I CAN SENSE THE MOVEMENT OF FIRESTORM. THEY'RE NOT TRAVELING MUCH FASTER THAN US.
WELL. LET ME KNOW IF IT STARTS HEADING AWAY FROM THE WEST COAST. WE'LL GO OUR SEPARATE WAYS THEN. BUT FOR NOW WE MIGHT AS WELL STICK TOGETHER.
IN OTHER CIRCUMSTANCES. WITH THE EARTH BACK TO THE WAY IT WAS...
...I WOULD BE PROUD OF COURTNEY. I CAN SEE IN HER THE ATTRIBUTES THAT MAKE HER GREATER THAN THE REST OF HER GENERATION.
SHE IS DRIVEN. NOT BY THE NEED TO PROVE HERSELF. THAT IS THE OUTER SHELL--THE MOTIVATION SHE HIDES BEHIND--THE EASY ANSWER. BUT I CAN SEE IT NOW. HER REAL MOTIVATION...IS MUCH LIKE MY OWN.
IT IS AN UNFATHOMABLE SADNESS.

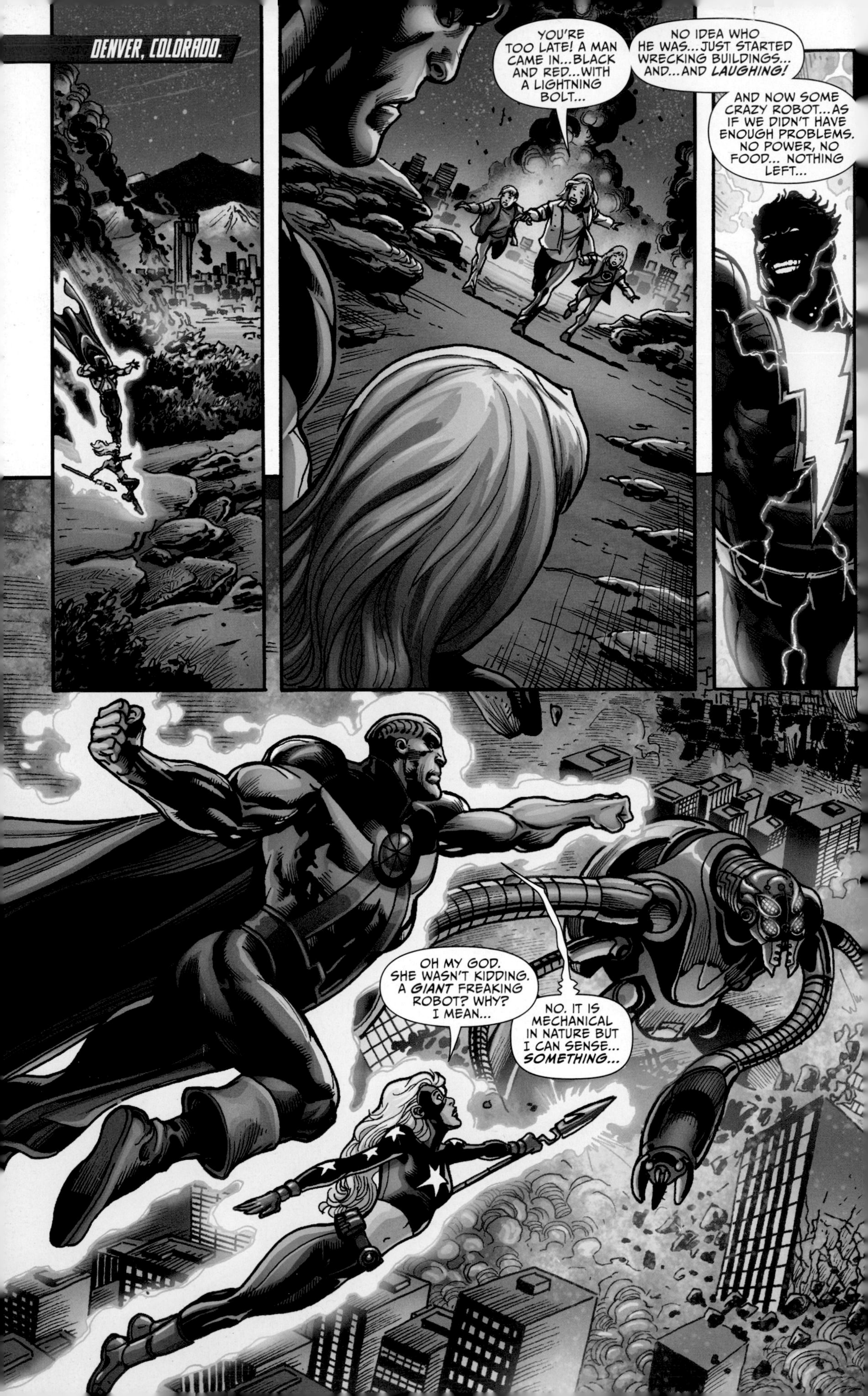
DENVER, COLORADO.
YOU'RE TOO LATE! A MAN CAME IN...BLACK AND RED...WITH A LIGHTNING BOLT...
NO IDEA WHO HE WAS...JUST STARTED WRECKING BUILDINGS... AND...AND *LAUGHING!*
AND NOW SOME CRAZY ROBOT...AS IF WE DIDN'T HAVE ENOUGH PROBLEMS. NO POWER, NO FOOD... NOTHING LEFT...
OH MY GOD. SHE WASN'T KIDDING. A *GIANT* FREAKING ROBOT? WHY? I MEAN...
NO. IT IS MECHANICAL IN NATURE BUT I CAN SENSE... *SOMETHING...*

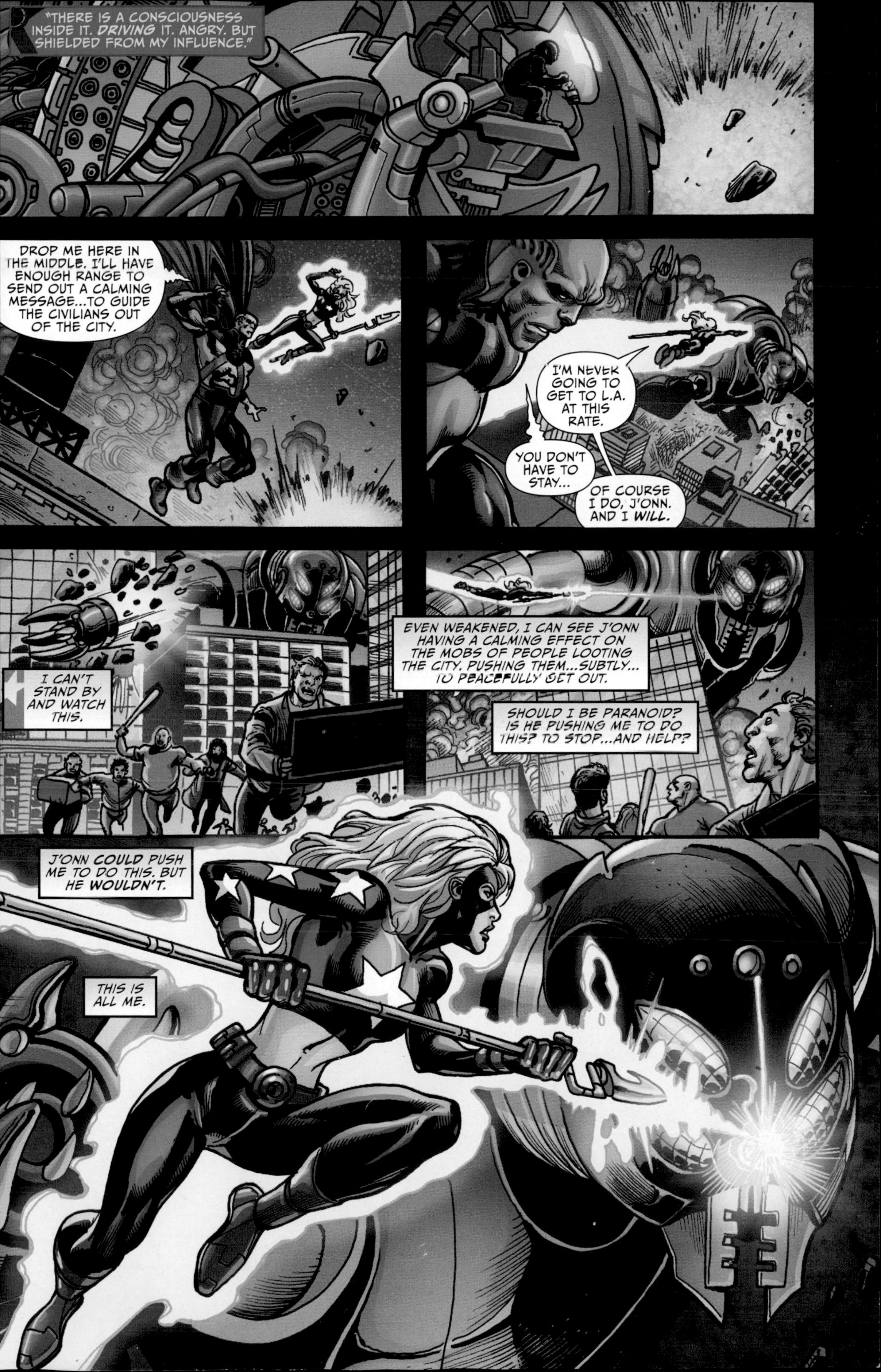
"THERE IS A CONSCIOUSNESS INSIDE IT. DRIVING IT. ANGRY. BUT SHIELDED FROM MY INFLUENCE."
DROP ME HERE IN THE MIDDLE. I'LL HAVE ENOUGH RANGE TO SEND OUT A CALMING MESSAGE...TO GUIDE THE CIVILIANS OUT OF THE CITY.
I'M NEVER GOING TO GET TO L.A. AT THIS RATE.
YOU DON'T HAVE TO STAY...
OF COURSE I DO, J'ONN. AND I WILL.
I CAN'T STAND BY AND WATCH THIS.
EVEN WEAKENED, I CAN SEE J'ONN HAVING A CALMING EFFECT ON THE MOBS OF PEOPLE LOOTING THE CITY. PUSHING THEM...SUBTLY... TO PEACEFULLY GET OUT.
SHOULD I BE PARANOID? IS HE PUSHING ME TO DO THIS? TO STOP...AND HELP?
J'ONN COULD PUSH ME TO DO THIS. BUT HE WOULDN'T.
THIS IS ALL ME.

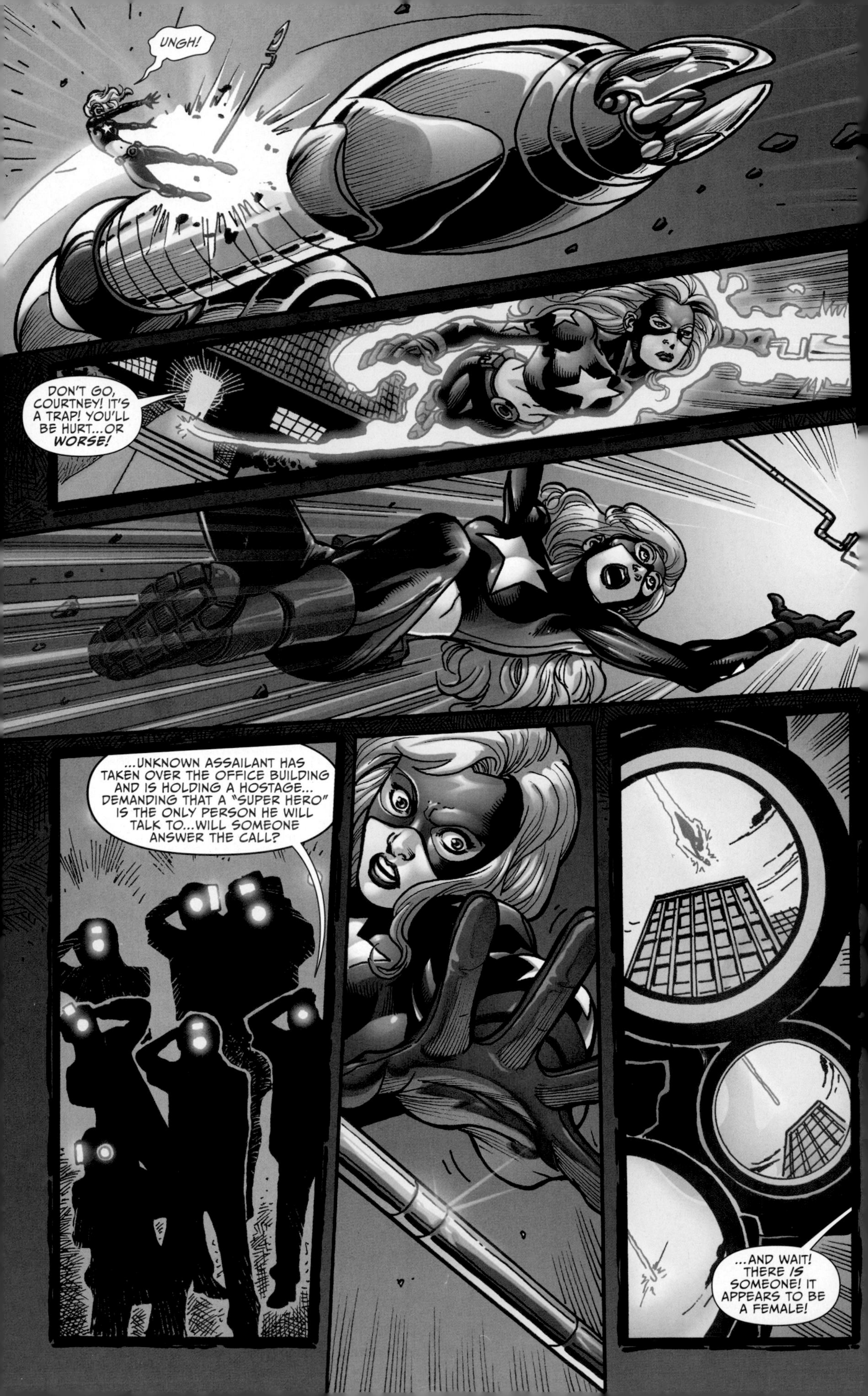
UNGH!
DON'T GO, COURTNEY! IT'S A TRAP! YOU'LL BE HURT...OR WORSE!
...UNKNOWN ASSAILANT HAS TAKEN OVER THE OFFICE BUILDING AND IS HOLDING A HOSTAGE... DEMANDING THAT A "SUPER HERO" IS THE ONLY PERSON HE WILL TALK TO...WILL SOMEONE ANSWER THE CALL?
...AND WAIT! THERE IS SOMEONE! IT APPEARS TO BE A FEMALE!

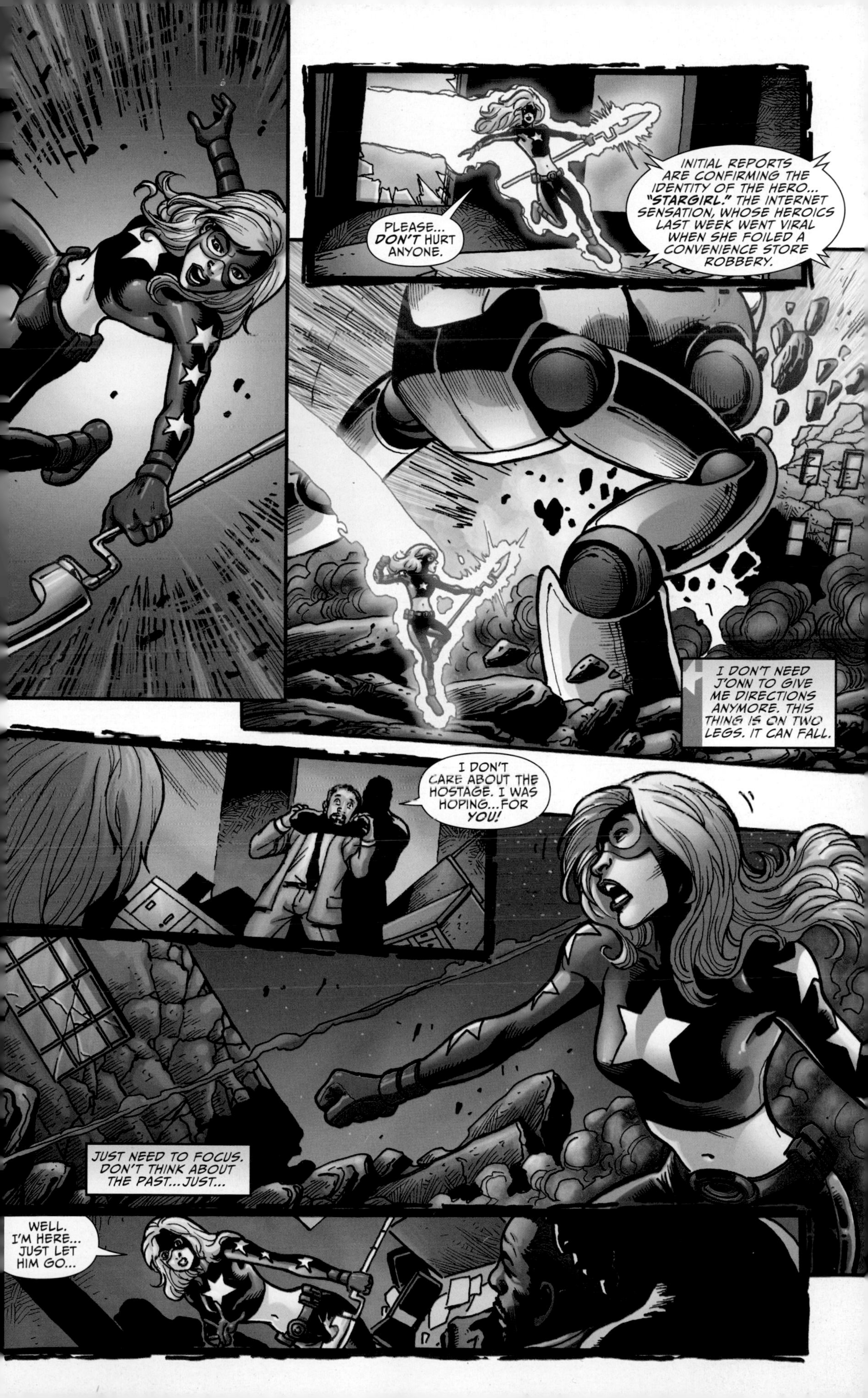
PLEASE... DON'T HURT ANYONE.
INITIAL REPORTS ARE CONFIRMING THE IDENTITY OF THE HERO... "STARGIRL." THE INTERNET SENSATION, WHOSE HEROICS LAST WEEK WENT VIRAL WHEN SHE FOILED A CONVENIENCE STORE ROBBERY.
I DON'T NEED J'ONN TO GIVE ME DIRECTIONS ANYMORE. THIS THING IS ON TWO LEGS. IT CAN FALL.
I DON'T CARE ABOUT THE HOSTAGE. I WAS HOPING...FOR YOU!
JUST NEED TO FOCUS. DON'T THINK ABOUT THE PAST...JUST...
WELL. I'M HERE... JUST LET HIM GO...

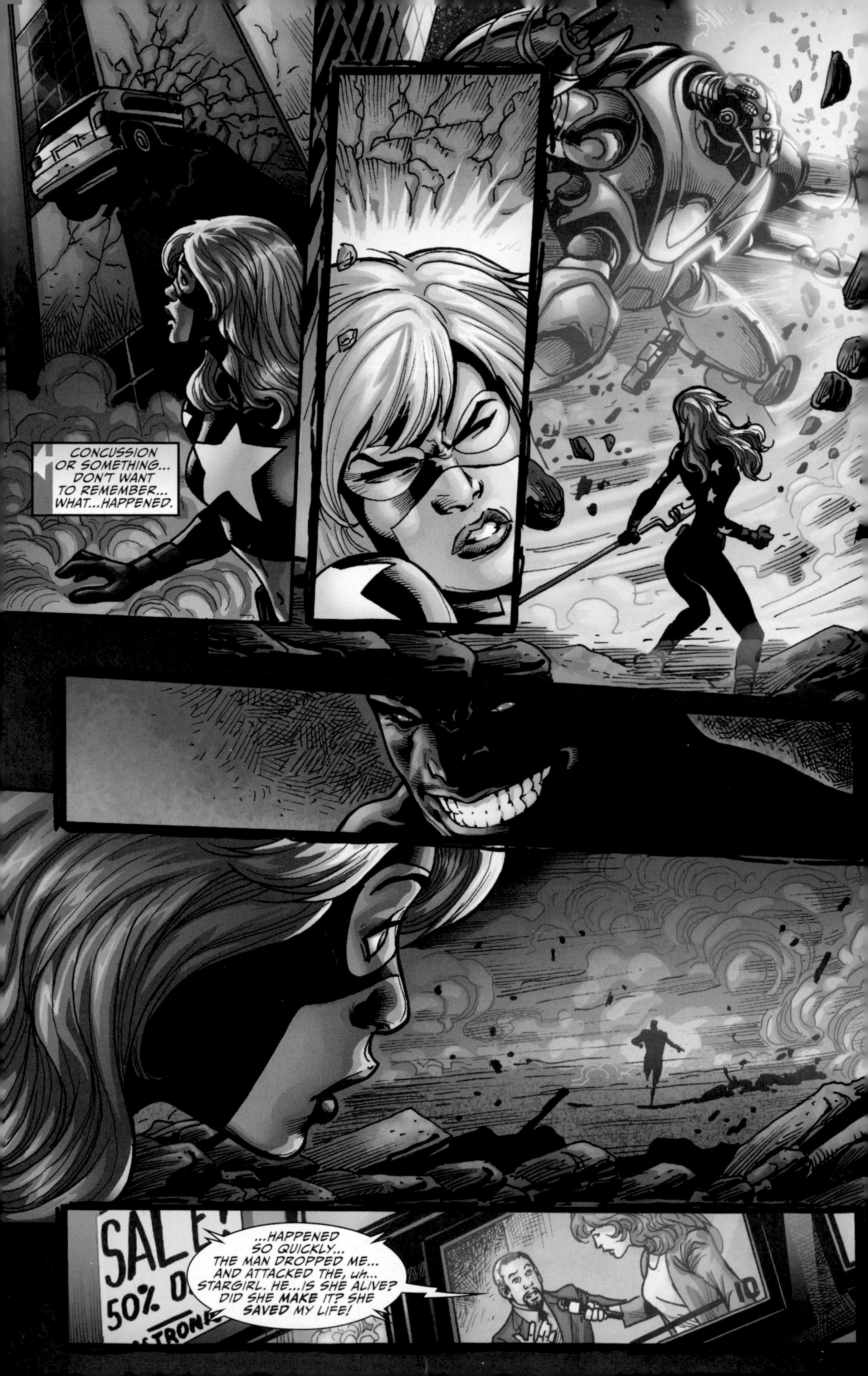
CONCUSSION OR SOMETHING... DON'T WANT TO REMEMBER... WHAT...HAPPENED.
...HAPPENED SO QUICKLY... THE MAN DROPPED ME... AND ATTACKED THE, uh... STARGIRL. HE...IS SHE ALIVE? DID SHE MAKE IT? SHE SAVED MY LIFE!
SALE!
50%

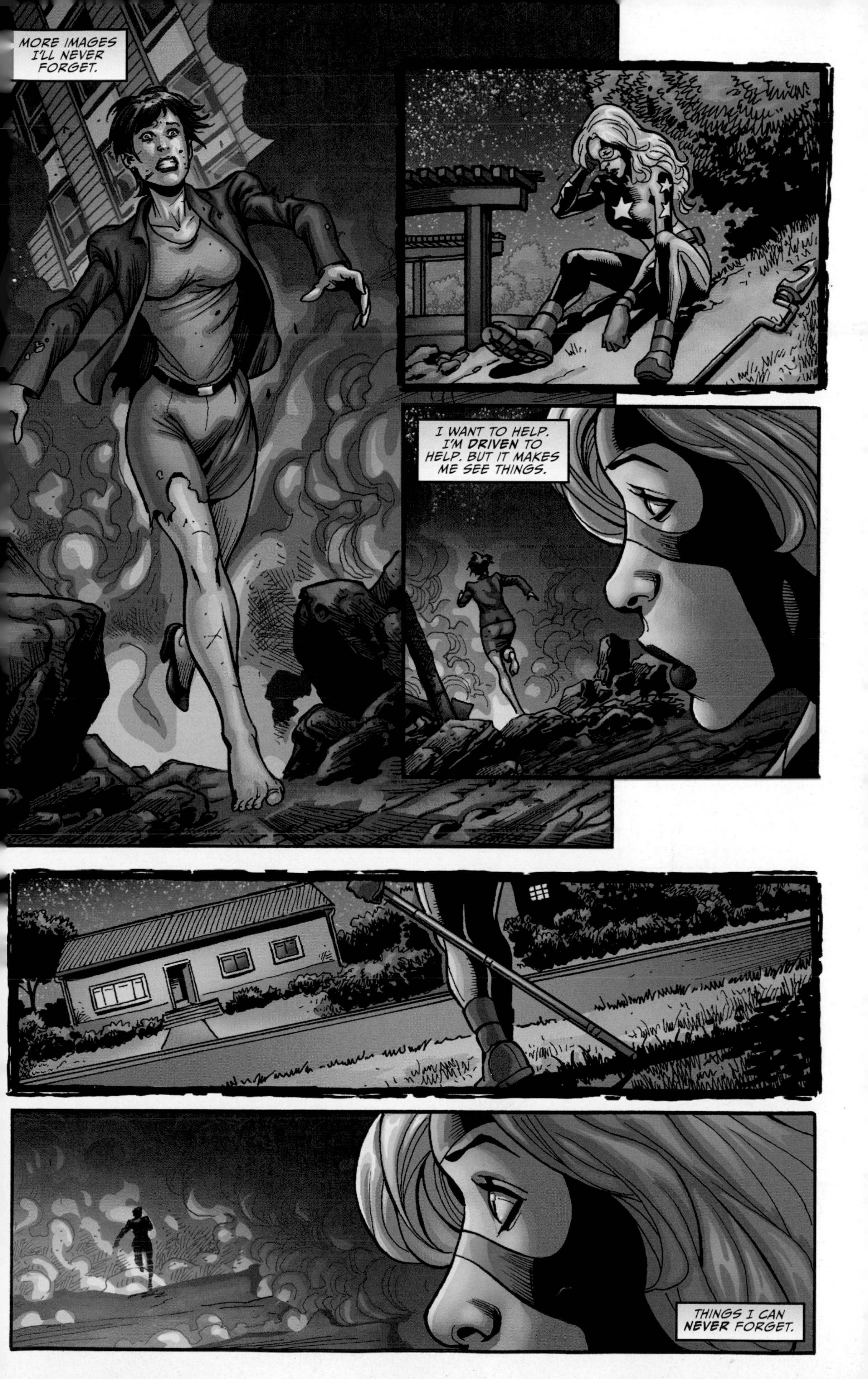
MORE IMAGES I'LL NEVER FORGET.
I WANT TO HELP. I'M DRIVEN TO HELP. BUT IT MAKES ME SEE THINGS.
THINGS I CAN NEVER FORGET.

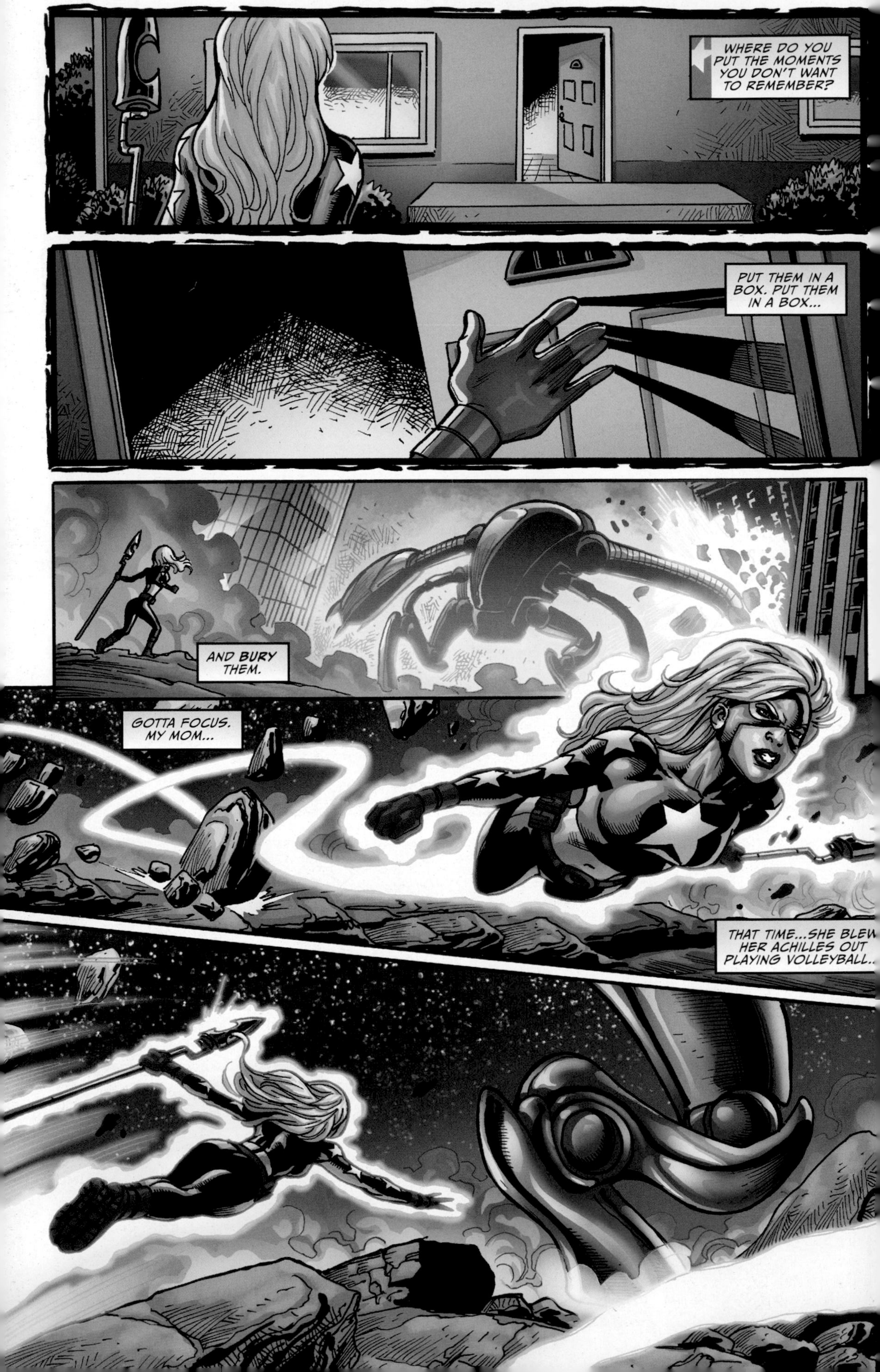
WHERE DO YOU PUT THE MOMENTS YOU DON'T WANT TO REMEMBER?
PUT THEM IN A BOX. PUT THEM IN A BOX...
AND BURY THEM.
GOTTA FOCUS. MY MOM...
THAT TIME...SHE BLEW HER ACHILLES OUT PLAYING VOLLEYBALL...

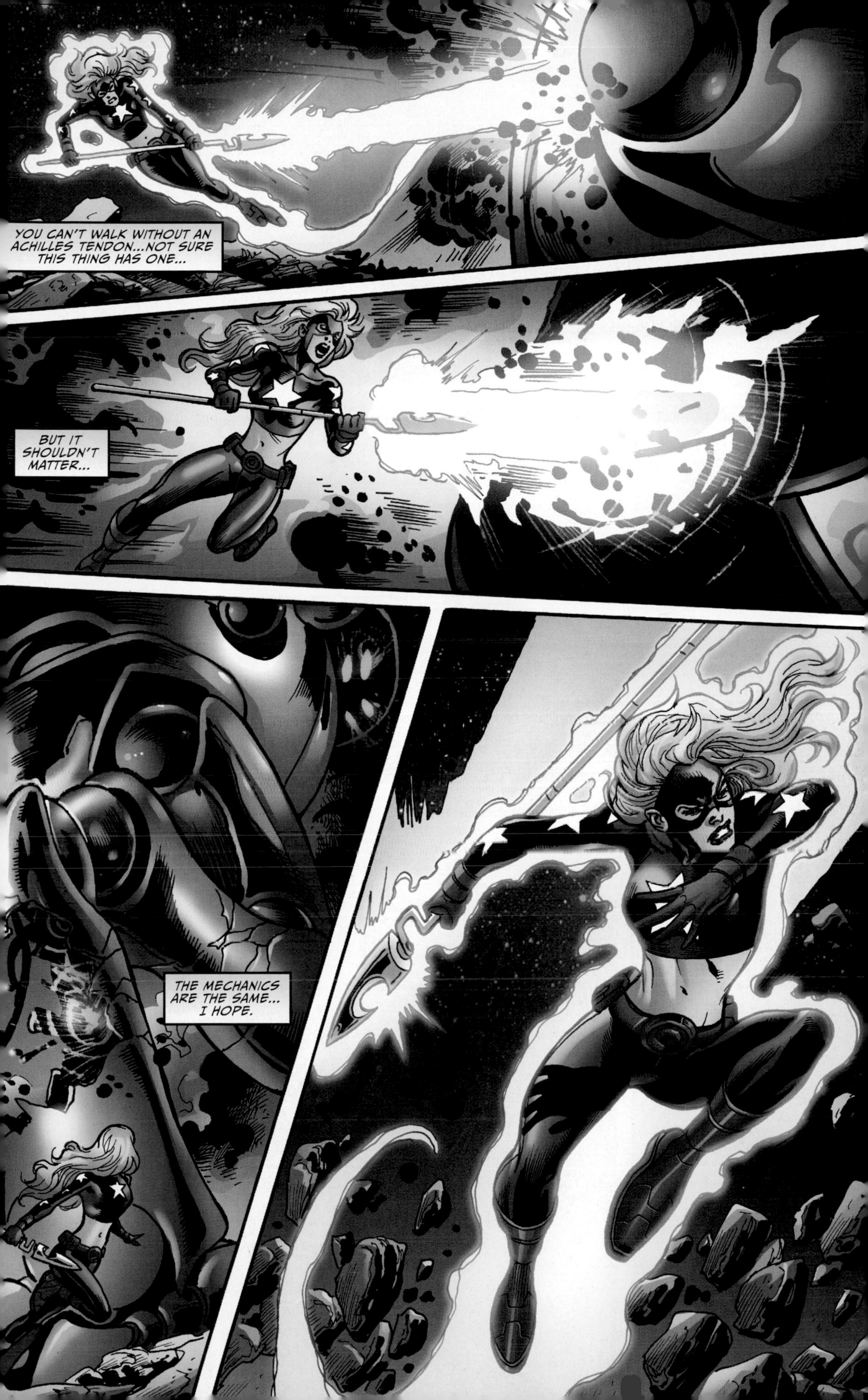

YOU CAN'T WALK WITHOUT AN ACHILLES TENDON...NOT SURE THIS THING HAS ONE...
BUT IT SHOULDN'T MATTER...
THE MECHANICS ARE THE SAME... I HOPE.

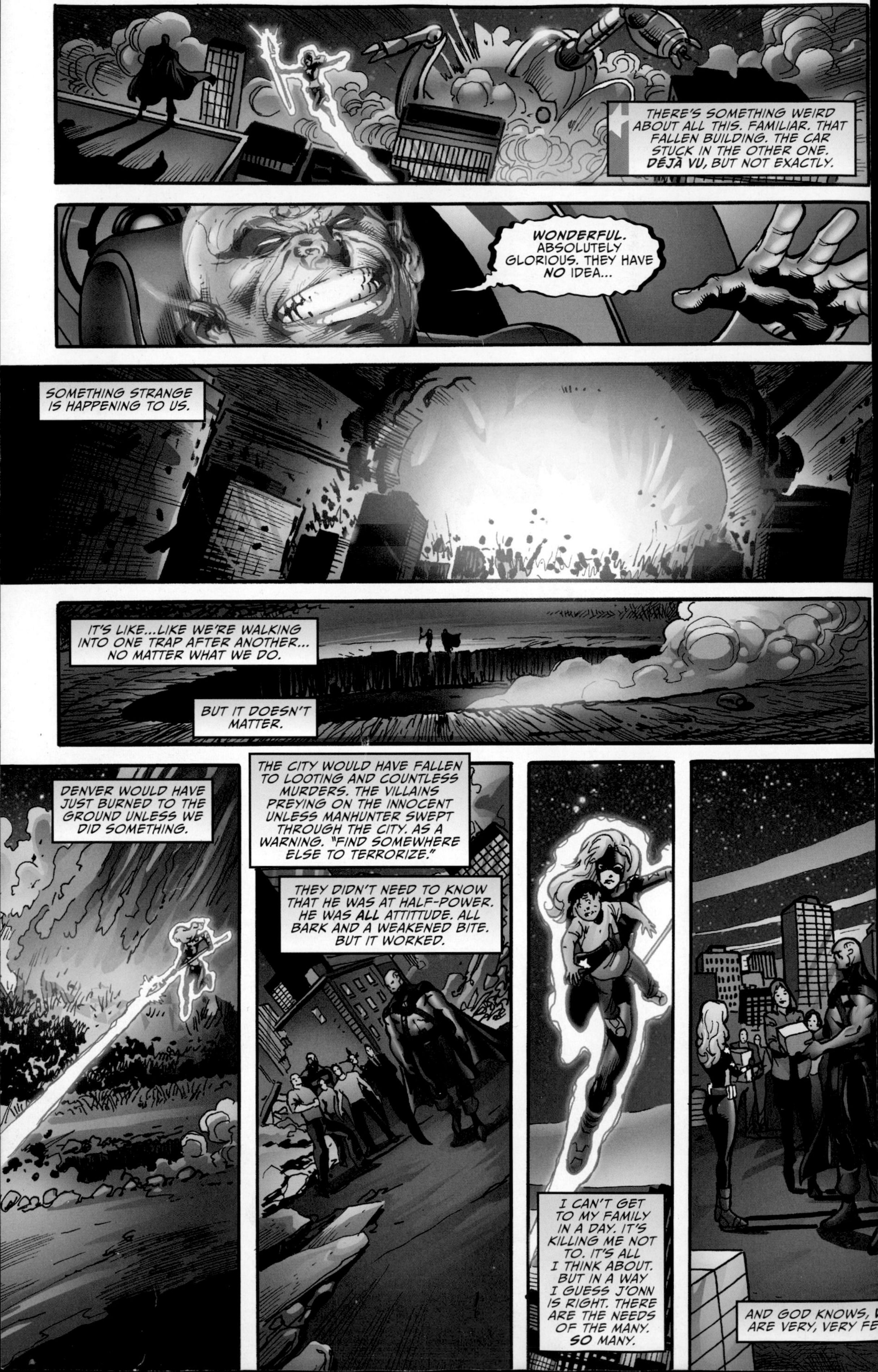
THERE'S SOMETHING WEIRD ABOUT ALL THIS. FAMILIAR. THAT FALLEN BUILDING. THE CAR STUCK IN THE OTHER ONE. **DÉJÀ VU,** BUT NOT EXACTLY.
WONDERFUL. ABSOLUTELY GLORIOUS. THEY HAVE **NO** IDEA...
SOMETHING STRANGE IS HAPPENING TO US.
IT'S LIKE...LIKE WE'RE WALKING INTO ONE TRAP AFTER ANOTHER... NO MATTER WHAT WE DO.
BUT IT DOESN'T MATTER.
DENVER WOULD HAVE JUST BURNED TO THE GROUND UNLESS WE DID SOMETHING.
THE CITY WOULD HAVE FALLEN TO LOOTING AND COUNTLESS MURDERS. THE VILLAINS PREYING ON THE INNOCENT UNLESS MANHUNTER SWEPT THROUGH THE CITY. AS A WARNING. "FIND SOMEWHERE ELSE TO TERRORIZE."
THEY DIDN'T NEED TO KNOW THAT HE WAS AT HALF-POWER. HE WAS **ALL** ATTITUDE. ALL BARK AND A WEAKENED BITE. BUT IT WORKED.
I CAN'T GET TO MY FAMILY IN A DAY. IT'S KILLING ME NOT TO. IT'S ALL I THINK ABOUT. BUT IN A WAY I GUESS J'ONN IS RIGHT. THERE ARE THE NEEDS OF THE MANY. **SO** MANY.
AND GOD KNOWS,
ARE VERY, VERY FE

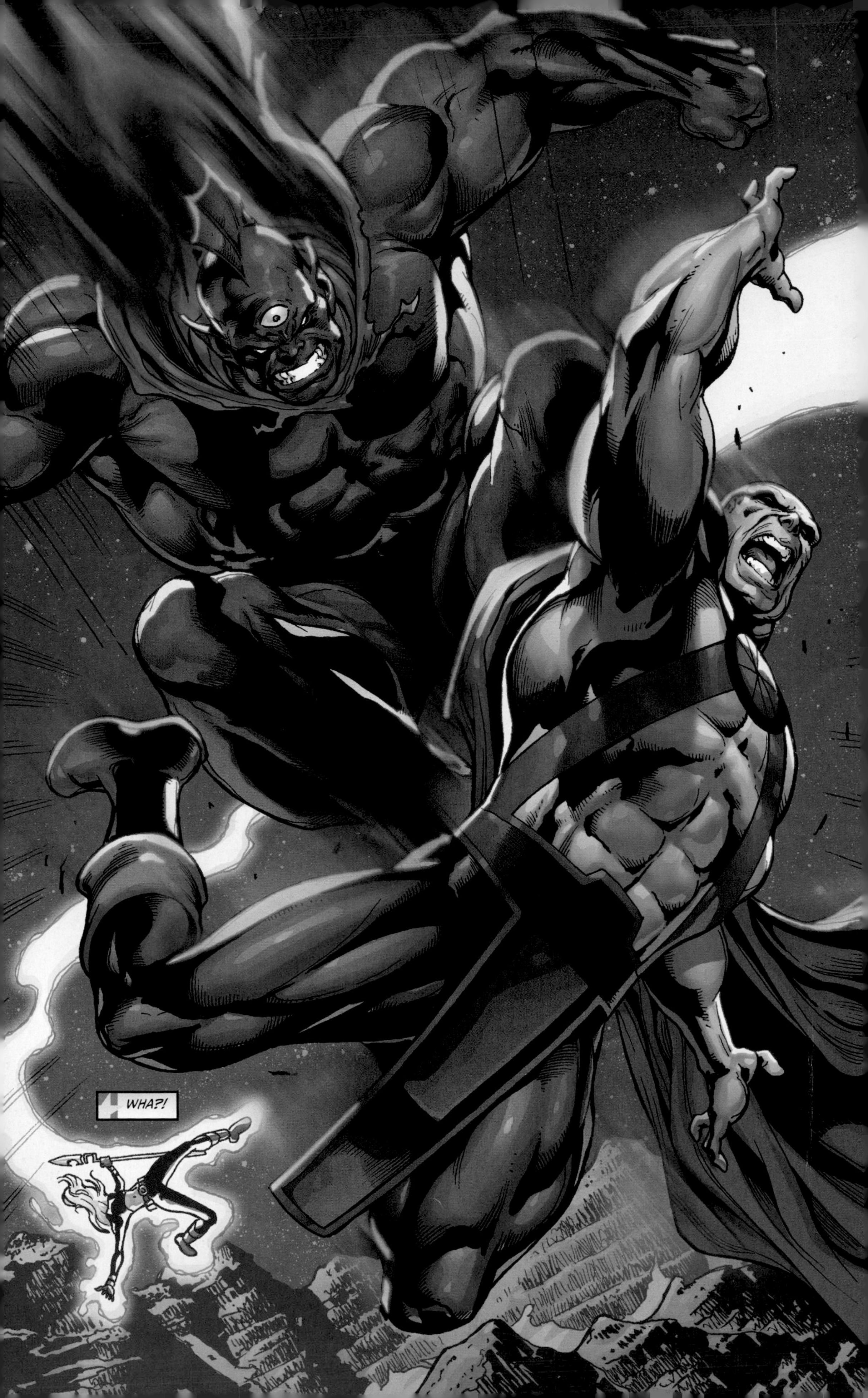
WHA?!

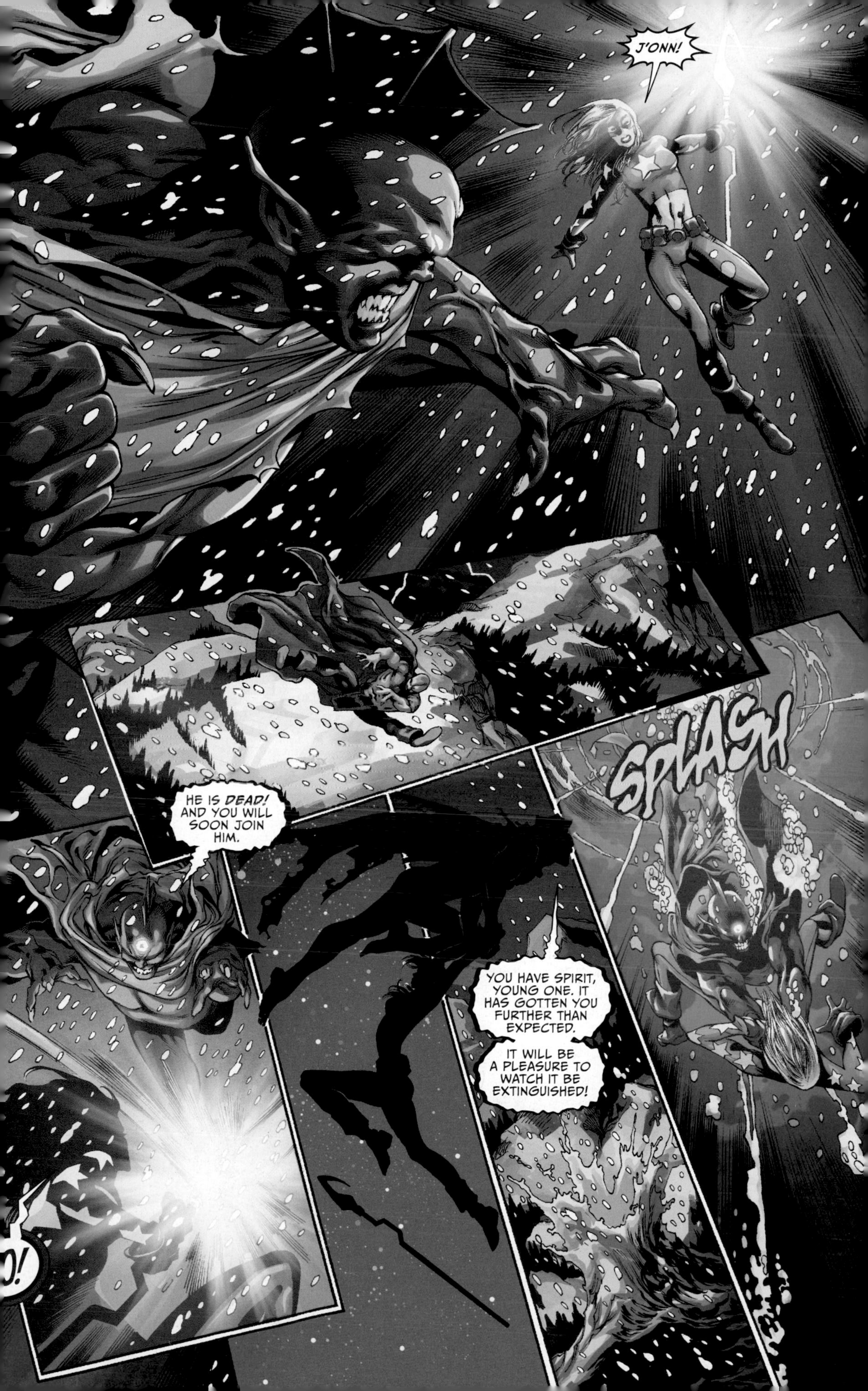
J'ONN!
HE IS DEAD! AND YOU WILL SOON JOIN HIM.
SPLASH
YOU HAVE SPIRIT, YOUNG ONE. IT HAS GOTTEN YOU FURTHER THAN EXPECTED.
IT WILL BE A PLEASURE TO WATCH IT BE EXTINGUISHED!

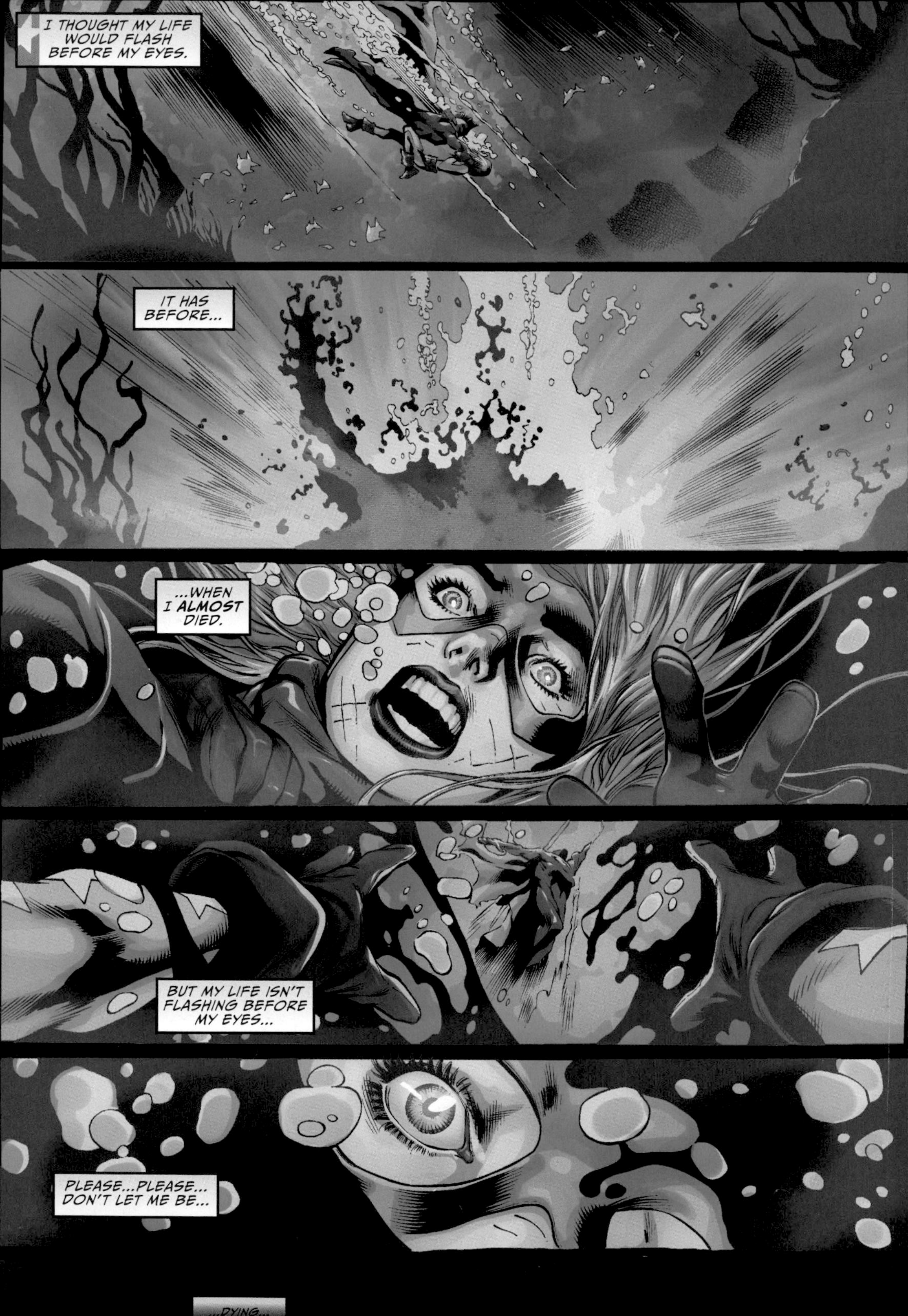
I THOUGHT MY LIFE WOULD FLASH BEFORE MY EYES.
IT HAS BEFORE...
...WHEN I ALMOST DIED.
BUT MY LIFE ISN'T FLASHING BEFORE MY EYES...
PLEASE...PLEASE... DON'T LET ME BE...
...DYING...

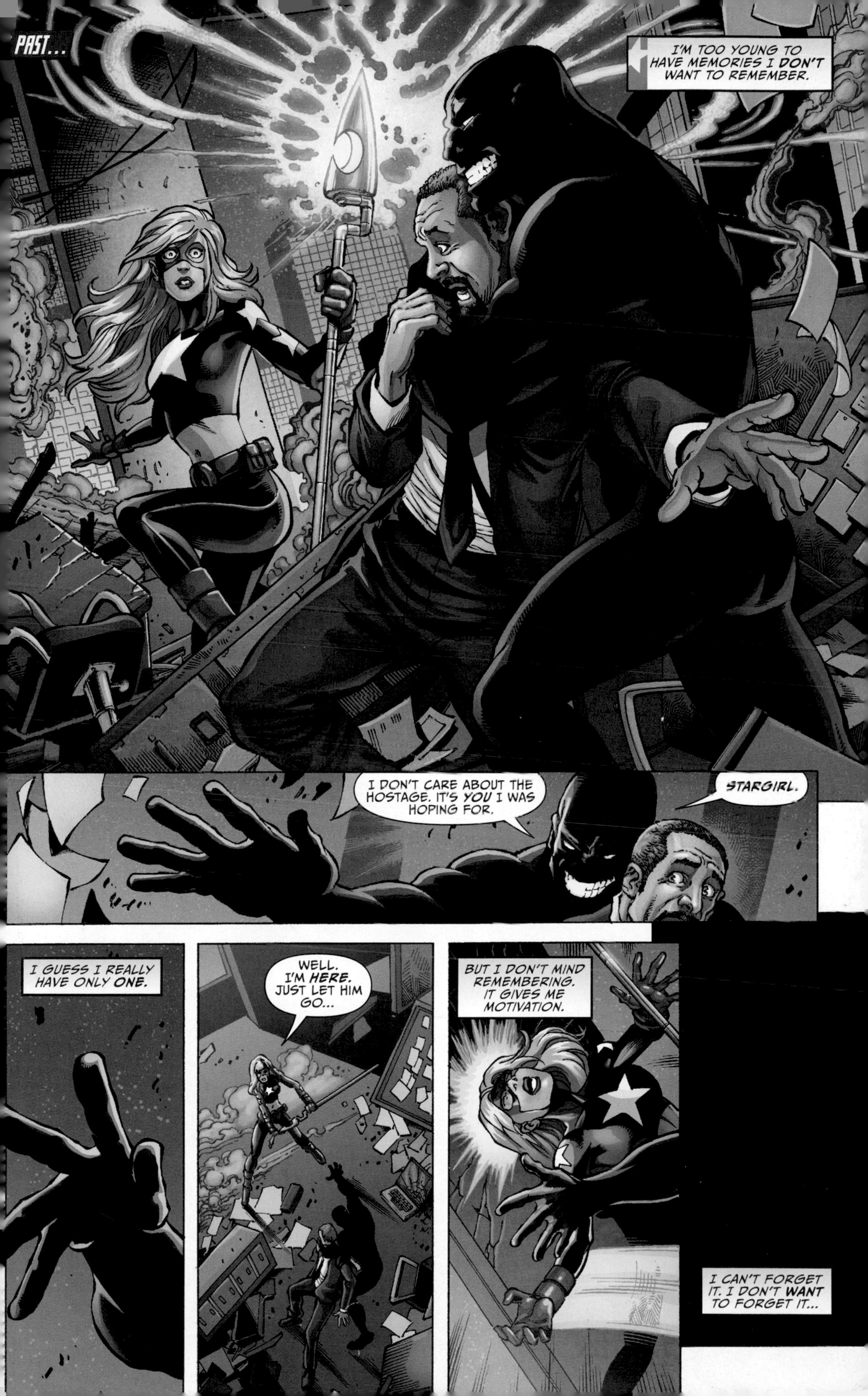
PAST...
I'M TOO YOUNG TO HAVE MEMORIES I DON'T WANT TO REMEMBER.
I DON'T CARE ABOUT THE HOSTAGE. IT'S YOU I WAS HOPING FOR.
STARGIRL.
I GUESS I REALLY HAVE ONLY ONE.
WELL. I'M HERE. JUST LET HIM GO...
BUT I DON'T MIND REMEMBERING. IT GIVES ME MOTIVATION.
I CAN'T FORGET IT. I DON'T WANT TO FORGET IT...

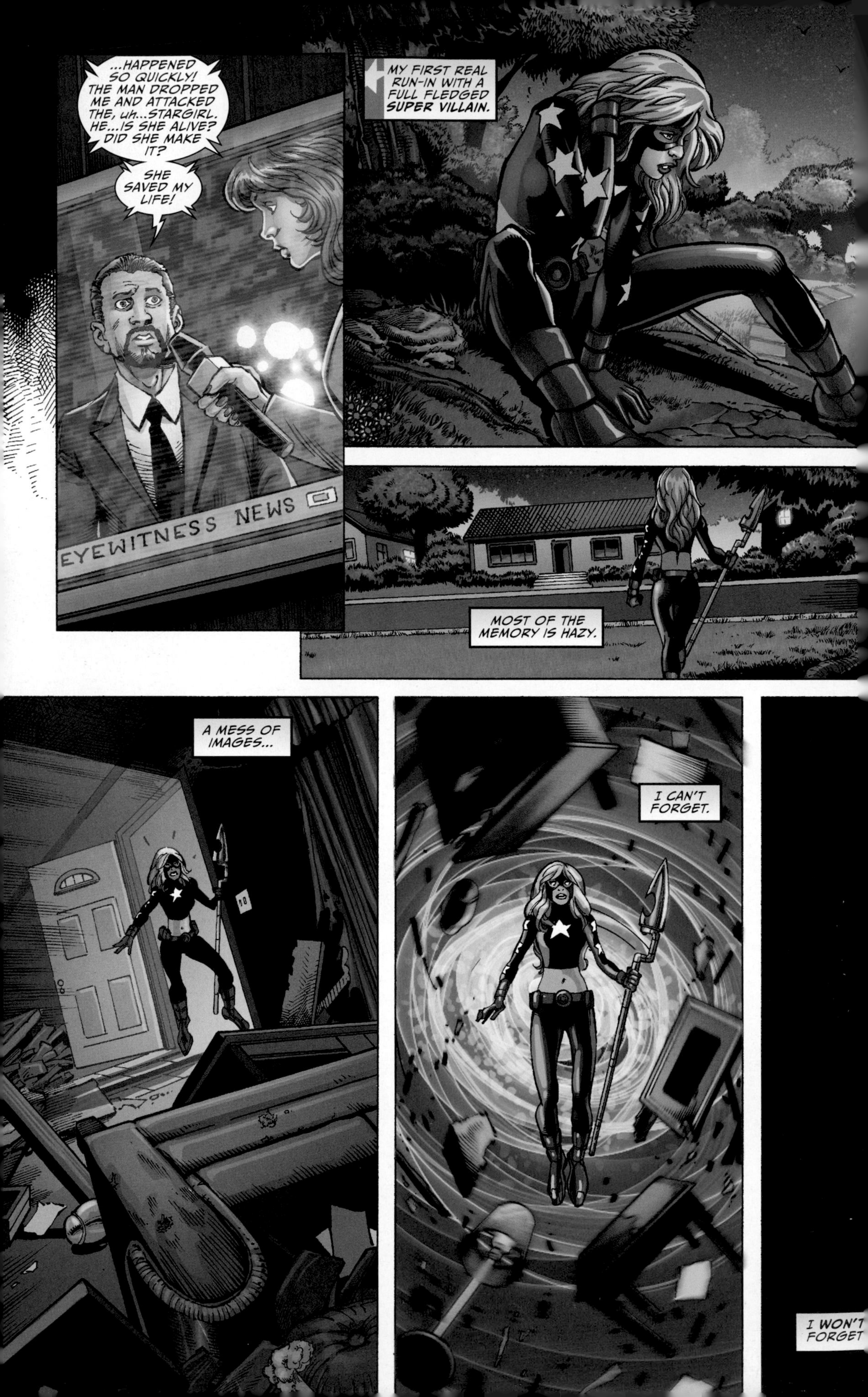
...HAPPENED SO QUICKLY! THE MAN DROPPED ME AND ATTACKED THE, uh...STARGIRL. HE...IS SHE ALIVE? DID SHE MAKE IT?
SHE SAVED MY LIFE!
EYEWITNESS NEWS
MY FIRST REAL RUN-IN WITH A FULL FLEDGED SUPER VILLAIN.
MOST OF THE MEMORY IS HAZY.
A MESS OF IMAGES...
I CAN'T FORGET.
I WON'T FORGET

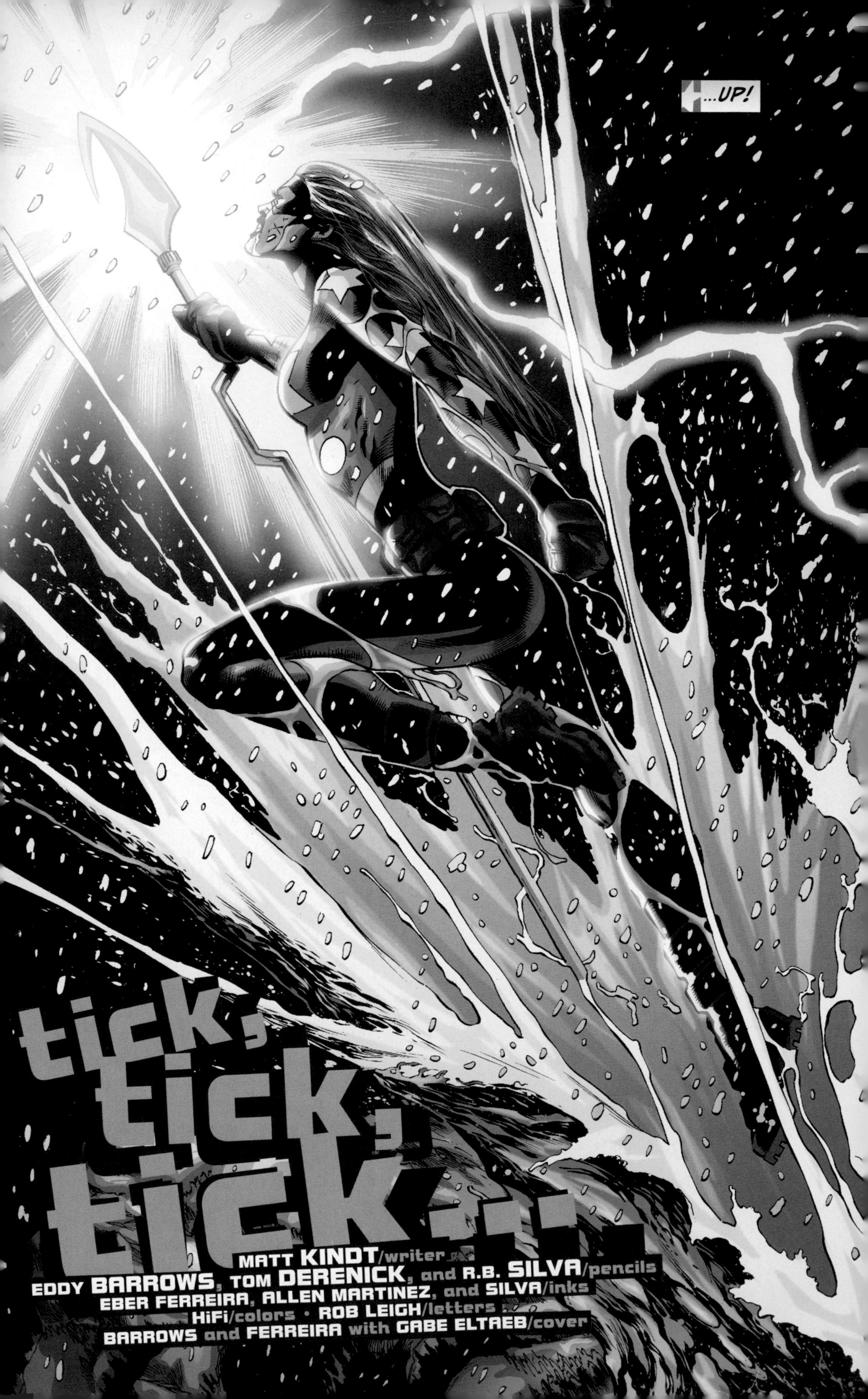
...UP!
tick, tick, tick...
MATT KINDT/writer
EDDY BARROWS, TOM DERENICK, and R.B. SILVA/pencils
EBER FERREIRA, ALLEN MARTINEZ, and SILVA/inks
HiFi/colors • ROB LEIGH/letters
BARROWS and FERREIRA with GABE ELTAEB/cover

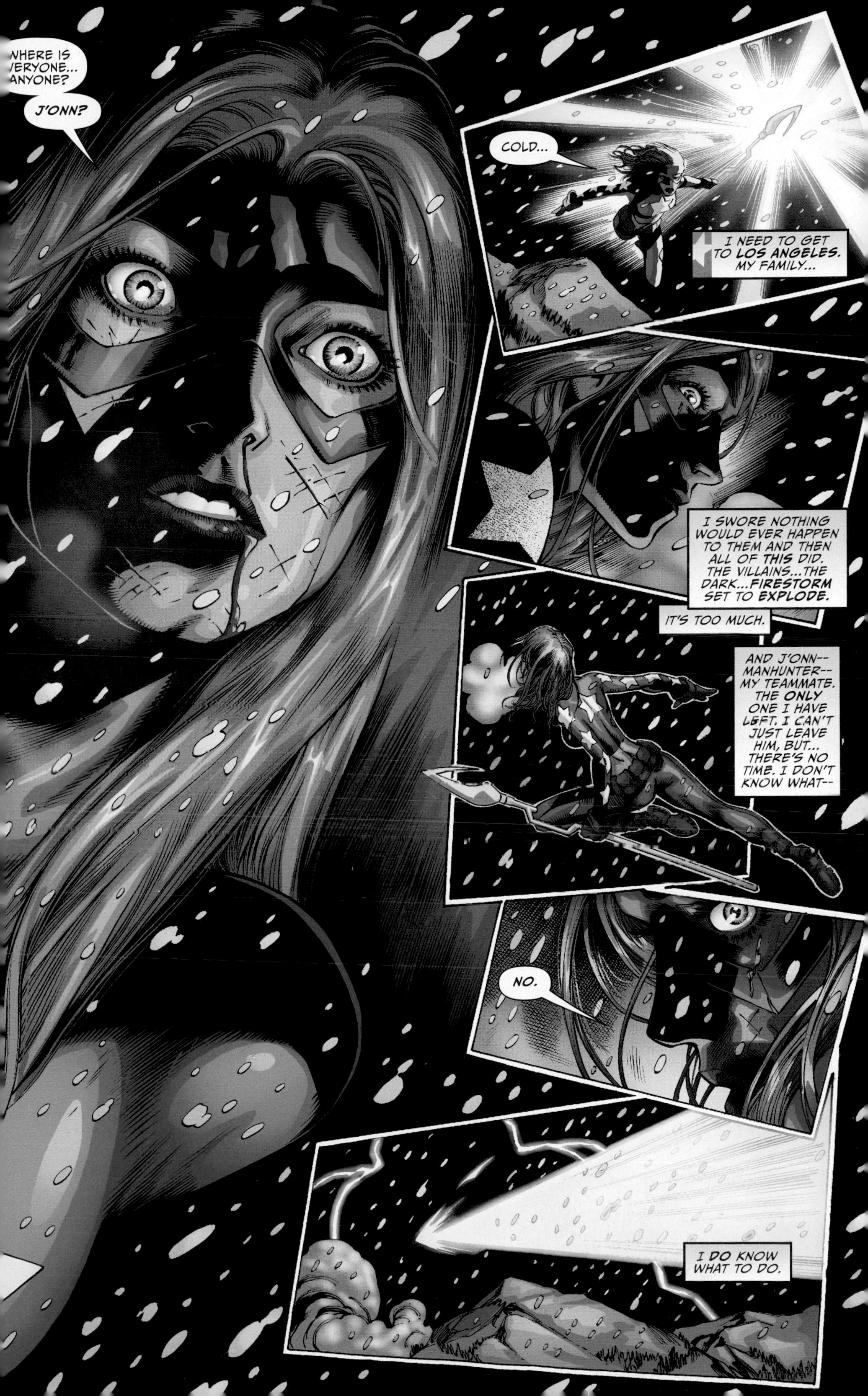

WHERE IS
VERYONE...
ANYONE?
J'ONN?
COLD...
I NEED TO GET TO **LOS ANGELES.** MY FAMILY...
I SWORE NOTHING WOULD EVER HAPPEN TO THEM AND THEN ALL OF **THIS** DID. THE VILLAINS...THE DARK...**FIRESTORM** SET TO **EXPLODE.**
IT'S TOO MUCH.
AND J'ONN-- MANHUNTER-- MY TEAMMATE. THE **ONLY** ONE I HAVE LEFT. I CAN'T JUST LEAVE HIM, BUT... THERE'S NO TIME. I DON'T KNOW WHAT--
NO.
I **DO** KNOW WHAT TO DO.

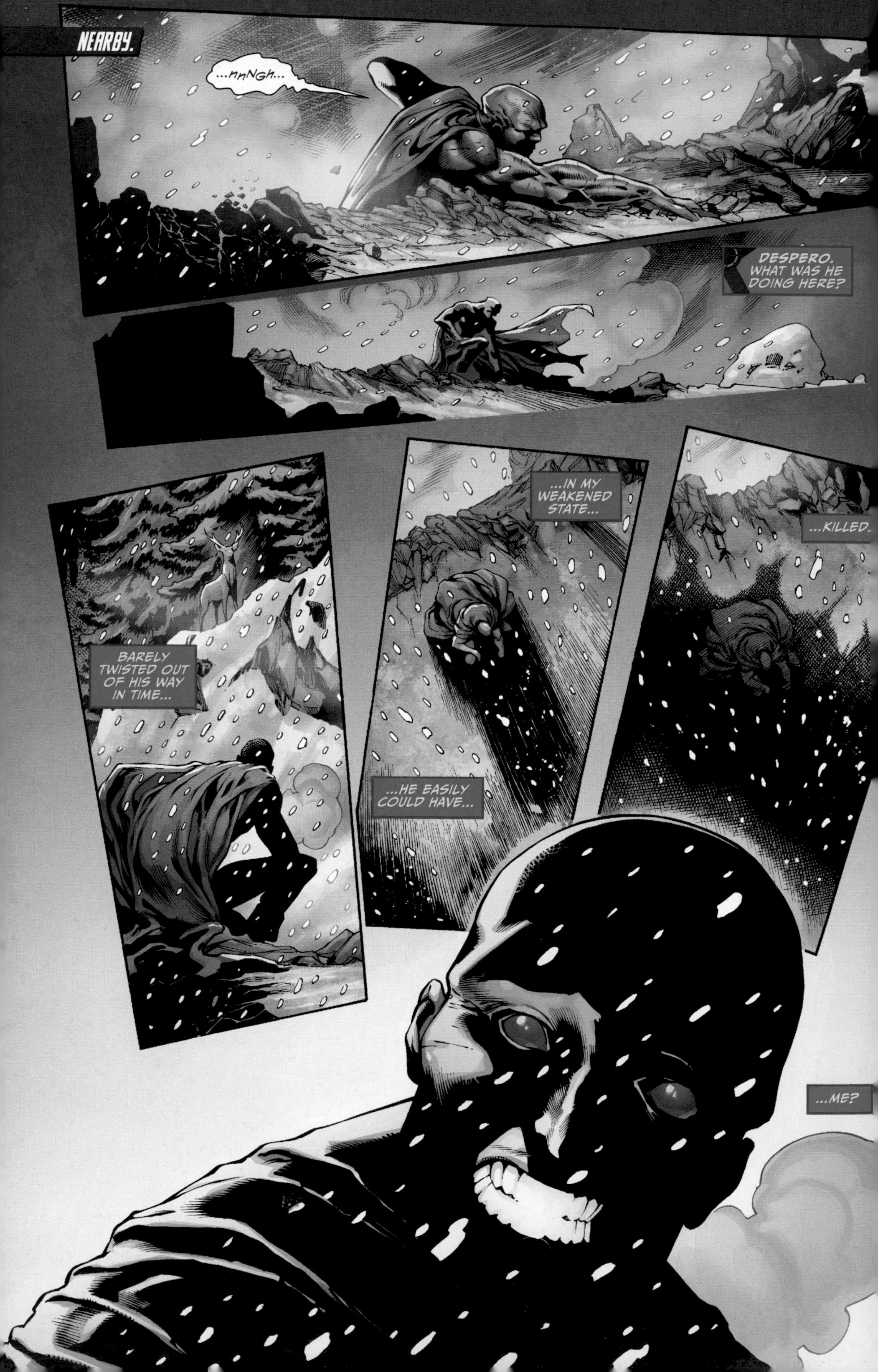
NEARBY.
...nnNGH...
DESPERO. WHAT WAS HE DOING HERE?
BARELY TWISTED OUT OF HIS WAY IN TIME...
...IN MY WEAKENED STATE...
...HE EASILY COULD HAVE...
...KILLED.
...ME?

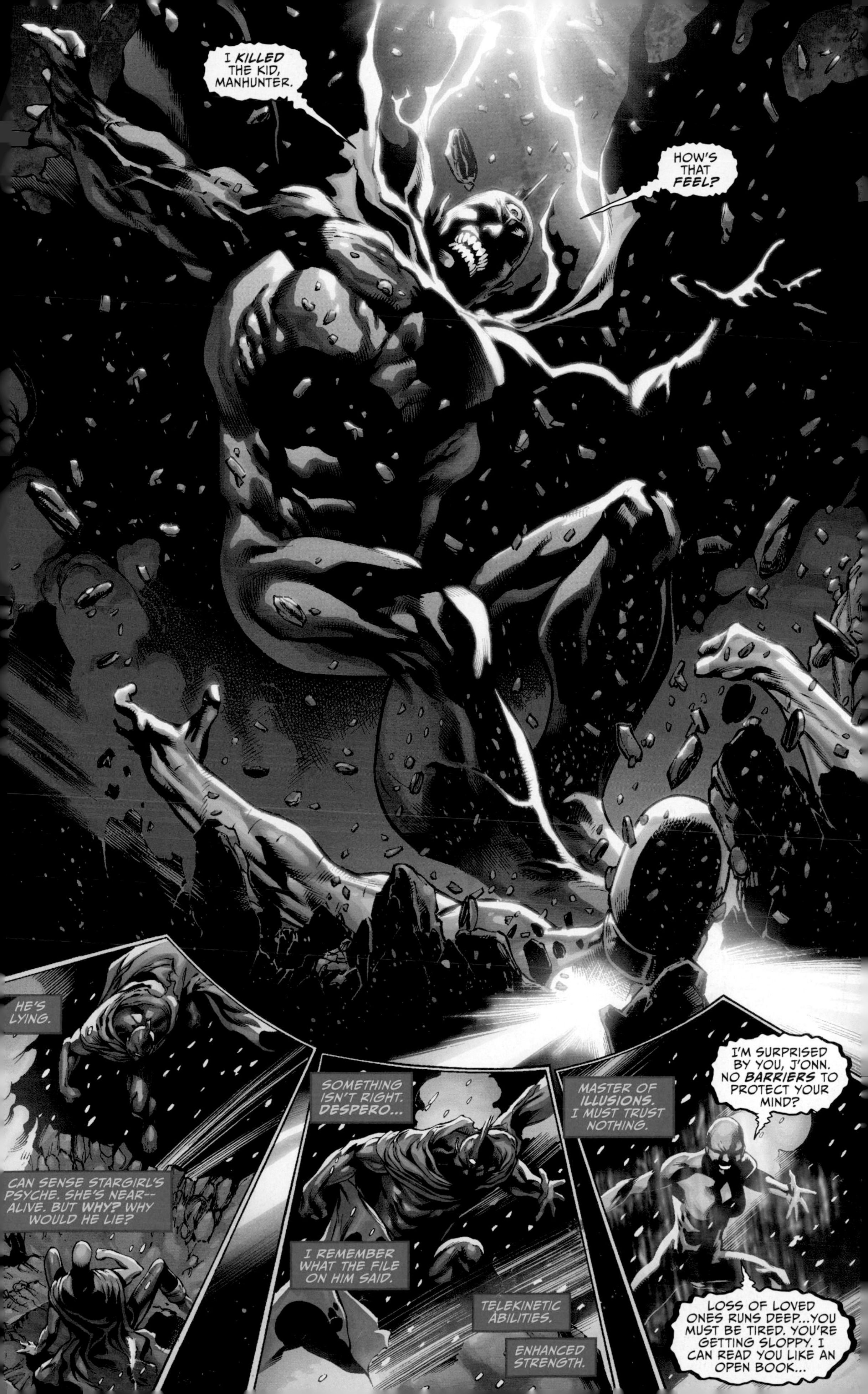
I KILLED THE KID, MANHUNTER.
HOW'S THAT FEEL?
HE'S LYING.
CAN SENSE STARGIRL'S PSYCHE. SHE'S NEAR--ALIVE. BUT WHY? WHY WOULD HE LIE?
SOMETHING ISN'T RIGHT. DESPERO...
I REMEMBER WHAT THE FILE ON HIM SAID.
TELEKINETIC ABILITIES.
ENHANCED STRENGTH.
MASTER OF ILLUSIONS. I MUST TRUST NOTHING.
I'M SURPRISED BY YOU, J'ONN. NO BARRIERS TO PROTECT YOUR MIND?
LOSS OF LOVED ONES RUNS DEEP...YOU MUST BE TIRED. YOU'RE GETTING SLOPPY. I CAN READ YOU LIKE AN OPEN BOOK...

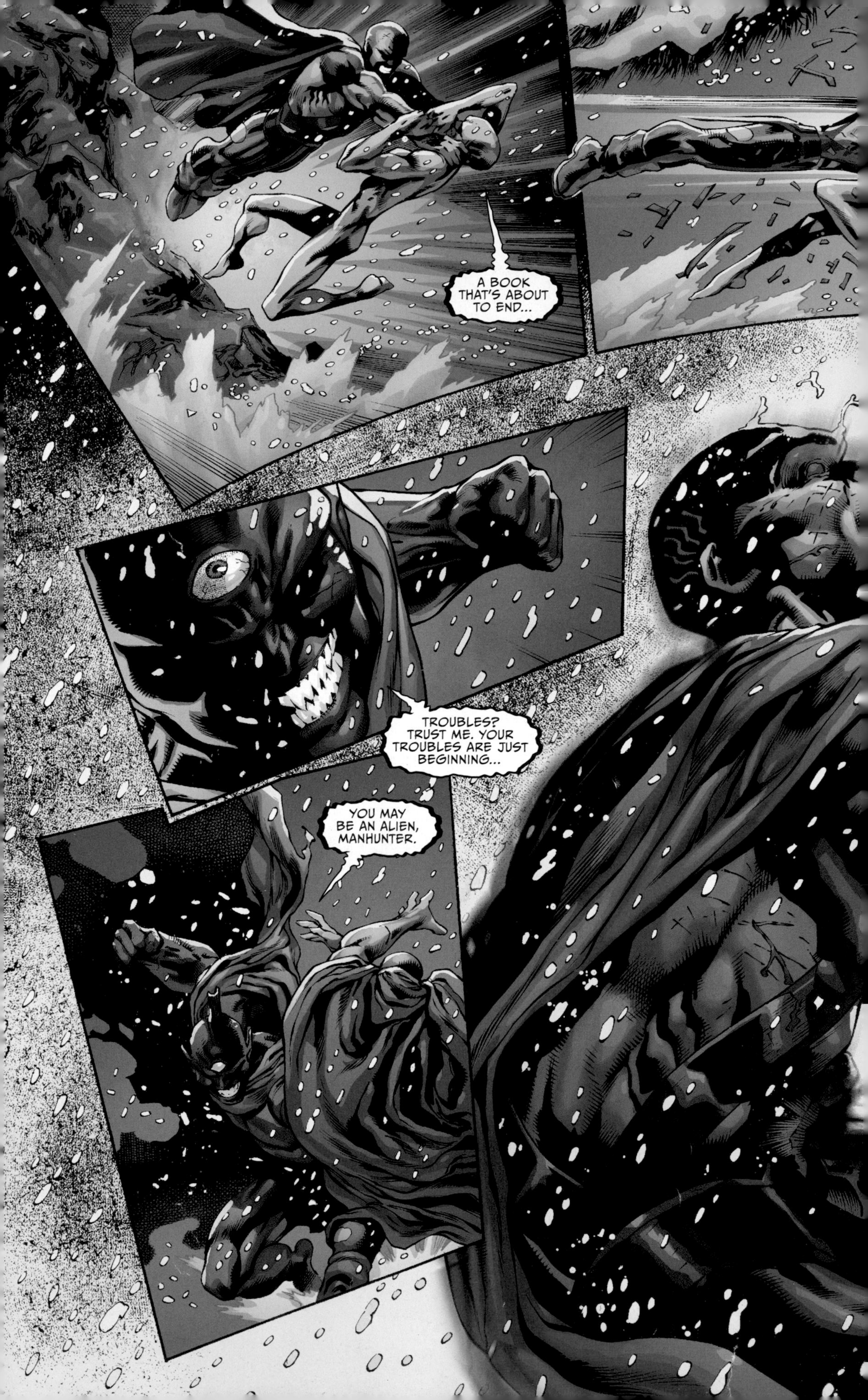
A BOOK THAT'S ABOUT TO END...
TROUBLES? TRUST ME. YOUR TROUBLES ARE JUST BEGINNING...
YOU MAY BE AN ALIEN, MANHUNTER.

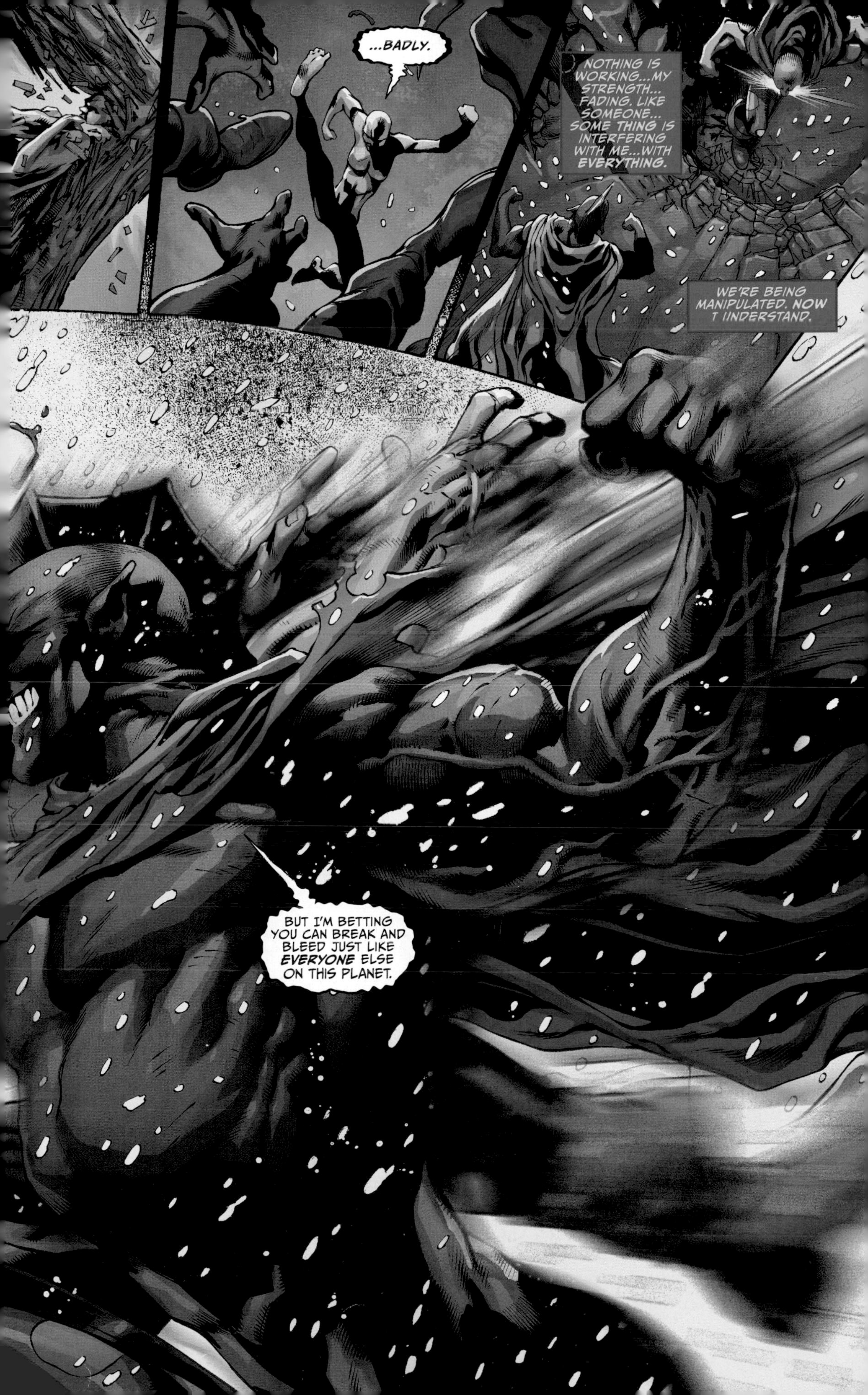
...BADLY.
NOTHING IS WORKING...MY STRENGTH... FADING. LIKE SOMEONE... SOME THING IS INTERFERING WITH ME...WITH EVERYTHING.
WE'RE BEING MANIPULATED. NOW I UNDERSTAND.
BUT I'M BETTING YOU CAN BREAK AND BLEED JUST LIKE EVERYONE ELSE ON THIS PLANET.

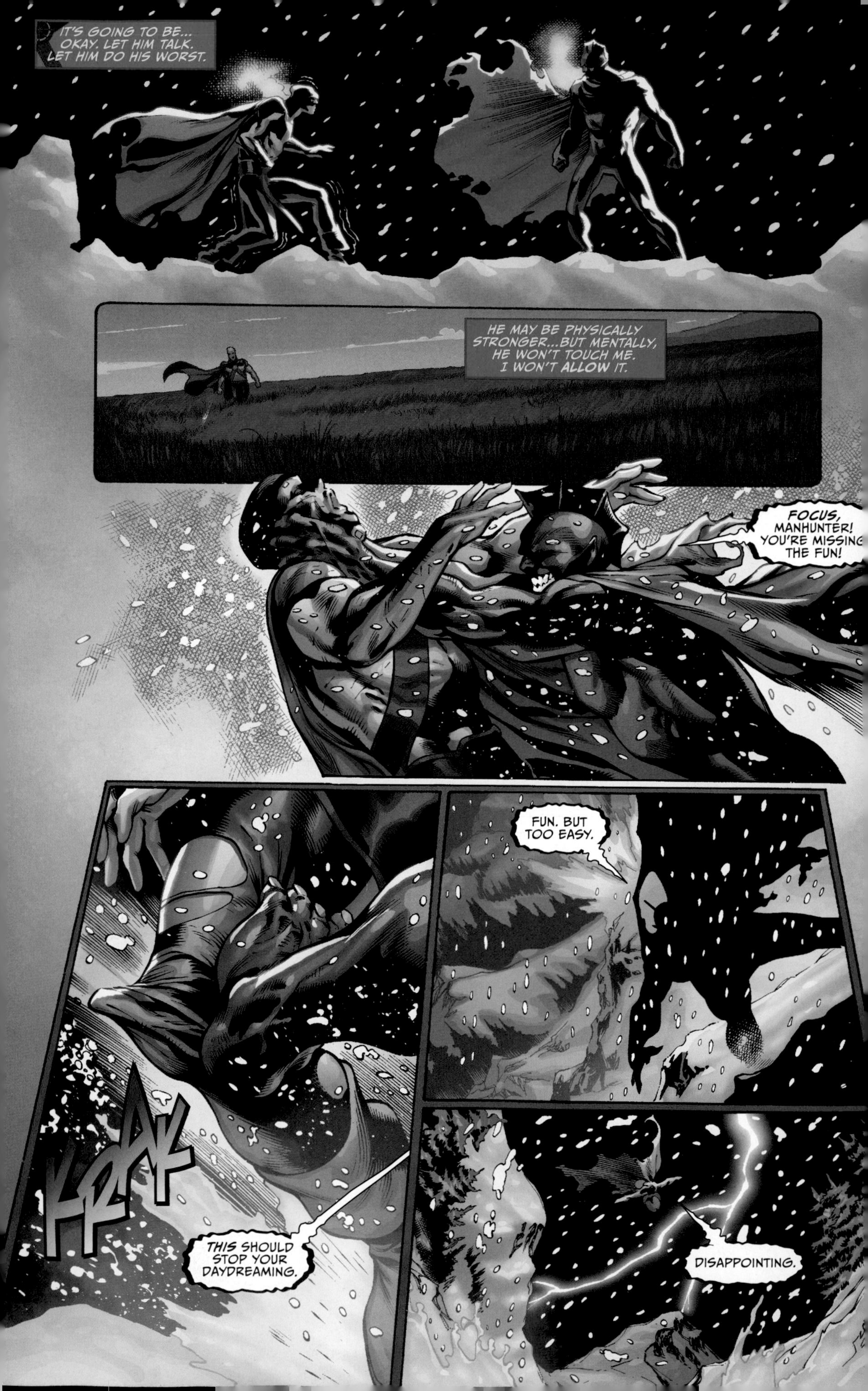
IT'S GOING TO BE... OKAY. LET HIM TALK. LET HIM DO HIS WORST.
HE MAY BE PHYSICALLY STRONGER...BUT MENTALLY, HE WON'T TOUCH ME. I WON'T ALLOW IT.
FOCUS, MANHUNTER! YOU'RE MISSING THE FUN!
KRAK
THIS SHOULD STOP YOUR DAYDREAMING.
FUN. BUT TOO EASY.
DISAPPOINTING.

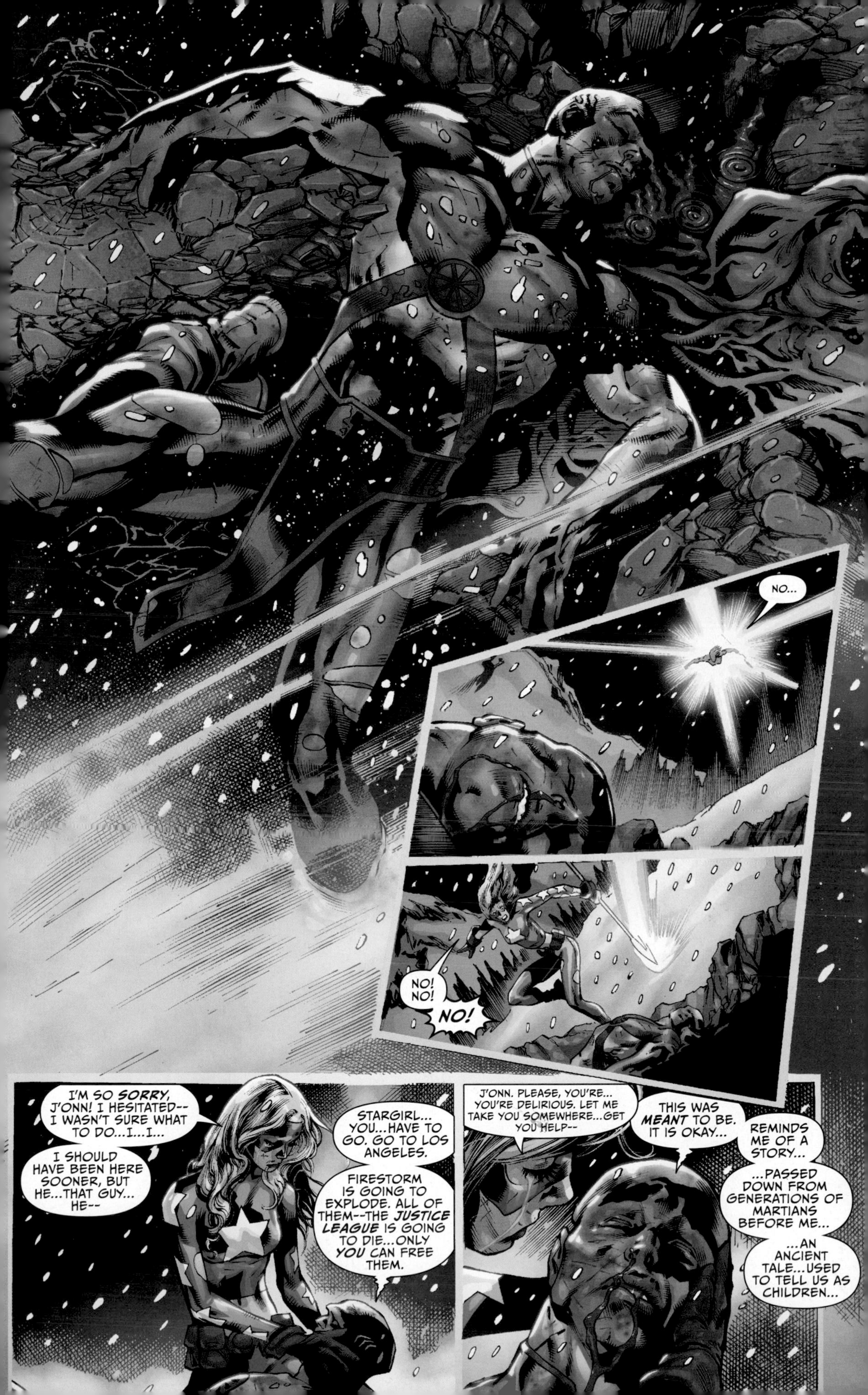
NO...
NO! NO! NO!
I'M SO SORRY, J'ONN! I HESITATED-- I WASN'T SURE WHAT TO DO...I...I...
I SHOULD HAVE BEEN HERE SOONER, BUT HE...THAT GUY... HE--
STARGIRL... YOU...HAVE TO GO. GO TO LOS ANGELES.
FIRESTORM IS GOING TO EXPLODE. ALL OF THEM--THE JUSTICE LEAGUE IS GOING TO DIE...ONLY YOU CAN FREE THEM.
J'ONN. PLEASE, YOU'RE... YOU'RE DELIRIOUS. LET ME TAKE YOU SOMEWHERE...GET YOU HELP--
THIS WAS MEANT TO BE. IT IS OKAY...
REMINDS ME OF A STORY...
...PASSED DOWN FROM GENERATIONS OF MARTIANS BEFORE ME...
...AN ANCIENT TALE...USED TO TELL US AS CHILDREN...

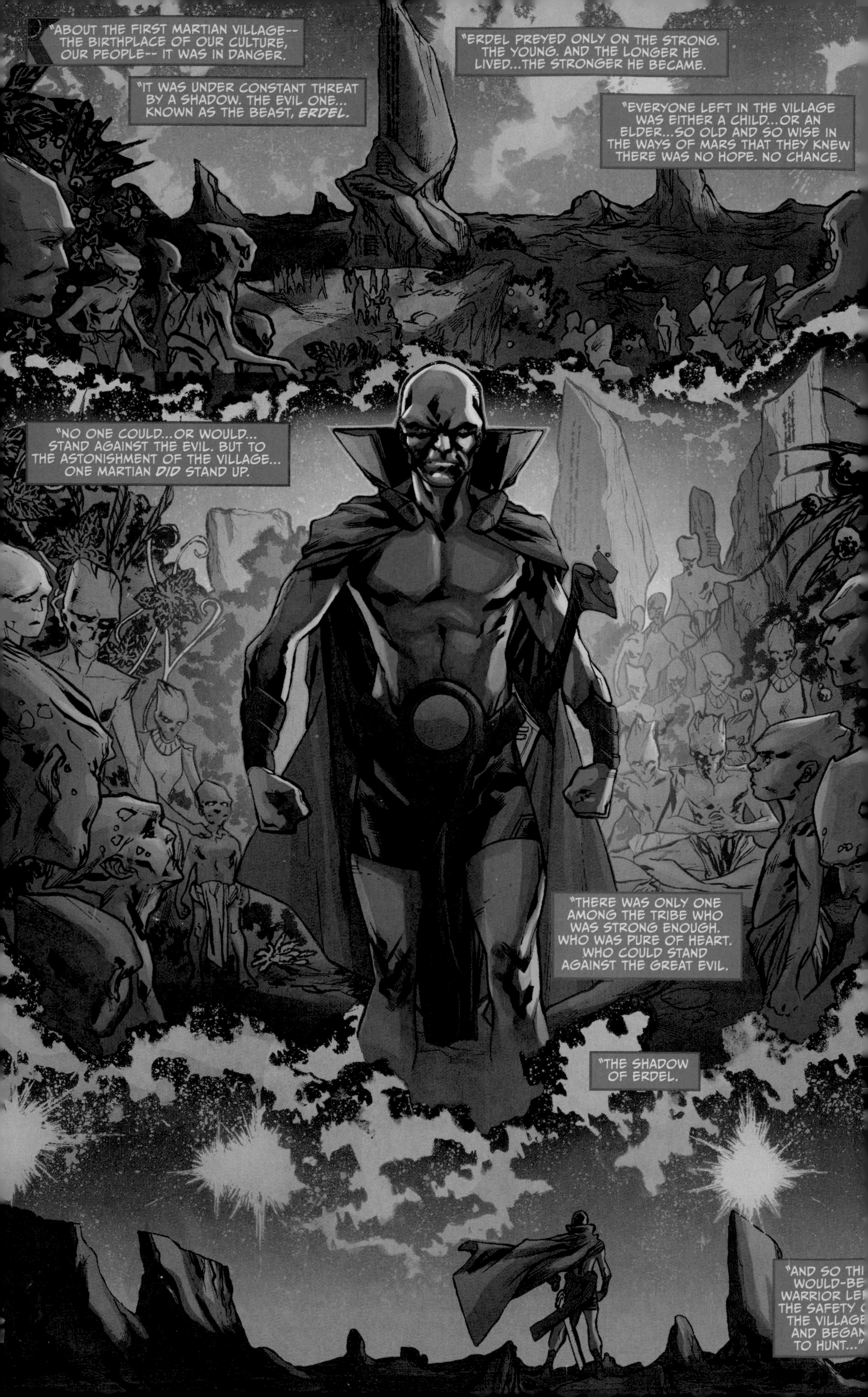
"ABOUT THE FIRST MARTIAN VILLAGE-- THE BIRTHPLACE OF OUR CULTURE, OUR PEOPLE-- IT WAS IN DANGER.
"IT WAS UNDER CONSTANT THREAT BY A SHADOW. THE EVIL ONE... KNOWN AS THE BEAST, *ERDEL.*
"ERDEL PREYED ONLY ON THE STRONG. THE YOUNG. AND THE LONGER HE LIVED...THE STRONGER HE BECAME.
"EVERYONE LEFT IN THE VILLAGE WAS EITHER A CHILD...OR AN ELDER...SO OLD AND SO WISE IN THE WAYS OF MARS THAT THEY KNEW THERE WAS NO HOPE. NO CHANCE.
"NO ONE COULD...OR WOULD... STAND AGAINST THE EVIL. BUT TO THE ASTONISHMENT OF THE VILLAGE... ONE MARTIAN *DID* STAND UP.
"THERE WAS ONLY ONE AMONG THE TRIBE WHO WAS STRONG ENOUGH. WHO WAS PURE OF HEART. WHO COULD STAND AGAINST THE GREAT EVIL.
"THE SHADOW OF ERDEL.
"AND SO THI WOULD-BE WARRIOR LE THE SAFETY THE VILLAGE AND BEGAN TO HUNT..."

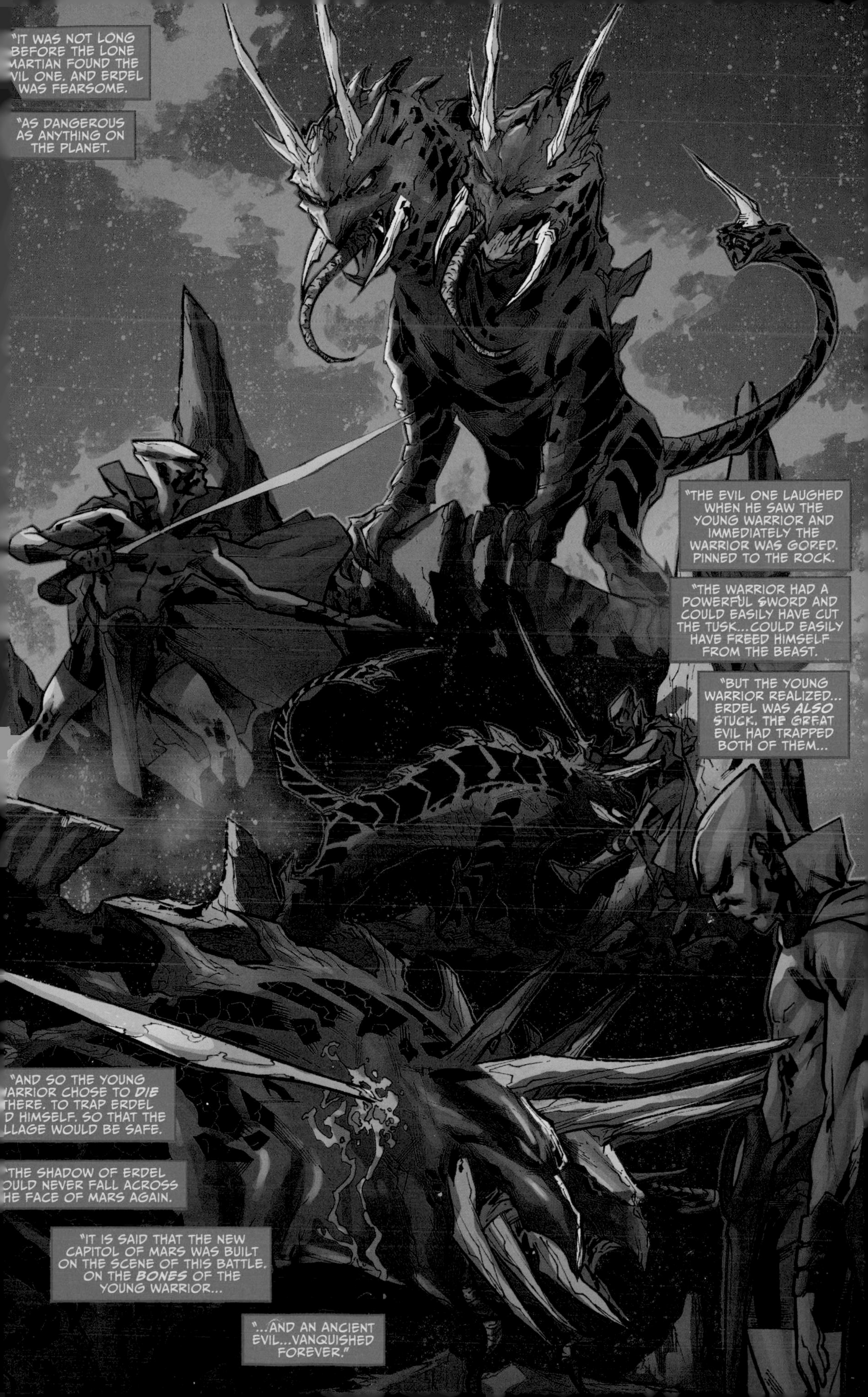
"IT WAS NOT LONG BEFORE THE LONE MARTIAN FOUND THE VIL ONE. AND ERDEL WAS FEARSOME.
"AS DANGEROUS AS ANYTHING ON THE PLANET.
"THE EVIL ONE LAUGHED WHEN HE SAW THE YOUNG WARRIOR AND IMMEDIATELY THE WARRIOR WAS GORED. PINNED TO THE ROCK.
"THE WARRIOR HAD A POWERFUL SWORD AND COULD EASILY HAVE CUT THE TUSK...COULD EASILY HAVE FREED HIMSELF FROM THE BEAST.
"BUT THE YOUNG WARRIOR REALIZED... ERDEL WAS ALSO STUCK. THE GREAT EVIL HAD TRAPPED BOTH OF THEM...
"AND SO THE YOUNG ARRIOR CHOSE TO DIE HERE. TO TRAP ERDEL D HIMSELF. SO THAT THE LLAGE WOULD BE SAFE.
"THE SHADOW OF ERDEL OULD NEVER FALL ACROSS HE FACE OF MARS AGAIN.
"IT IS SAID THAT THE NEW CAPITOL OF MARS WAS BUILT ON THE SCENE OF THIS BATTLE. ON THE BONES OF THE YOUNG WARRIOR...
"...AND AN ANCIENT EVIL...VANQUISHED FOREVER."

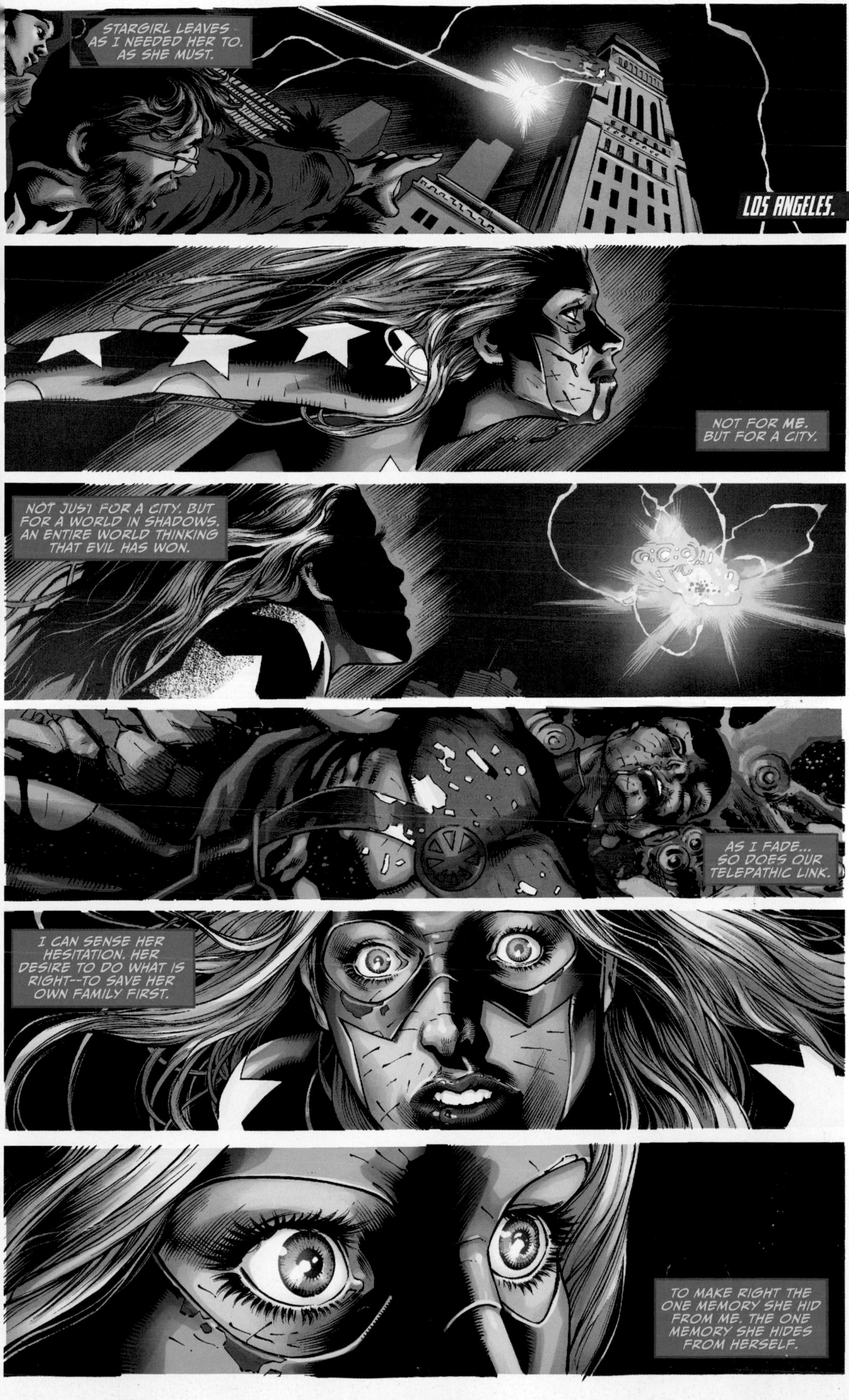
STARGIRL LEAVES AS I NEEDED HER TO. AS SHE MUST.
LOS ANGELES.
NOT FOR ME. BUT FOR A CITY.
NOT JUST FOR A CITY. BUT FOR A WORLD IN SHADOWS. AN ENTIRE WORLD THINKING THAT EVIL HAS WON.
AS I FADE... SO DOES OUR TELEPATHIC LINK.
I CAN SENSE HER HESITATION. HER DESIRE TO DO WHAT IS RIGHT--TO SAVE HER OWN FAMILY FIRST.
TO MAKE RIGHT THE ONE MEMORY SHE HID FROM ME. THE ONE MEMORY SHE HIDES FROM HERSELF.

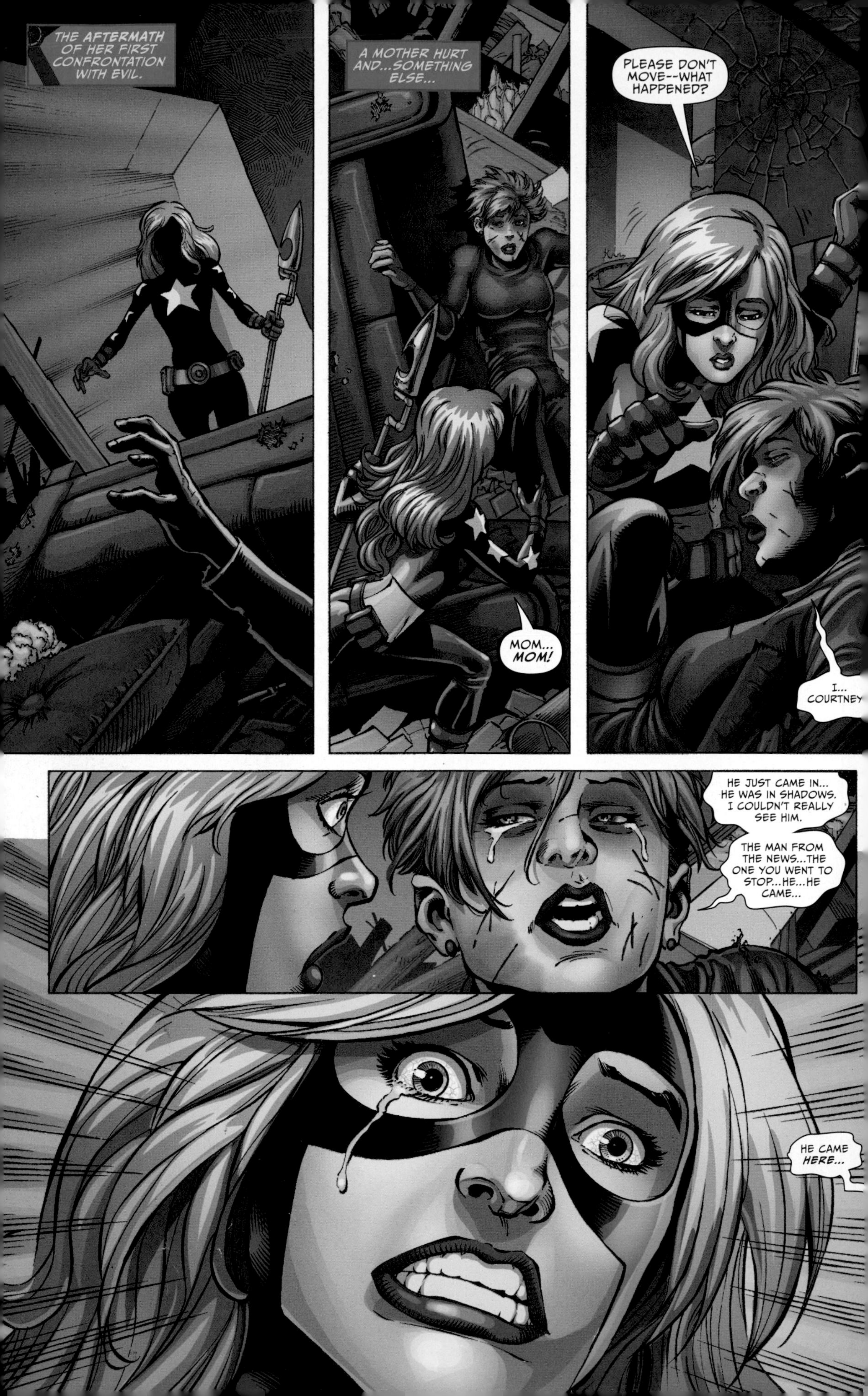
THE AFTERMATH OF HER FIRST CONFRONTATION WITH EVIL.
A MOTHER HURT AND...SOMETHING ELSE...
MOM... MOM!
PLEASE DON'T MOVE--WHAT HAPPENED?
I... COURTNEY
HE JUST CAME IN... HE WAS IN SHADOWS. I COULDN'T REALLY SEE HIM.
THE MAN FROM THE NEWS...THE ONE YOU WENT TO STOP...HE...HE CAME...
HE CAME HERE...

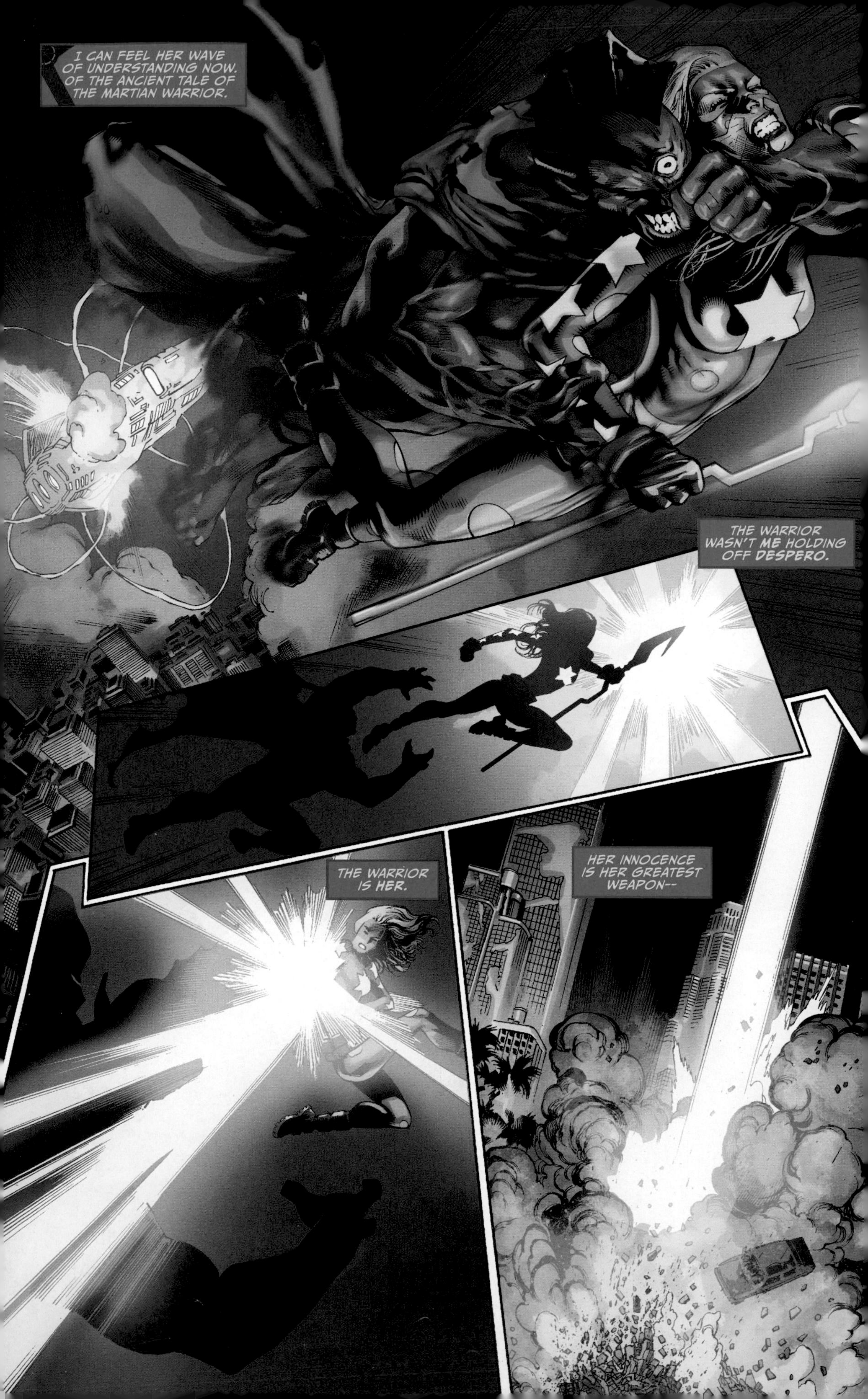
I CAN FEEL HER WAVE OF UNDERSTANDING NOW. OF THE ANCIENT TALE OF THE MARTIAN WARRIOR.
THE WARRIOR WASN'T ME HOLDING OFF DESPERO.
THE WARRIOR IS HER.
HER INNOCENCE IS HER GREATEST WEAPON--

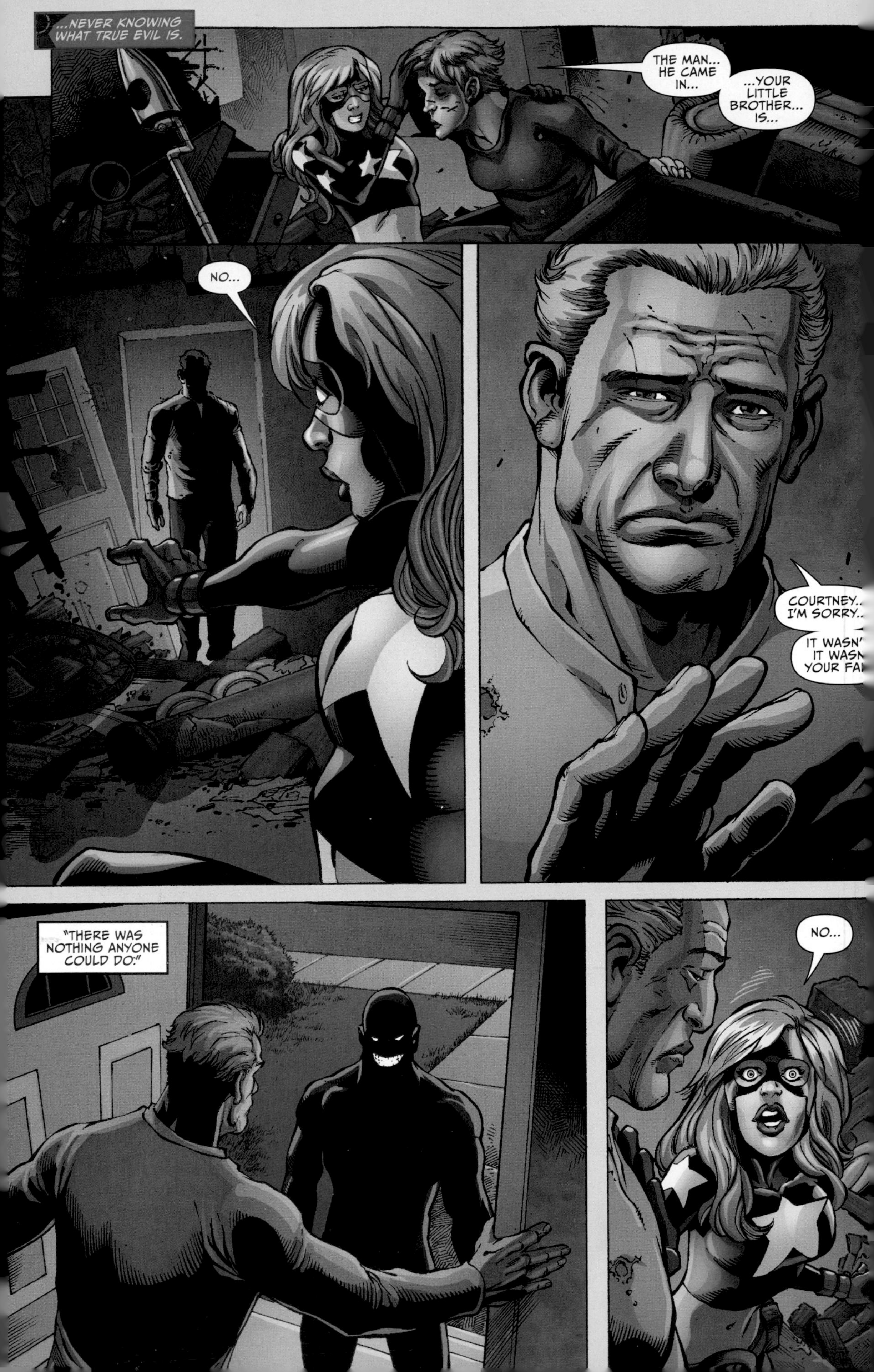
...NEVER KNOWING WHAT TRUE EVIL IS.
THE MAN... HE CAME IN...
...YOUR LITTLE BROTHER... IS...
NO...
COURTNEY... I'M SORRY...
"THERE WAS NOTHING ANYONE COULD DO."
NO...

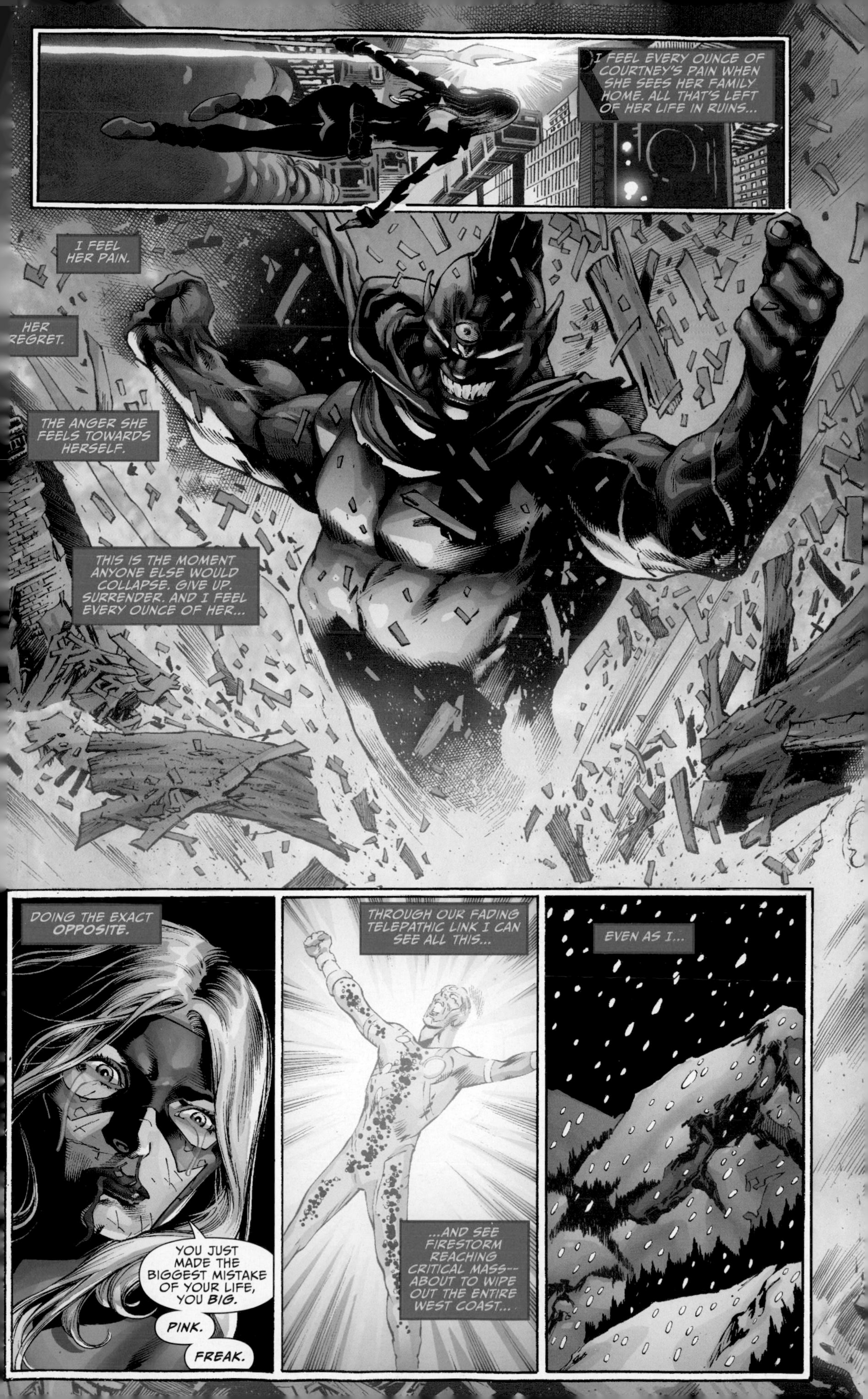

I FEEL EVERY OUNCE OF COURTNEY'S PAIN WHEN SHE SEES HER FAMILY HOME. ALL THAT'S LEFT OF HER LIFE IN RUINS...
I FEEL HER PAIN.
HER REGRET.
THE ANGER SHE FEELS TOWARDS HERSELF.
THIS IS THE MOMENT ANYONE ELSE WOULD COLLAPSE. GIVE UP. SURRENDER. AND I FEEL EVERY OUNCE OF HER...
DOING THE EXACT OPPOSITE.
YOU JUST MADE THE BIGGEST MISTAKE OF YOUR LIFE, YOU BIG.
PINK.
FREAK.
THROUGH OUR FADING TELEPATHIC LINK I CAN SEE ALL THIS...
...AND SEE FIRESTORM REACHING CRITICAL MASS--ABOUT TO WIPE OUT THE ENTIRE WEST COAST...
EVEN AS I...

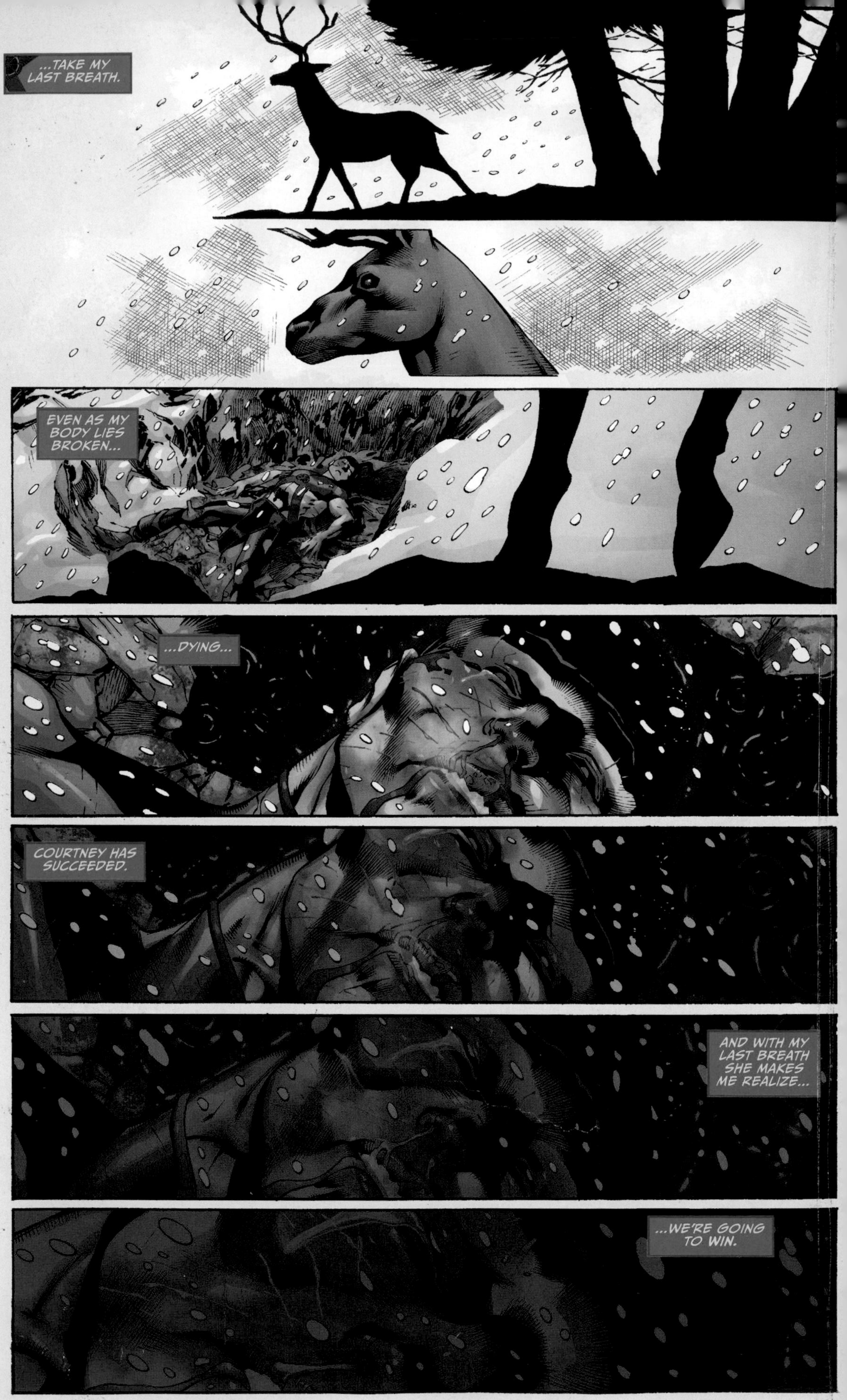
...TAKE MY LAST BREATH.
EVEN AS MY BODY LIES BROKEN...
...DYING...
COURTNEY HAS SUCCEEDED.
AND WITH MY LAST BREATH SHE MAKES ME REALIZE...
...WE'RE GOING TO WIN.

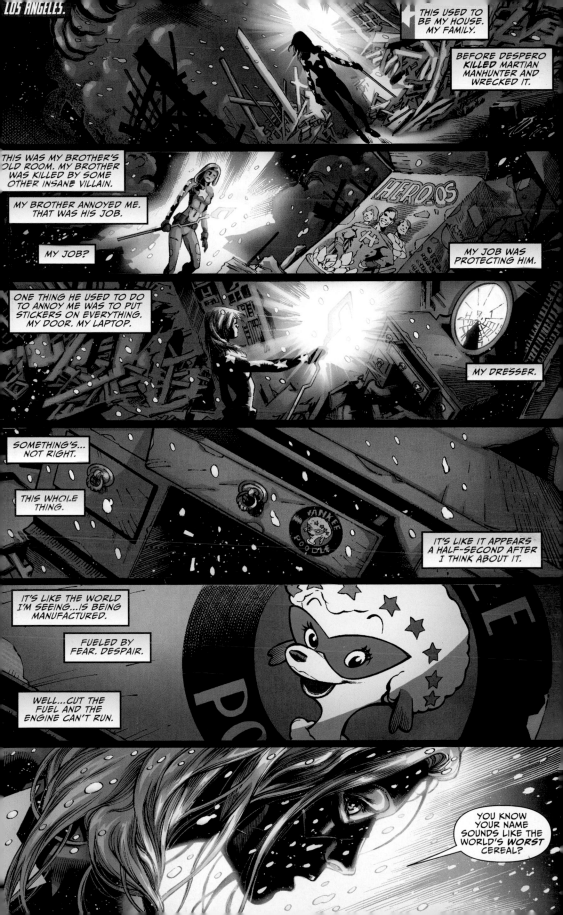

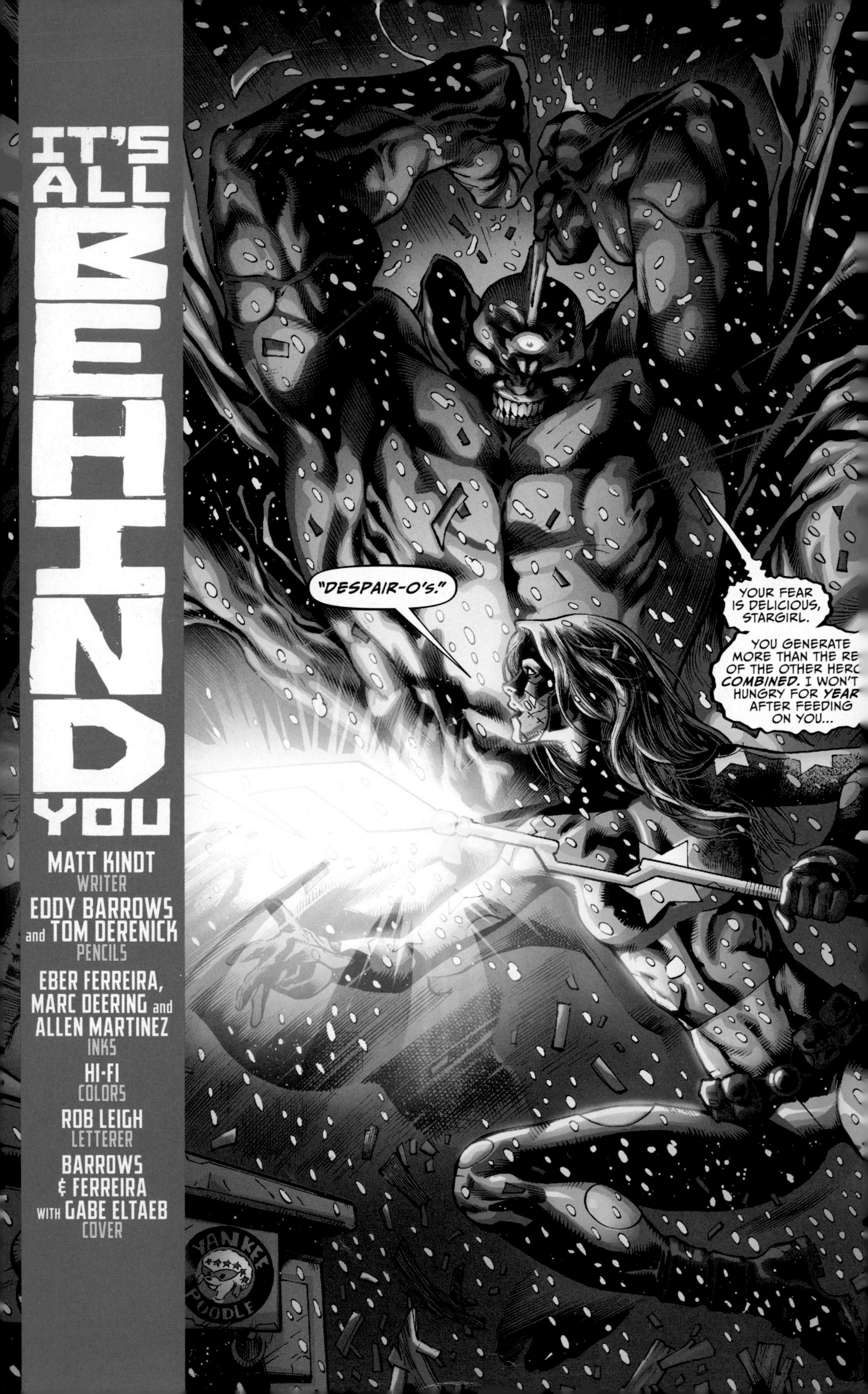

IT'S ALL BEHIND YOU
MATT KINDT WRITER
EDDY BARROWS and TOM DERENICK PENCILS
EBER FERREIRA, MARC DEERING and ALLEN MARTINEZ INKS
HI-FI COLORS
ROB LEIGH LETTERER
BARROWS & FERREIRA with GABE ELTAEB COVER
"DESPAIR-O'S."
YOUR FEAR IS DELICIOUS, STARGIRL.
YOU GENERATE MORE THAN THE RE OF THE OTHER HERC COMBINED. I WON'T HUNGRY FOR YEAR AFTER FEEDING ON YOU...
YANKEE POODLE

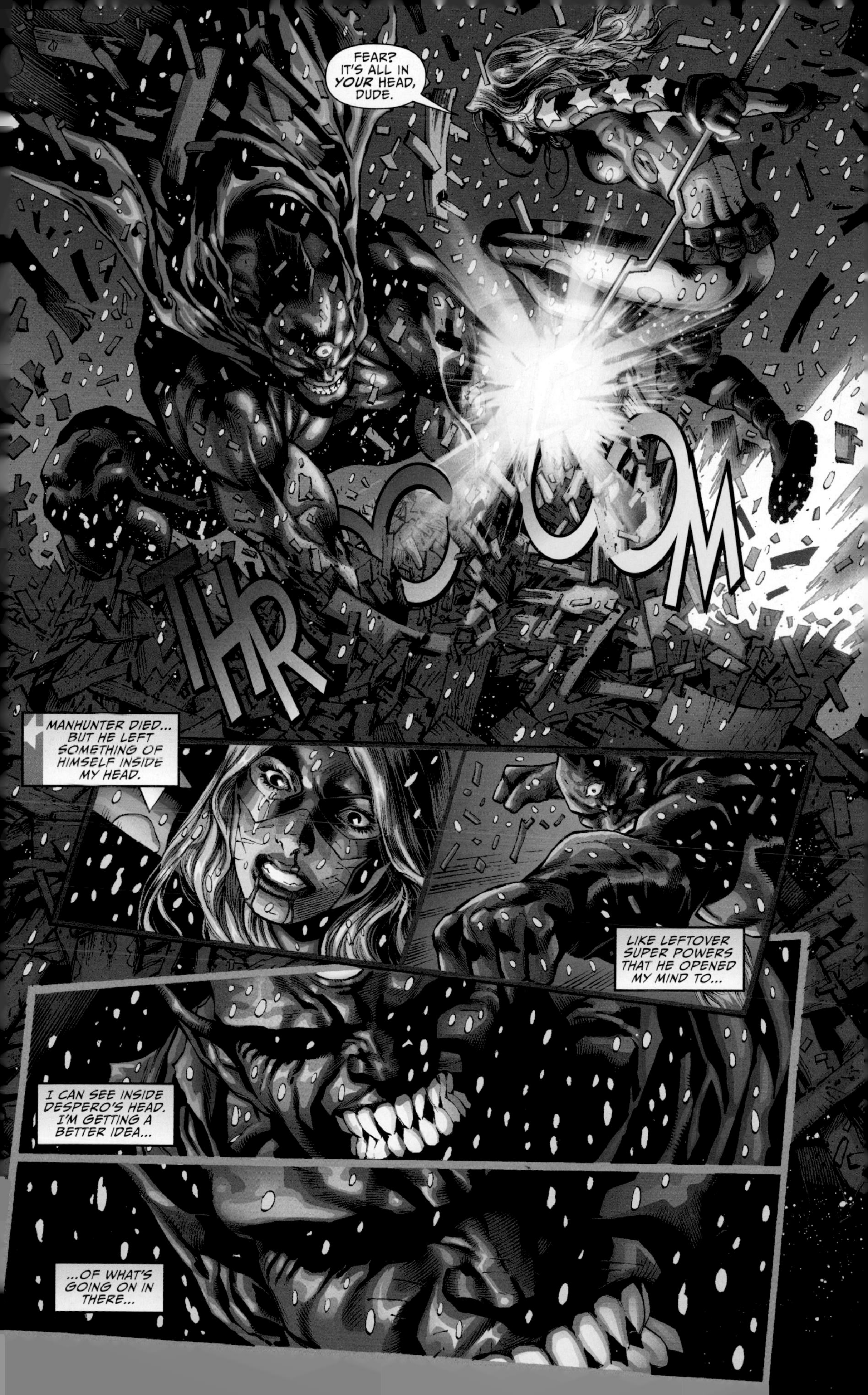
FEAR? IT'S ALL IN YOUR HEAD, DUDE.
THROOOM
MANHUNTER DIED... BUT HE LEFT SOMETHING OF HIMSELF INSIDE MY HEAD.
LIKE LEFTOVER SUPER POWERS THAT HE OPENED MY MIND TO...
I CAN SEE INSIDE DESPERO'S HEAD. I'M GETTING A BETTER IDEA...
...OF WHAT'S GOING ON IN THERE...

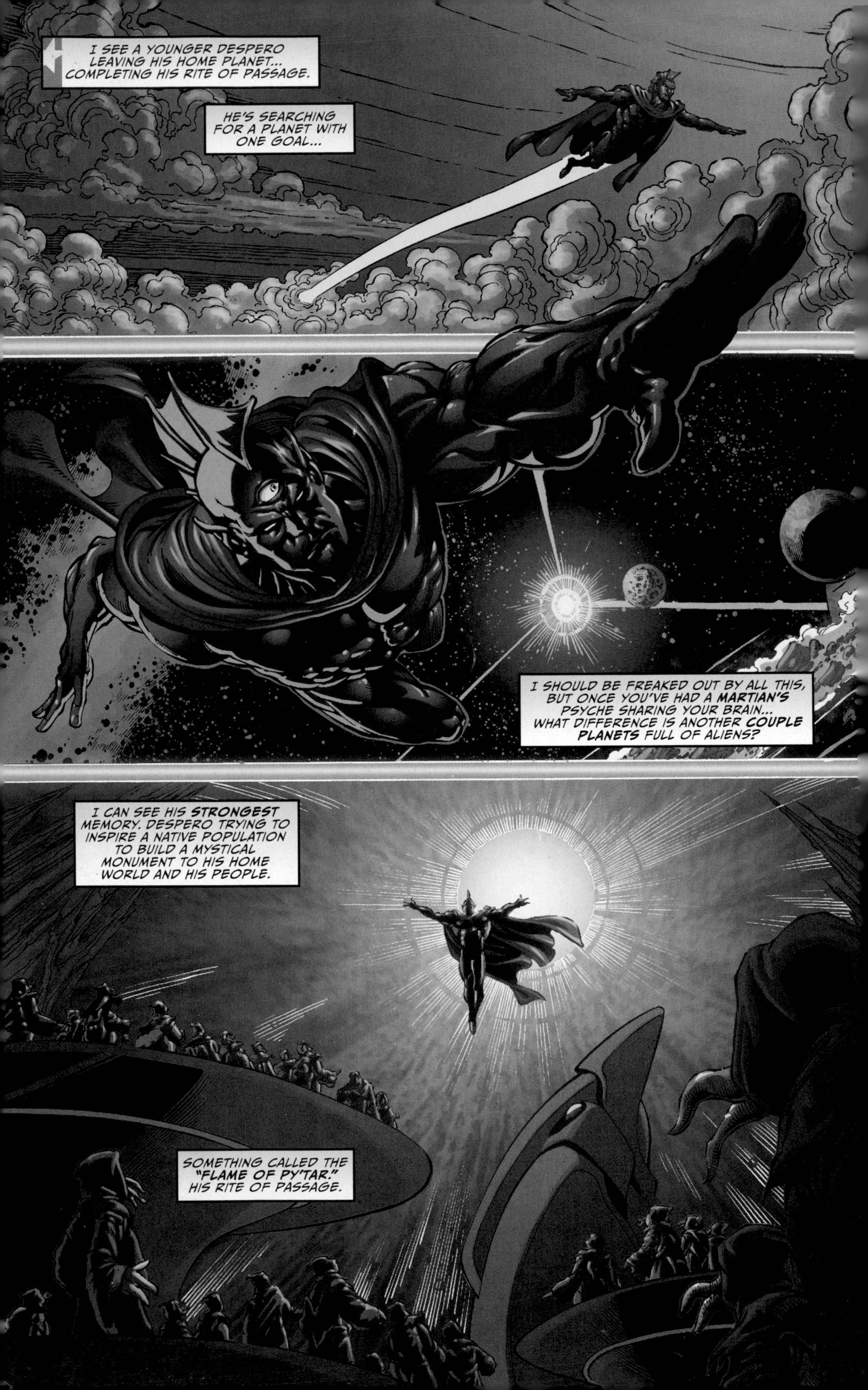
I SEE A YOUNGER DESPERO LEAVING HIS HOME PLANET... COMPLETING HIS RITE OF PASSAGE.
HE'S SEARCHING FOR A PLANET WITH ONE GOAL...
I SHOULD BE FREAKED OUT BY ALL THIS, BUT ONCE YOU'VE HAD A MARTIAN'S PSYCHE SHARING YOUR BRAIN... WHAT DIFFERENCE IS ANOTHER COUPLE PLANETS FULL OF ALIENS?
I CAN SEE HIS STRONGEST MEMORY. DESPERO TRYING TO INSPIRE A NATIVE POPULATION TO BUILD A MYSTICAL MONUMENT TO HIS HOME WORLD AND HIS PEOPLE.
SOMETHING CALLED THE "FLAME OF PY'TAR." HIS RITE OF PASSAGE.

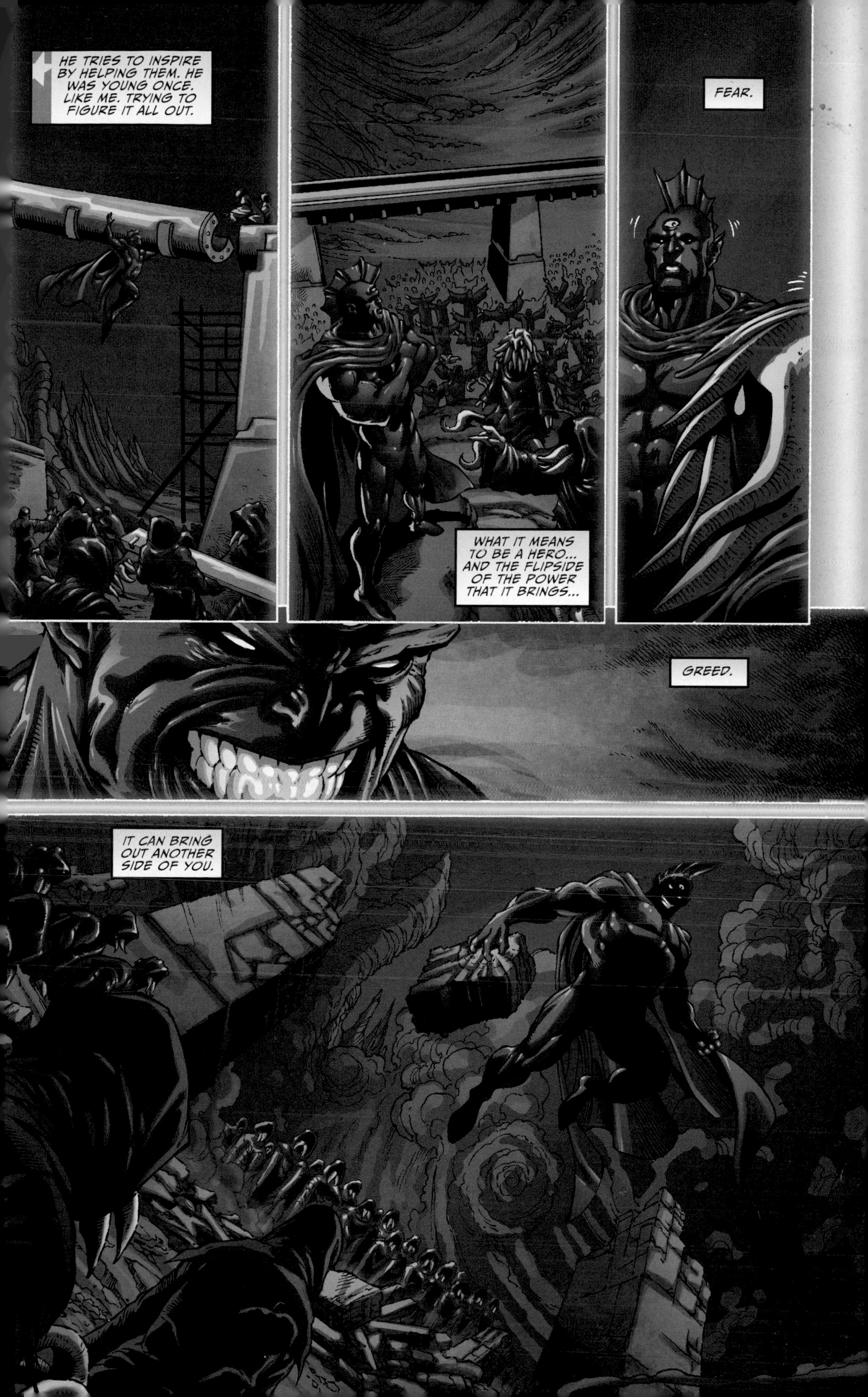
HE TRIES TO INSPIRE BY HELPING THEM. HE WAS YOUNG ONCE. LIKE ME. TRYING TO FIGURE IT ALL OUT.
WHAT IT MEANS TO BE A HERO... AND THE FLIPSIDE OF THE POWER THAT IT BRINGS...
FEAR.
GREED.
IT CAN BRING OUT ANOTHER SIDE OF YOU.

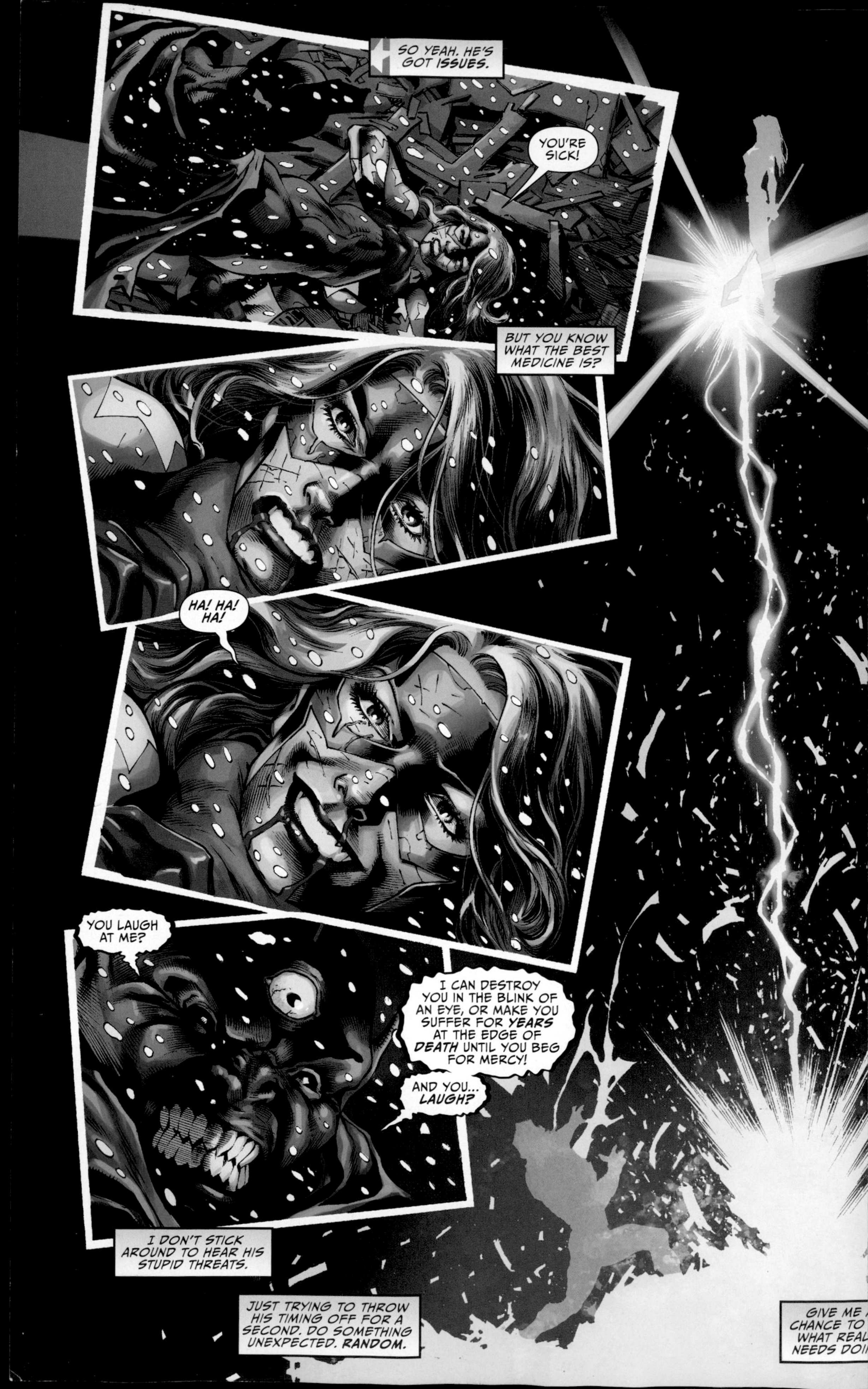

SO YEAH. HE'S GOT ISSUES.
YOU'RE SICK!
BUT YOU KNOW WHAT THE BEST MEDICINE IS?
HA! HA! HA!
YOU LAUGH AT ME?
I CAN DESTROY YOU IN THE BLINK OF AN EYE, OR MAKE YOU SUFFER FOR YEARS AT THE EDGE OF DEATH UNTIL YOU BEG FOR MERCY!
AND YOU... LAUGH?
I DON'T STICK AROUND TO HEAR HIS STUPID THREATS.
JUST TRYING TO THROW HIS TIMING OFF FOR A SECOND. DO SOMETHING UNEXPECTED. RANDOM.

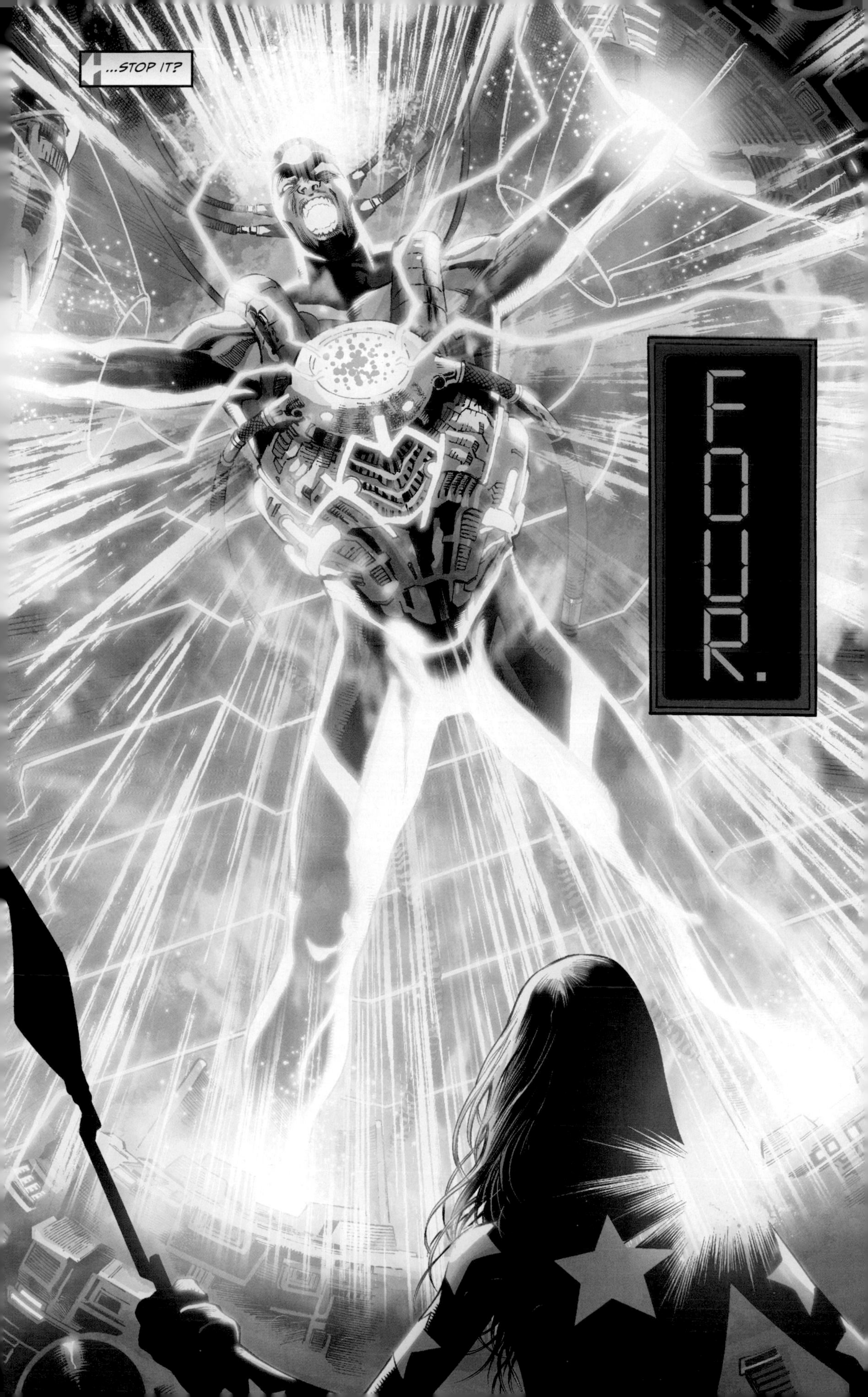
...STOP IT?
FOUR.

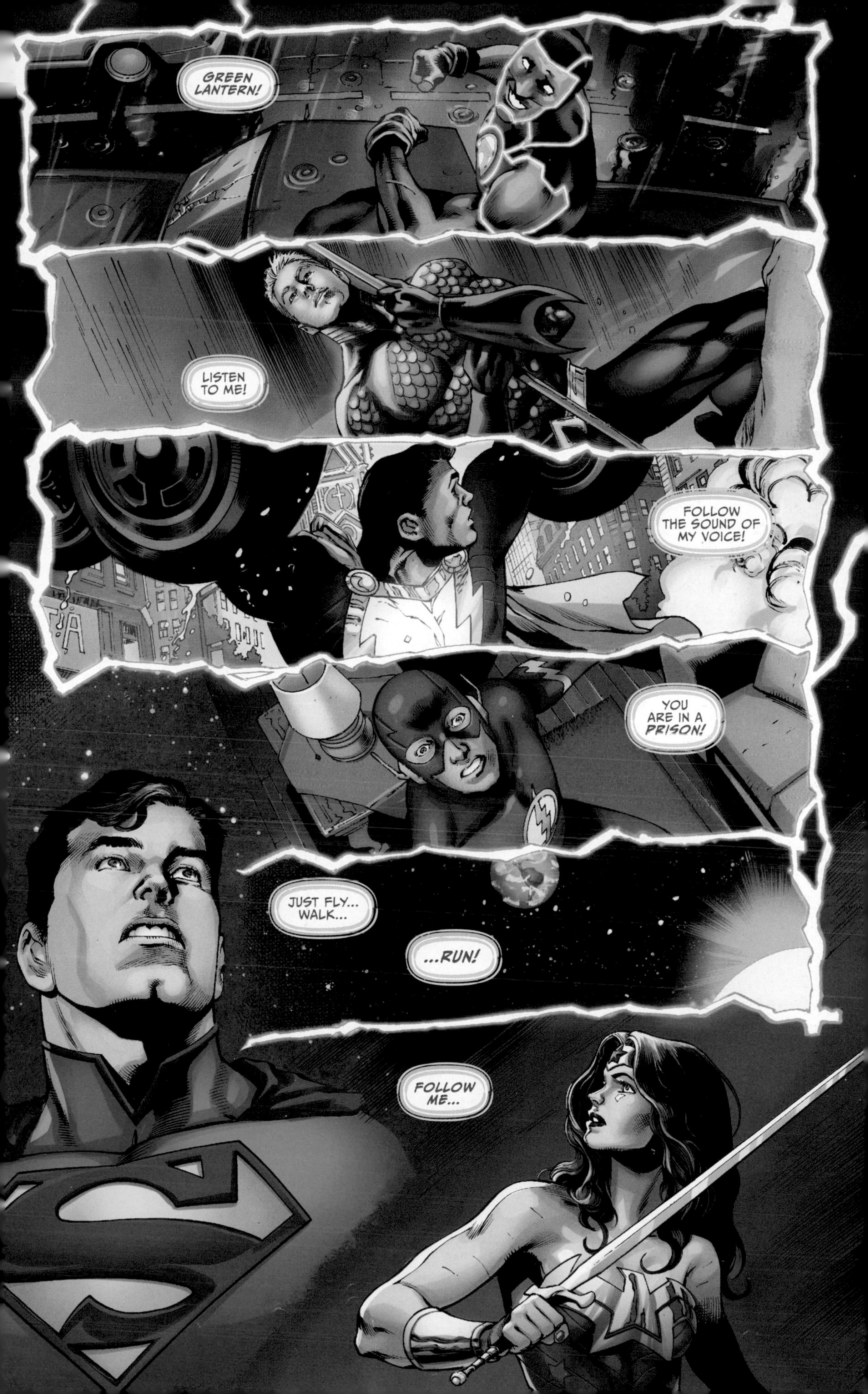
GREEN LANTERN!
LISTEN TO ME!
FOLLOW THE SOUND OF MY VOICE!
YOU ARE IN A PRISON!
JUST FLY... WALK...
...RUN!
FOLLOW ME...

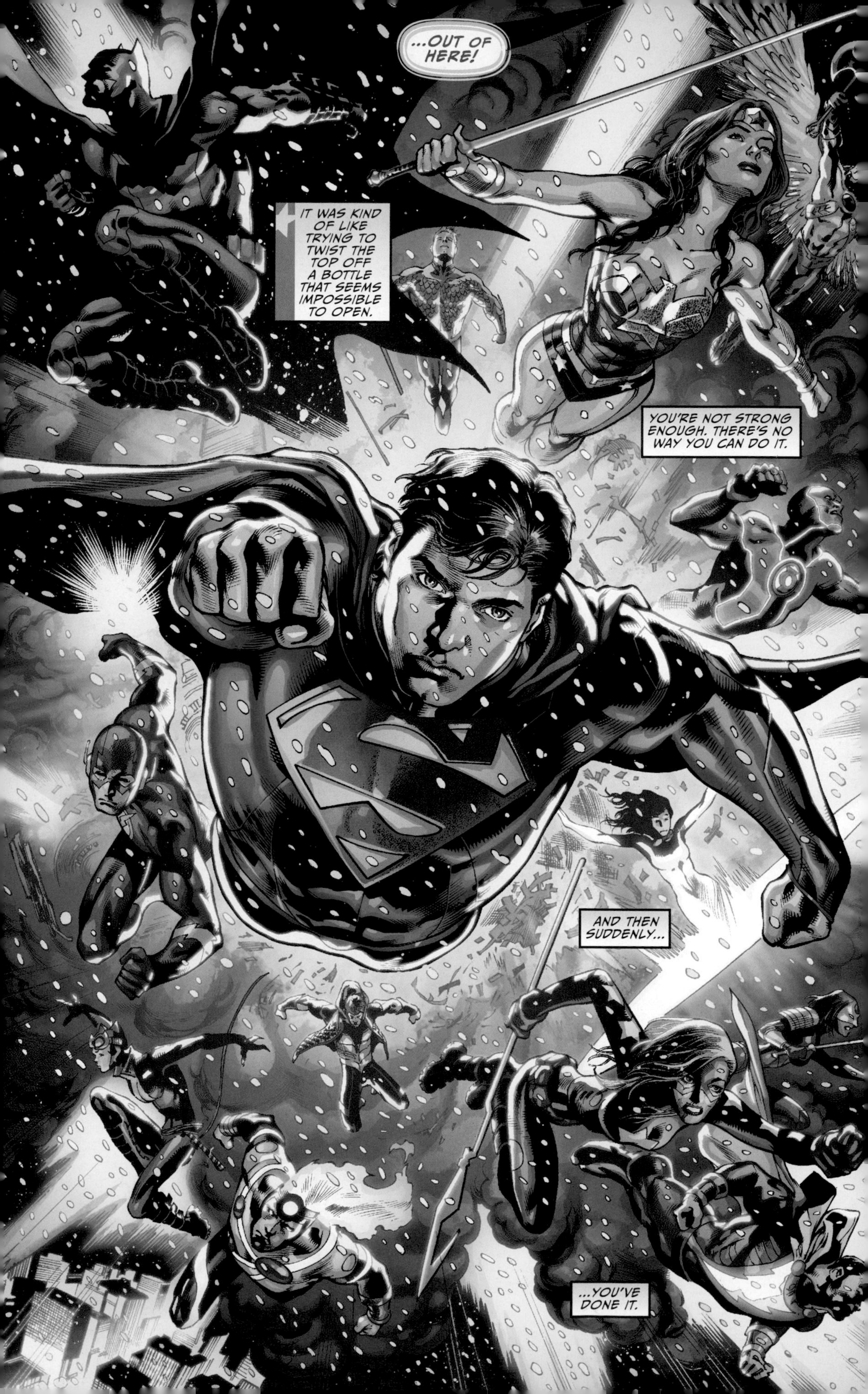
...OUT OF HERE!
IT WAS KIND OF LIKE TRYING TO TWIST THE TOP OFF A BOTTLE THAT SEEMS IMPOSSIBLE TO OPEN.
YOU'RE NOT STRONG ENOUGH. THERE'S NO WAY YOU CAN DO IT.
AND THEN SUDDENLY...
...YOU'VE DONE IT.

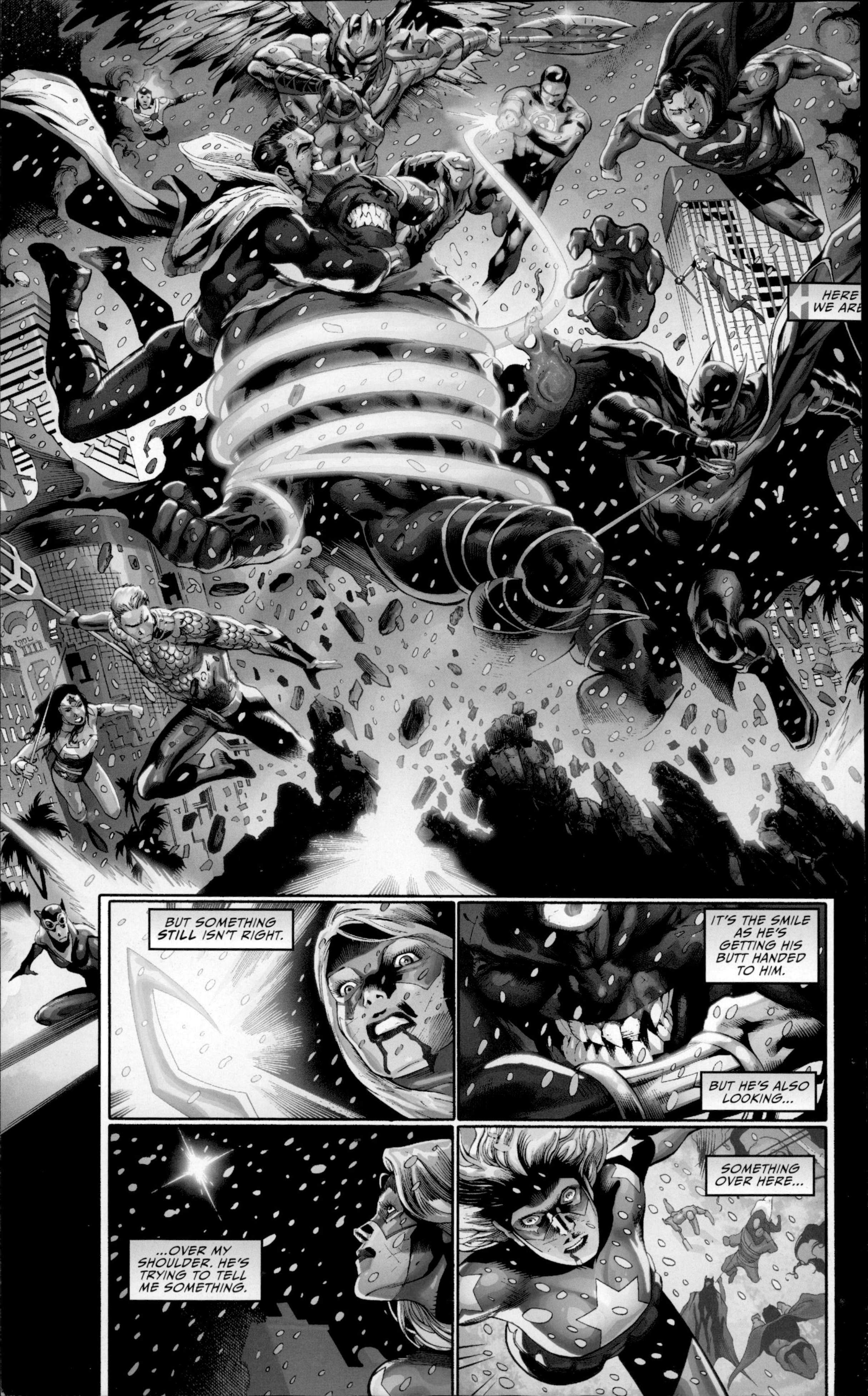
HERE WE ARE
BUT SOMETHING STILL ISN'T RIGHT.
IT'S THE SMILE AS HE'S GETTING HIS BUTT HANDED TO HIM.
BUT HE'S ALSO LOOKING...
...OVER MY SHOULDER. HE'S TRYING TO TELL ME SOMETHING.
SOMETHING OVER HERE...

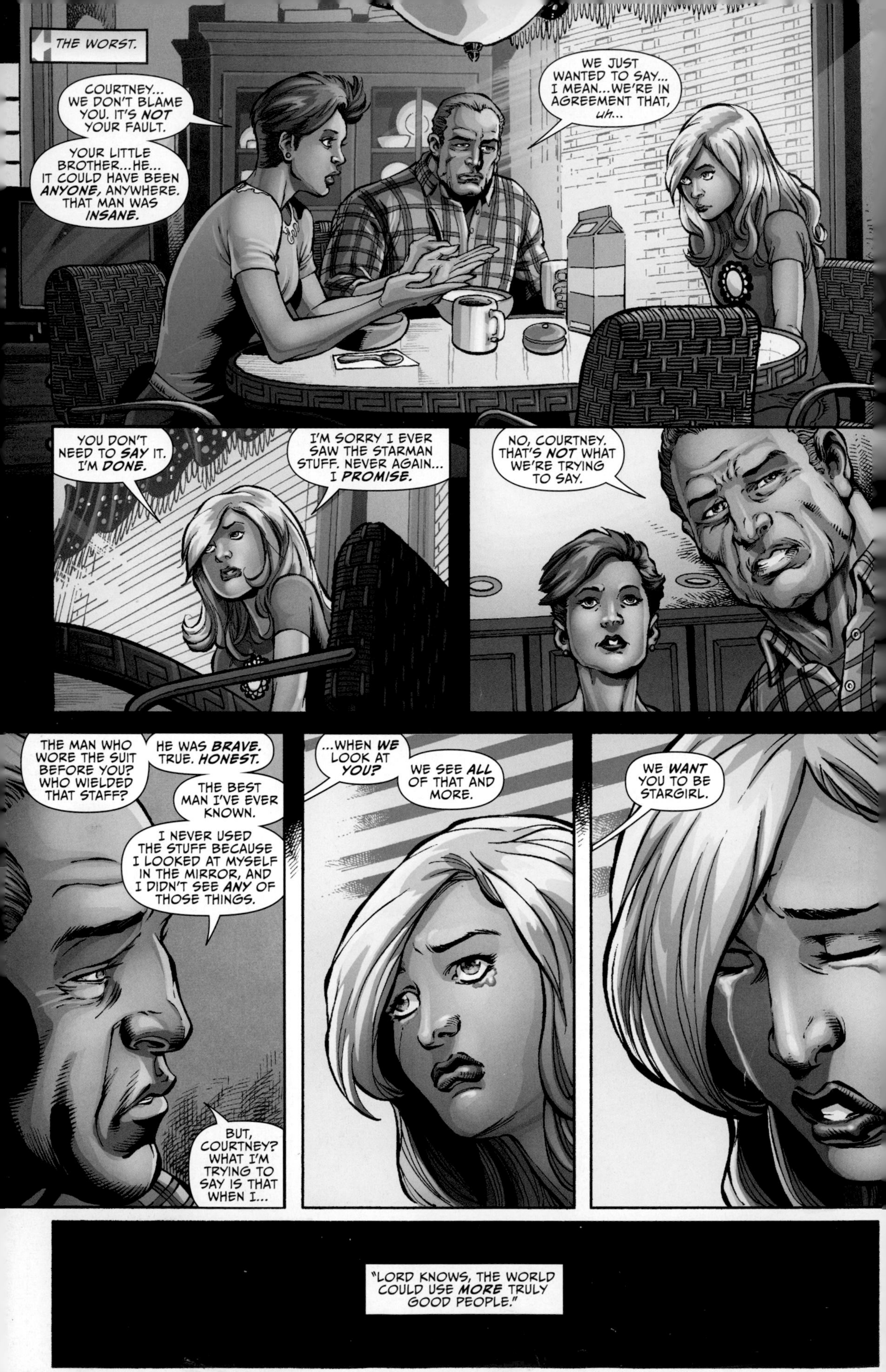

THE WORST.
COURTNEY... WE DON'T BLAME YOU. IT'S NOT YOUR FAULT.
YOUR LITTLE BROTHER...HE... IT COULD HAVE BEEN ANYONE, ANYWHERE. THAT MAN WAS INSANE.
WE JUST WANTED TO SAY... I MEAN...WE'RE IN AGREEMENT THAT, uh...
YOU DON'T NEED TO SAY IT. I'M DONE.
I'M SORRY I EVER SAW THE STARMAN STUFF. NEVER AGAIN... I PROMISE.
NO, COURTNEY. THAT'S NOT WHAT WE'RE TRYING TO SAY.
THE MAN WHO WORE THE SUIT BEFORE YOU? WHO WIELDED THAT STAFF?
HE WAS BRAVE. TRUE. HONEST.
THE BEST MAN I'VE EVER KNOWN.
I NEVER USED THE STUFF BECAUSE I LOOKED AT MYSELF IN THE MIRROR, AND I DIDN'T SEE ANY OF THOSE THINGS.
BUT, COURTNEY? WHAT I'M TRYING TO SAY IS THAT WHEN I...
...WHEN WE LOOK AT YOU?
WE SEE ALL OF THAT AND MORE.
WE WANT YOU TO BE STARGIRL.
"LORD KNOWS, THE WORLD COULD USE MORE TRULY GOOD PEOPLE."

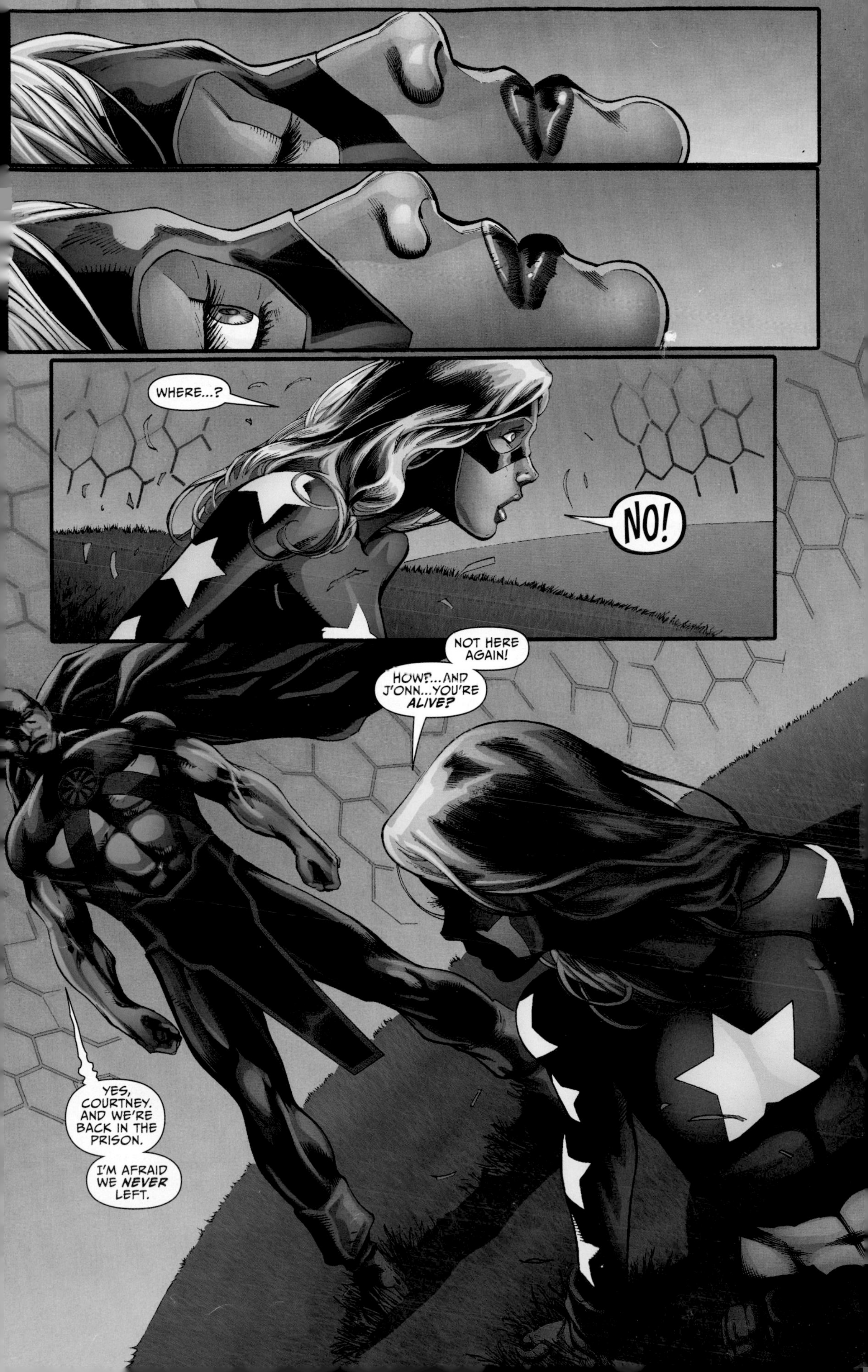
WHERE...?
NO!
NOT HERE AGAIN!
HOW?...AND J'ONN...YOU'RE ALIVE?
YES, COURTNEY. AND WE'RE BACK IN THE PRISON.
I'M AFRAID WE NEVER LEFT.

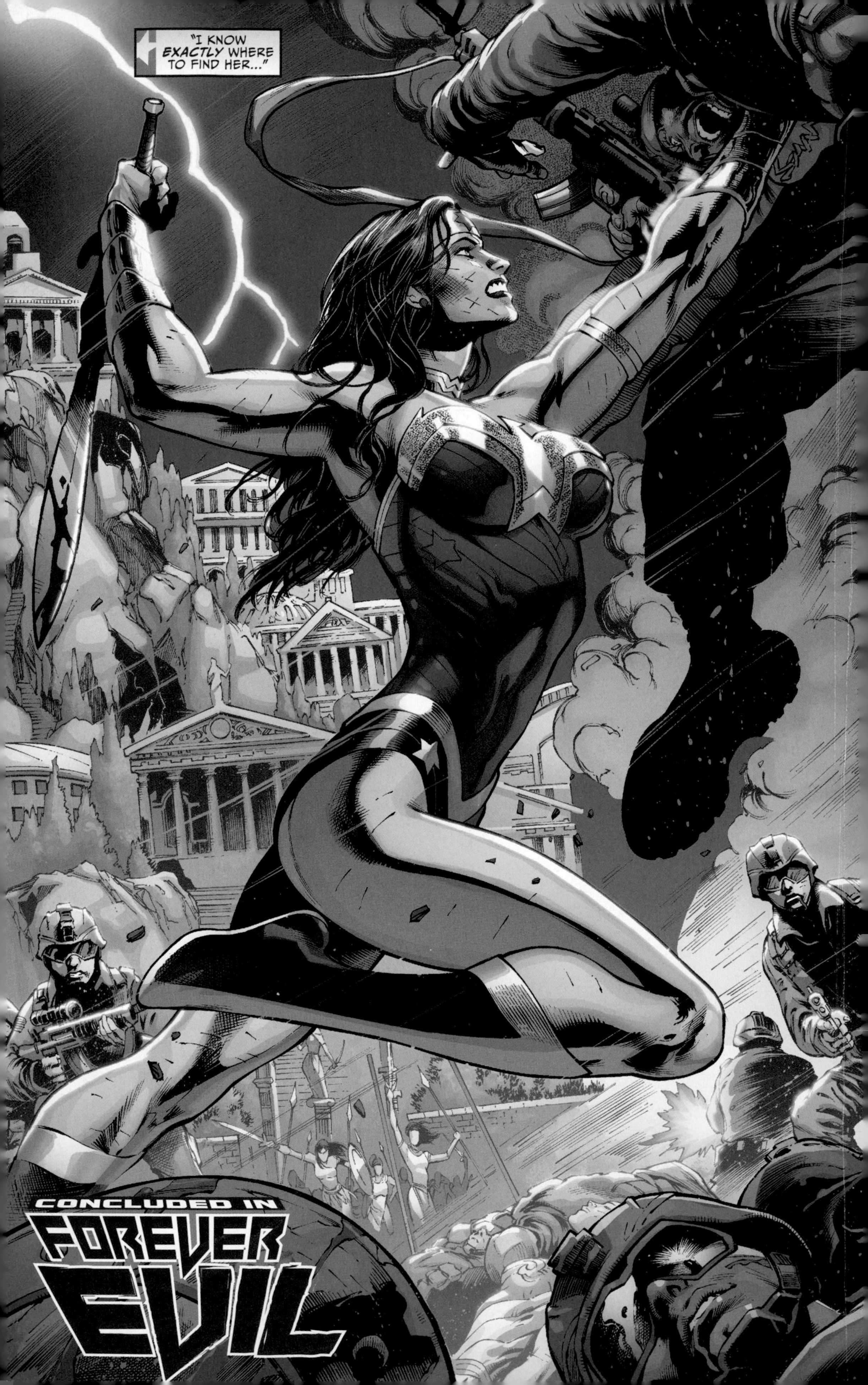
"I KNOW EXACTLY WHERE TO FIND HER..."
CONCLUDED IN
FOREVER EVIL

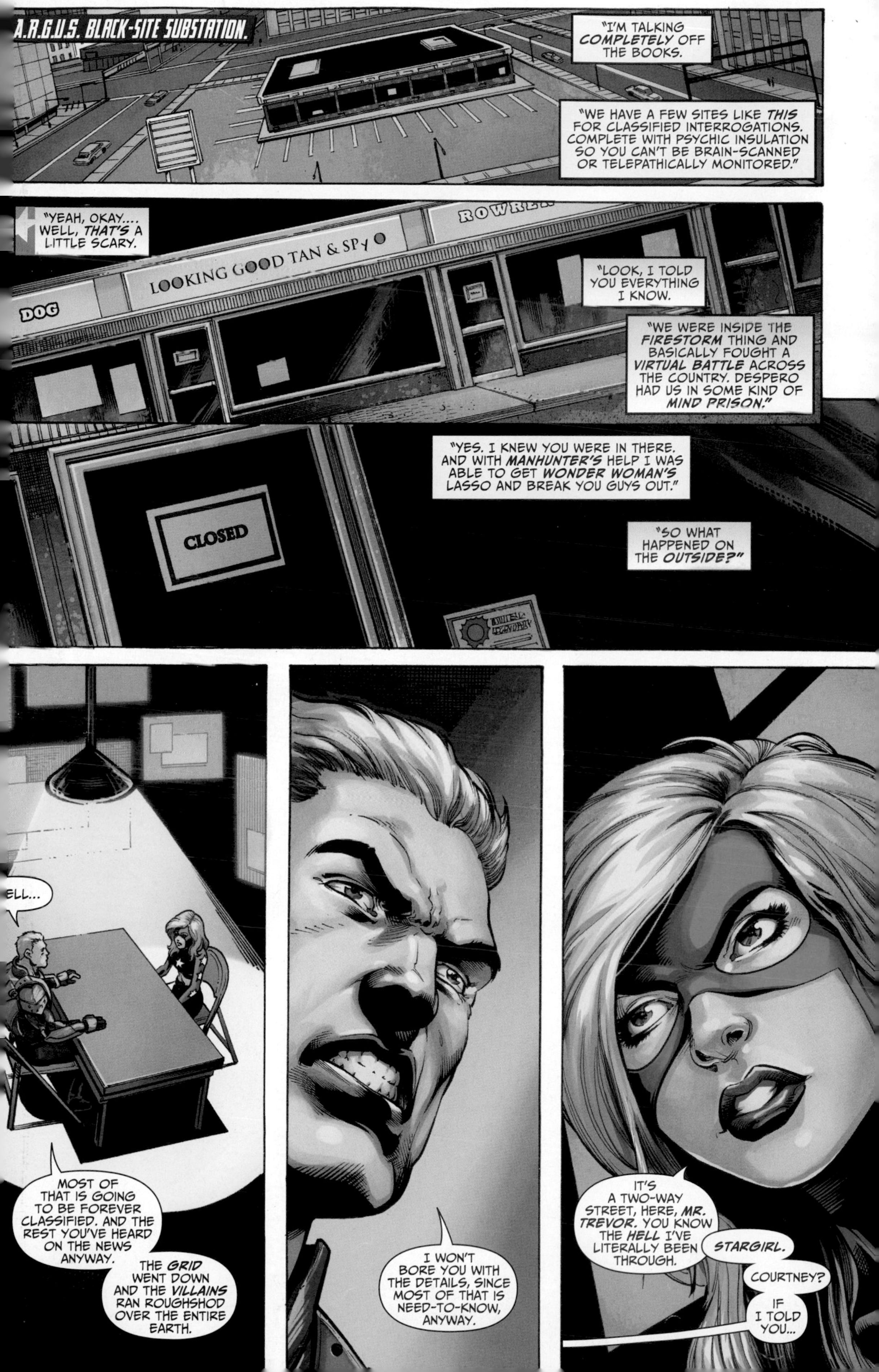
A.R.G.U.S. BLACK-SITE SUBSTATION.
"I'M TALKING COMPLETELY OFF THE BOOKS.
"WE HAVE A FEW SITES LIKE THIS FOR CLASSIFIED INTERROGATIONS. COMPLETE WITH PSYCHIC INSULATION SO YOU CAN'T BE BRAIN-SCANNED OR TELEPATHICALLY MONITORED."
"YEAH, OKAY.... WELL, THAT'S A LITTLE SCARY.
LOOKING GOOD TAN & SPA
DOG
"LOOK, I TOLD YOU EVERYTHING I KNOW.
"WE WERE INSIDE THE FIRESTORM THING AND BASICALLY FOUGHT A VIRTUAL BATTLE ACROSS THE COUNTRY. DESPERO HAD US IN SOME KIND OF MIND PRISON."
"YES. I KNEW YOU WERE IN THERE. AND WITH MANHUNTER'S HELP I WAS ABLE TO GET WONDER WOMAN'S LASSO AND BREAK YOU GUYS OUT."
CLOSED
"SO WHAT HAPPENED ON THE OUTSIDE?"
ELL...
MOST OF THAT IS GOING TO BE FOREVER CLASSIFIED. AND THE REST YOU'VE HEARD ON THE NEWS ANYWAY.
THE GRID WENT DOWN AND THE VILLAINS RAN ROUGHSHOD OVER THE ENTIRE EARTH.
I WON'T BORE YOU WITH THE DETAILS, SINCE MOST OF THAT IS NEED-TO-KNOW, ANYWAY.
IT'S A TWO-WAY STREET, HERE, MR. TREVOR. YOU KNOW THE HELL I'VE LITERALLY BEEN THROUGH.
STARGIRL.
COURTNEY?
IF I TOLD YOU...

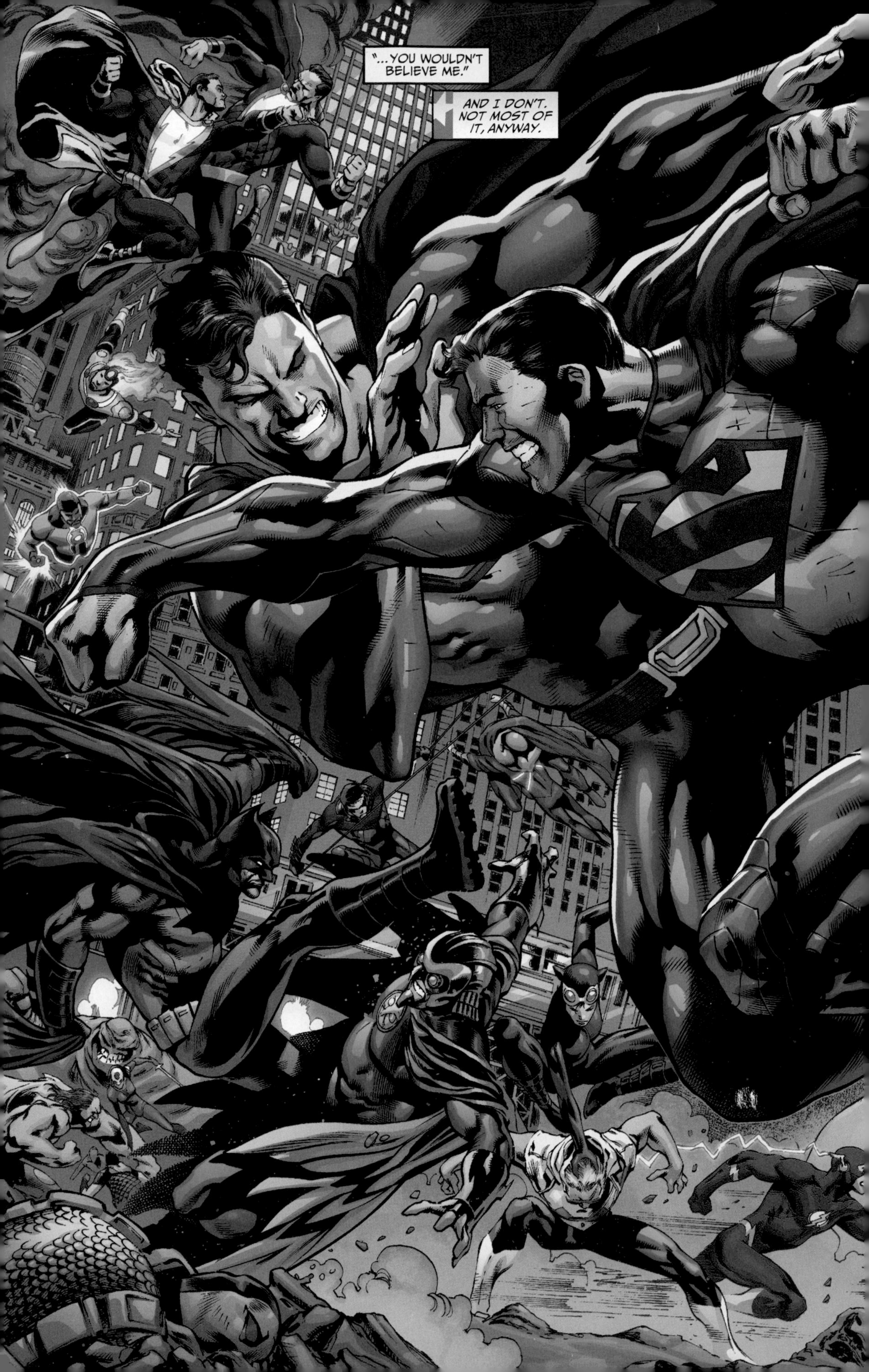

"...YOU WOULDN'T BELIEVE ME."
AND I DON'T. NOT MOST OF IT, ANYWAY.

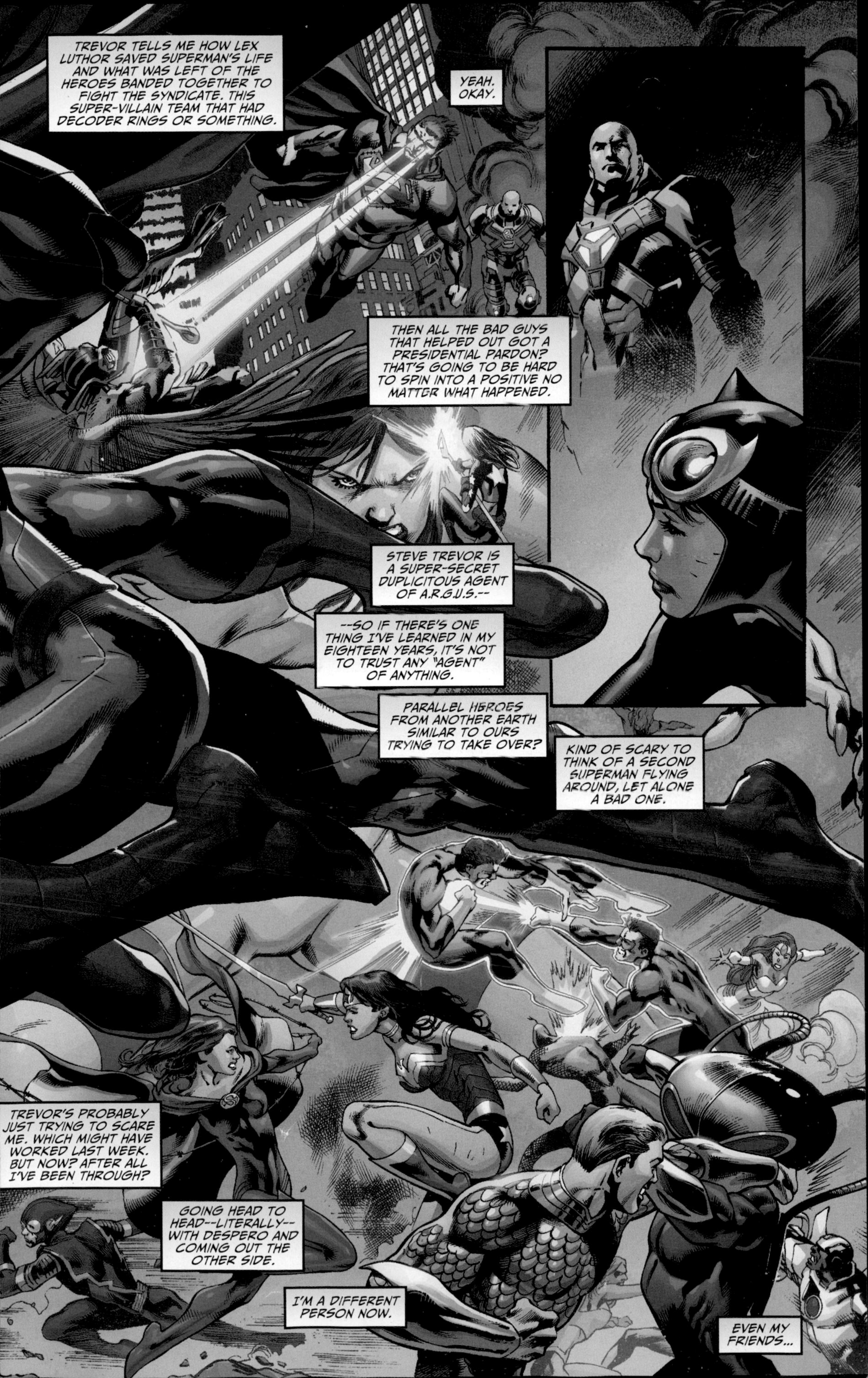
TREVOR TELLS ME HOW LEX LUTHOR SAVED SUPERMAN'S LIFE AND WHAT WAS LEFT OF THE HEROES BANDED TOGETHER TO FIGHT THE SYNDICATE. THIS SUPER-VILLAIN TEAM THAT HAD DECODER RINGS OR SOMETHING.
YEAH. OKAY.
THEN ALL THE BAD GUYS THAT HELPED OUT GOT A PRESIDENTIAL PARDON? THAT'S GOING TO BE HARD TO SPIN INTO A POSITIVE NO MATTER WHAT HAPPENED.
STEVE TREVOR IS A SUPER-SECRET DUPLICITOUS AGENT OF A.R.G.U.S.--
--SO IF THERE'S ONE THING I'VE LEARNED IN MY EIGHTEEN YEARS, IT'S NOT TO TRUST ANY "AGENT" OF ANYTHING.
PARALLEL HEROES FROM ANOTHER EARTH SIMILAR TO OURS TRYING TO TAKE OVER?
KIND OF SCARY TO THINK OF A SECOND SUPERMAN FLYING AROUND, LET ALONE A BAD ONE.
TREVOR'S PROBABLY JUST TRYING TO SCARE ME. WHICH MIGHT HAVE WORKED LAST WEEK. BUT NOW? AFTER ALL I'VE BEEN THROUGH?
GOING HEAD TO HEAD--LITERALLY--WITH DESPERO AND COMING OUT THE OTHER SIDE.
I'M A DIFFERENT PERSON NOW.
EVEN MY FRIENDS...

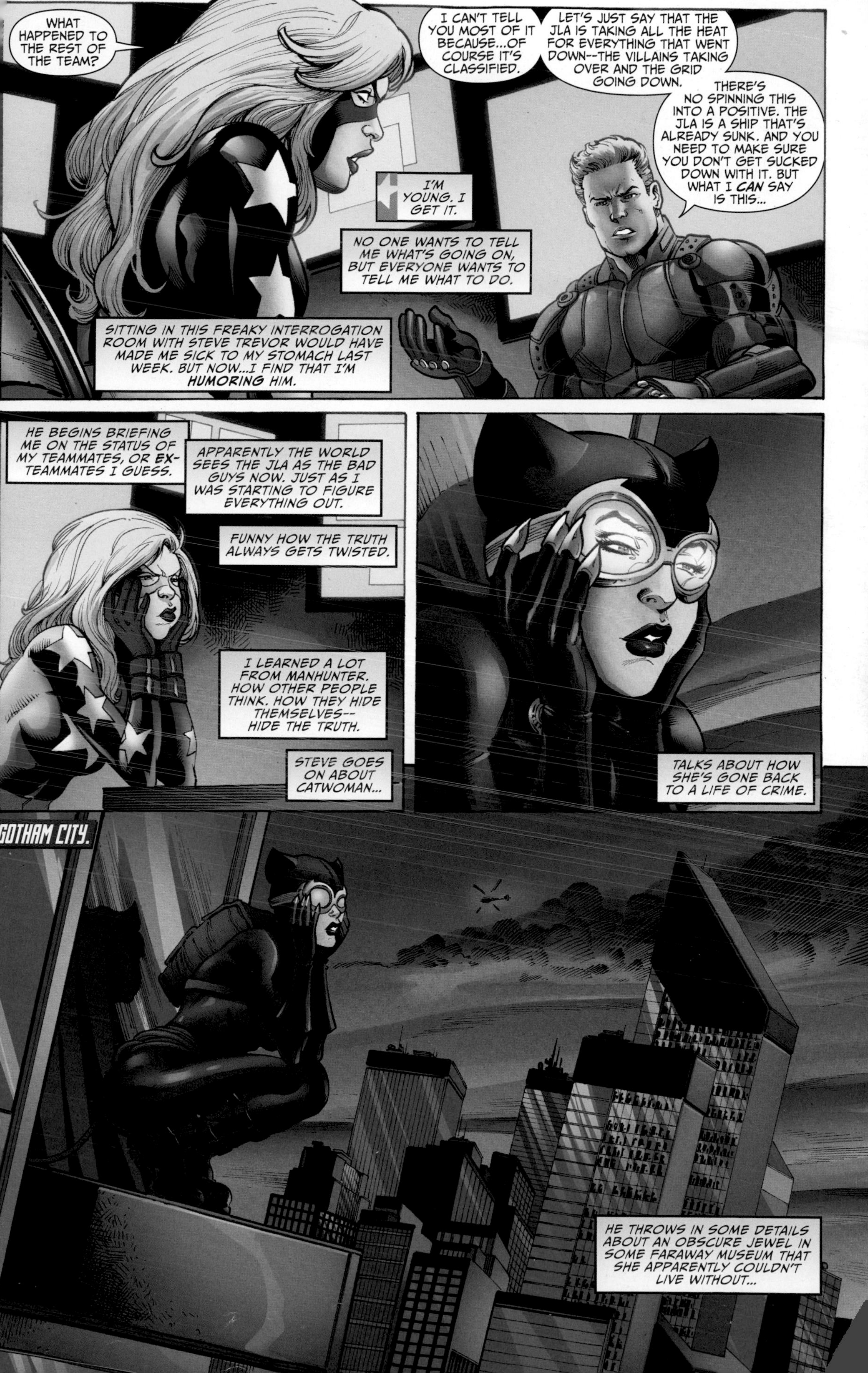
WHAT HAPPENED TO THE REST OF THE TEAM?
I CAN'T TELL YOU MOST OF IT BECAUSE...OF COURSE IT'S CLASSIFIED.
LET'S JUST SAY THAT THE JLA IS TAKING ALL THE HEAT FOR EVERYTHING THAT WENT DOWN--THE VILLAINS TAKING OVER AND THE GRID GOING DOWN.
THERE'S NO SPINNING THIS INTO A POSITIVE. THE JLA IS A SHIP THAT'S ALREADY SUNK. AND YOU NEED TO MAKE SURE YOU DON'T GET SUCKED DOWN WITH IT. BUT WHAT I CAN SAY IS THIS...
I'M YOUNG. I GET IT.
NO ONE WANTS TO TELL ME WHAT'S GOING ON, BUT EVERYONE WANTS TO TELL ME WHAT TO DO.
SITTING IN THIS FREAKY INTERROGATION ROOM WITH STEVE TREVOR WOULD HAVE MADE ME SICK TO MY STOMACH LAST WEEK. BUT NOW...I FIND THAT I'M HUMORING HIM.
HE BEGINS BRIEFING ME ON THE STATUS OF MY TEAMMATES, OR EX-TEAMMATES I GUESS.
APPARENTLY THE WORLD SEES THE JLA AS THE BAD GUYS NOW. JUST AS I WAS STARTING TO FIGURE EVERYTHING OUT.
FUNNY HOW THE TRUTH ALWAYS GETS TWISTED.
I LEARNED A LOT FROM MANHUNTER. HOW OTHER PEOPLE THINK. HOW THEY HIDE THEMSELVES--HIDE THE TRUTH.
STEVE GOES ON ABOUT CATWOMAN...
TALKS ABOUT HOW SHE'S GONE BACK TO A LIFE OF CRIME.
GOTHAM CITY.
HE THROWS IN SOME DETAILS ABOUT AN OBSCURE JEWEL IN SOME FARAWAY MUSEUM THAT SHE APPARENTLY COULDN'T LIVE WITHOUT...

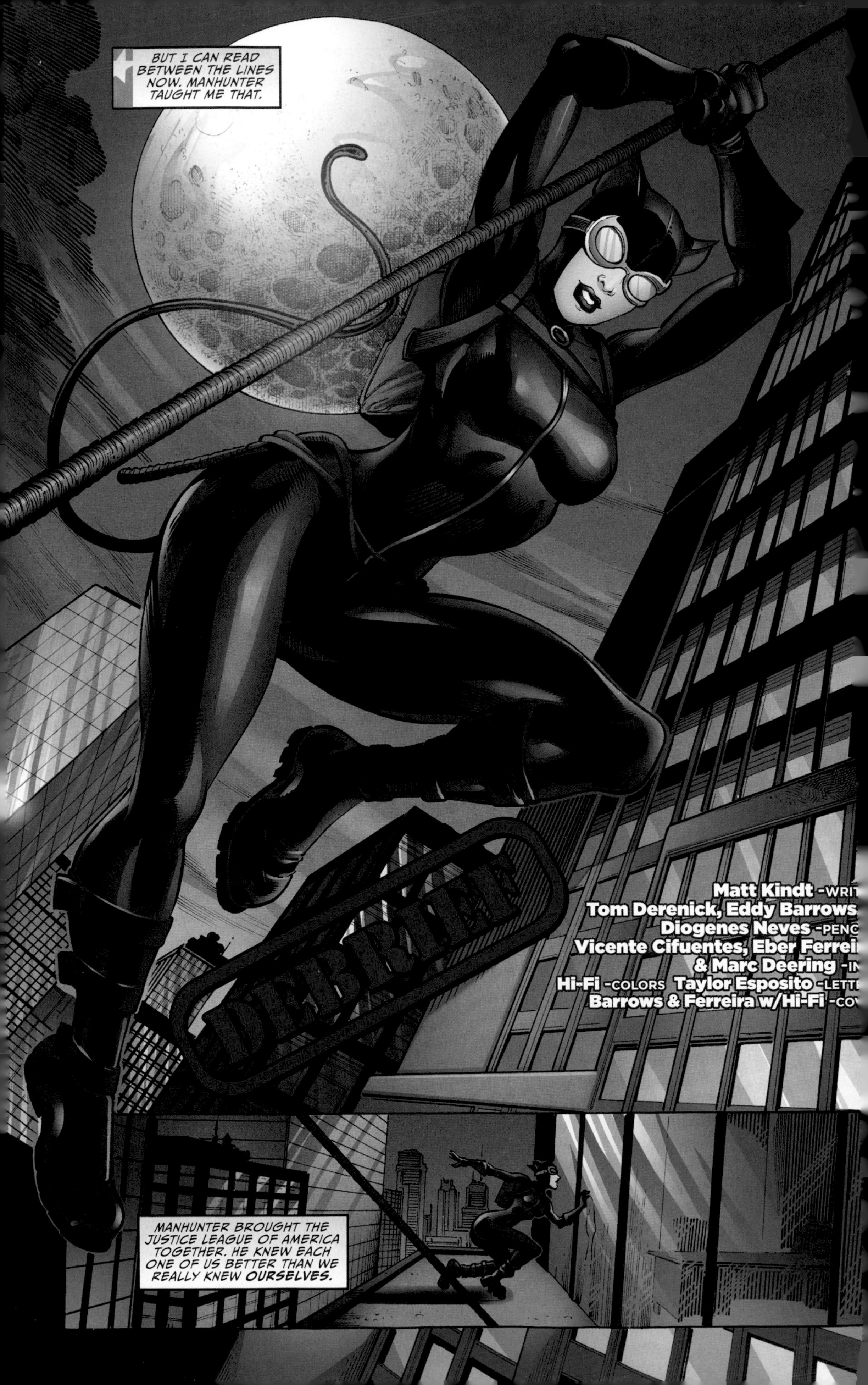
BUT I CAN READ BETWEEN THE LINES NOW. MANHUNTER TAUGHT ME THAT.
DEBRIEF
Matt Kindt -WRIT
Tom Derenick, Eddy Barrows,
Diogenes Neves -PENC
Vicente Cifuentes, Eber Ferrei
& Marc Deering -IN
Hi-Fi -COLORS Taylor Esposito -LETT
Barrows & Ferreira w/Hi-Fi -COV
MANHUNTER BROUGHT THE JUSTICE LEAGUE OF AMERICA TOGETHER. HE KNEW EACH ONE OF US BETTER THAN WE REALLY KNEW OURSELVES.

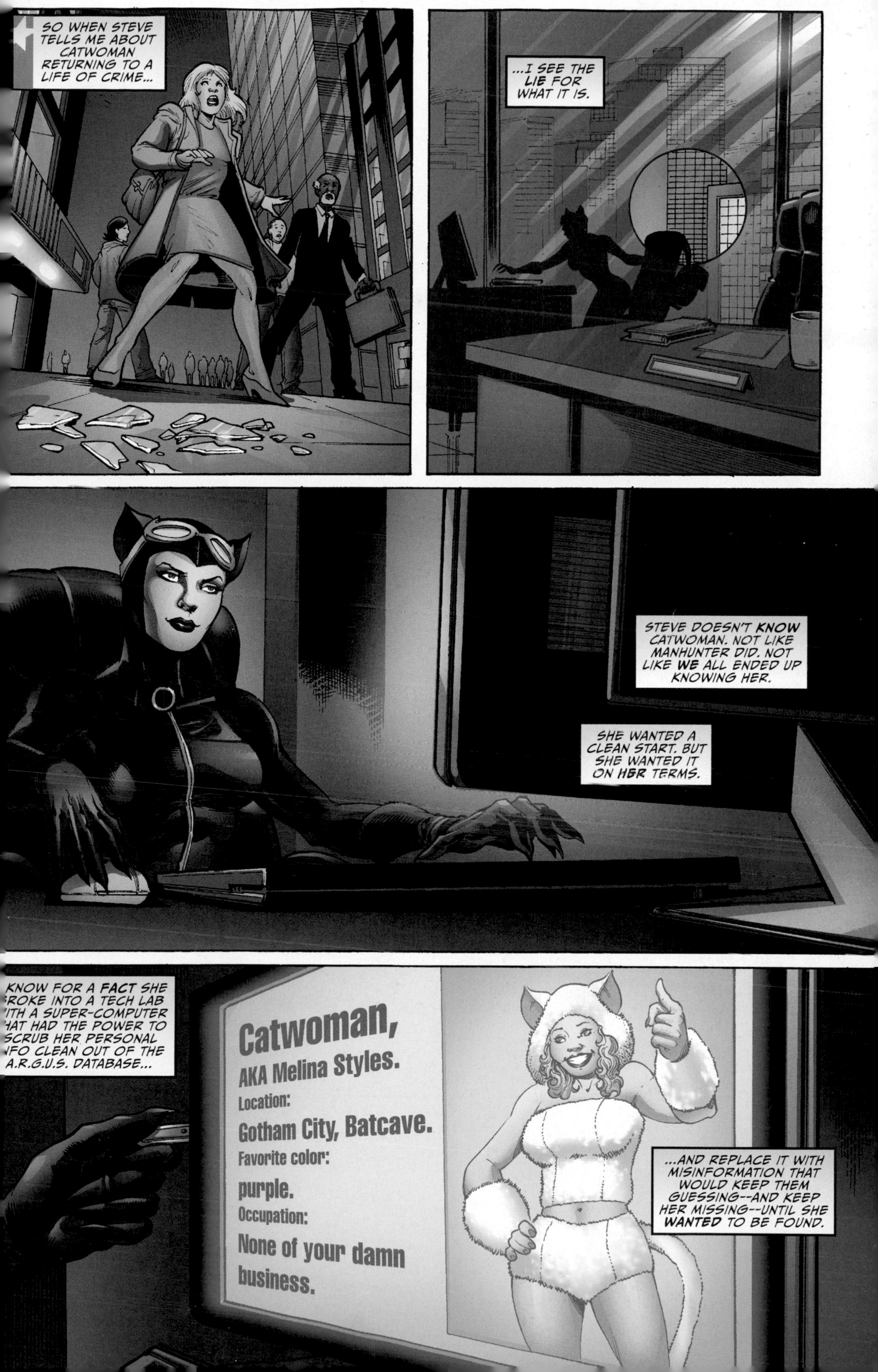
SO WHEN STEVE TELLS ME ABOUT CATWOMAN RETURNING TO A LIFE OF CRIME...
...I SEE THE LIE FOR WHAT IT IS.
STEVE DOESN'T KNOW CATWOMAN. NOT LIKE MANHUNTER DID. NOT LIKE WE ALL ENDED UP KNOWING HER.
SHE WANTED A CLEAN START. BUT SHE WANTED IT ON HER TERMS.
KNOW FOR A FACT SHE ROKE INTO A TECH LAB ITH A SUPER-COMPUTER HAT HAD THE POWER TO SCRUB HER PERSONAL NFO CLEAN OUT OF THE A.R.G.U.S. DATABASE...
Catwoman,
AKA Melina Styles.
Location:
Gotham City, Batcave.
Favorite color:
purple.
Occupation:
None of your damn business.
...AND REPLACE IT WITH MISINFORMATION THAT WOULD KEEP THEM GUESSING--AND KEEP HER MISSING--UNTIL SHE WANTED TO BE FOUND.

A LOT OF PEOPLE HAVE PROBLEMS WITH SUPER-POWERED GUYS FLYING AROUND TAKING CHARGE.

EASY ENOUGH TO UNDERSTAND...

PUT A BROWN-SKINNED GUY IN A **MASK** WITH THOSE KINDS OF **POWERS** IN AN UPSCALE NEIGHBORHOOD...AND IT JUST MULTIPLIED THE FEAR FACTOR.

I SAW FIRST-HAND WHAT SIMON FELT...

IT WASN'T PRETTY.

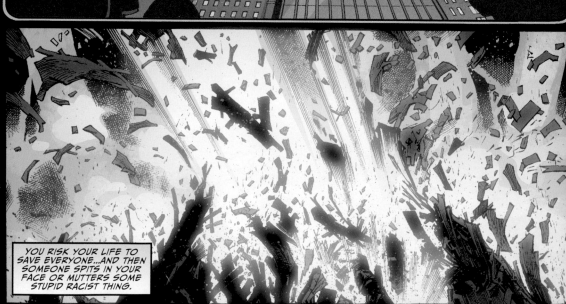

YOU RISK YOUR LIFE TO SAVE EVERYONE...AND THEN SOMEONE SPITS IN YOUR FACE OR MUTTERS SOME STUPID RACIST THING.

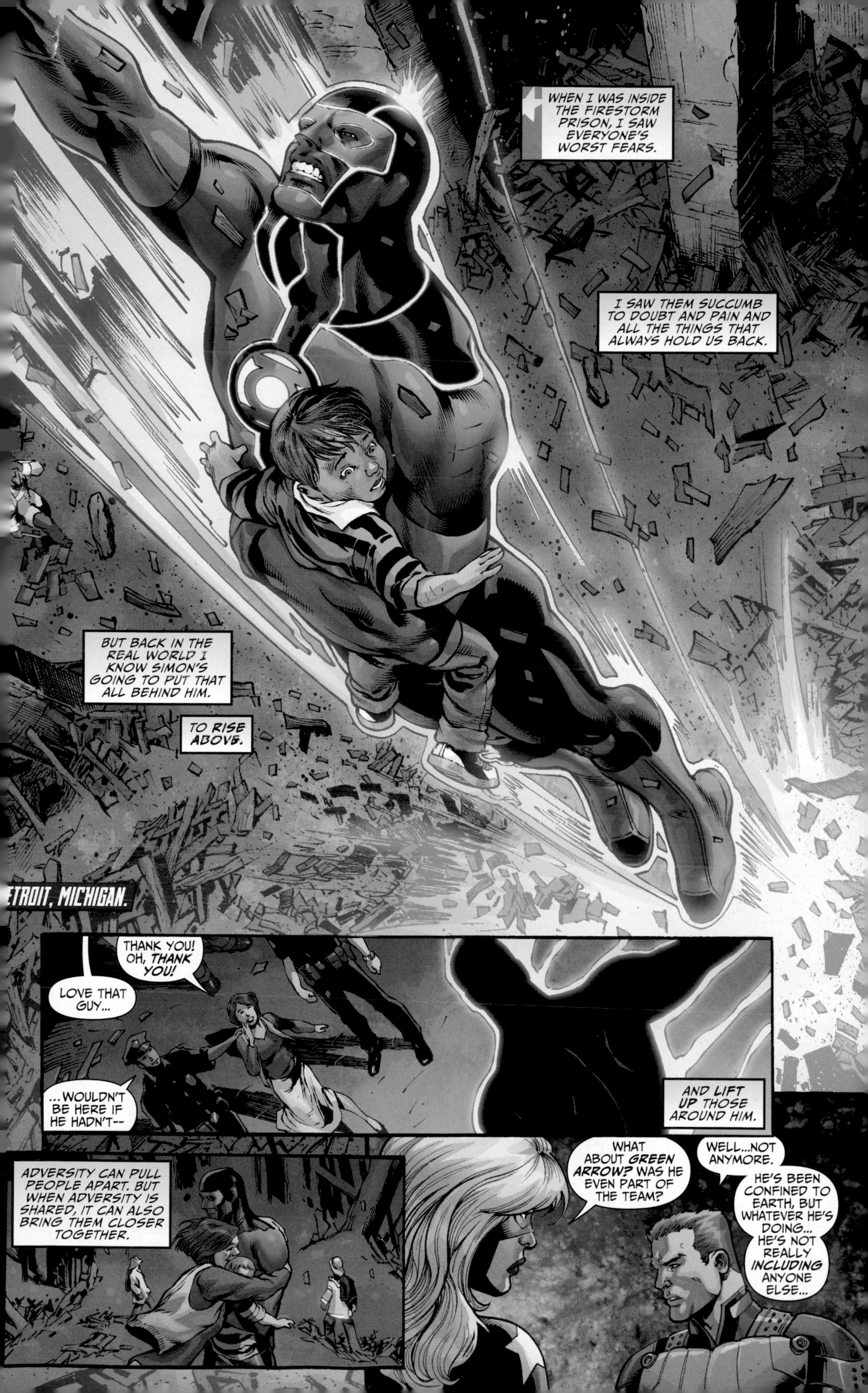
WHEN I WAS INSIDE THE FIRESTORM PRISON, I SAW EVERYONE'S WORST FEARS.
I SAW THEM SUCCUMB TO DOUBT AND PAIN AND ALL THE THINGS THAT ALWAYS HOLD US BACK.
BUT BACK IN THE REAL WORLD I KNOW SIMON'S GOING TO PUT THAT ALL BEHIND HIM.
TO RISE ABOVE.
ETROIT, MICHIGAN.
THANK YOU! OH, THANK YOU!
LOVE THAT GUY...
...WOULDN'T BE HERE IF HE HADN'T--
AND LIFT UP THOSE AROUND HIM.
ADVERSITY CAN PULL PEOPLE APART. BUT WHEN ADVERSITY IS SHARED, IT CAN ALSO BRING THEM CLOSER TOGETHER.
WHAT ABOUT GREEN ARROW? WAS HE EVEN PART OF THE TEAM?
WELL...NOT ANYMORE.
HE'S BEEN CONFINED TO EARTH, BUT WHATEVER HE'S DOING... HE'S NOT REALLY INCLUDING ANYONE ELSE...

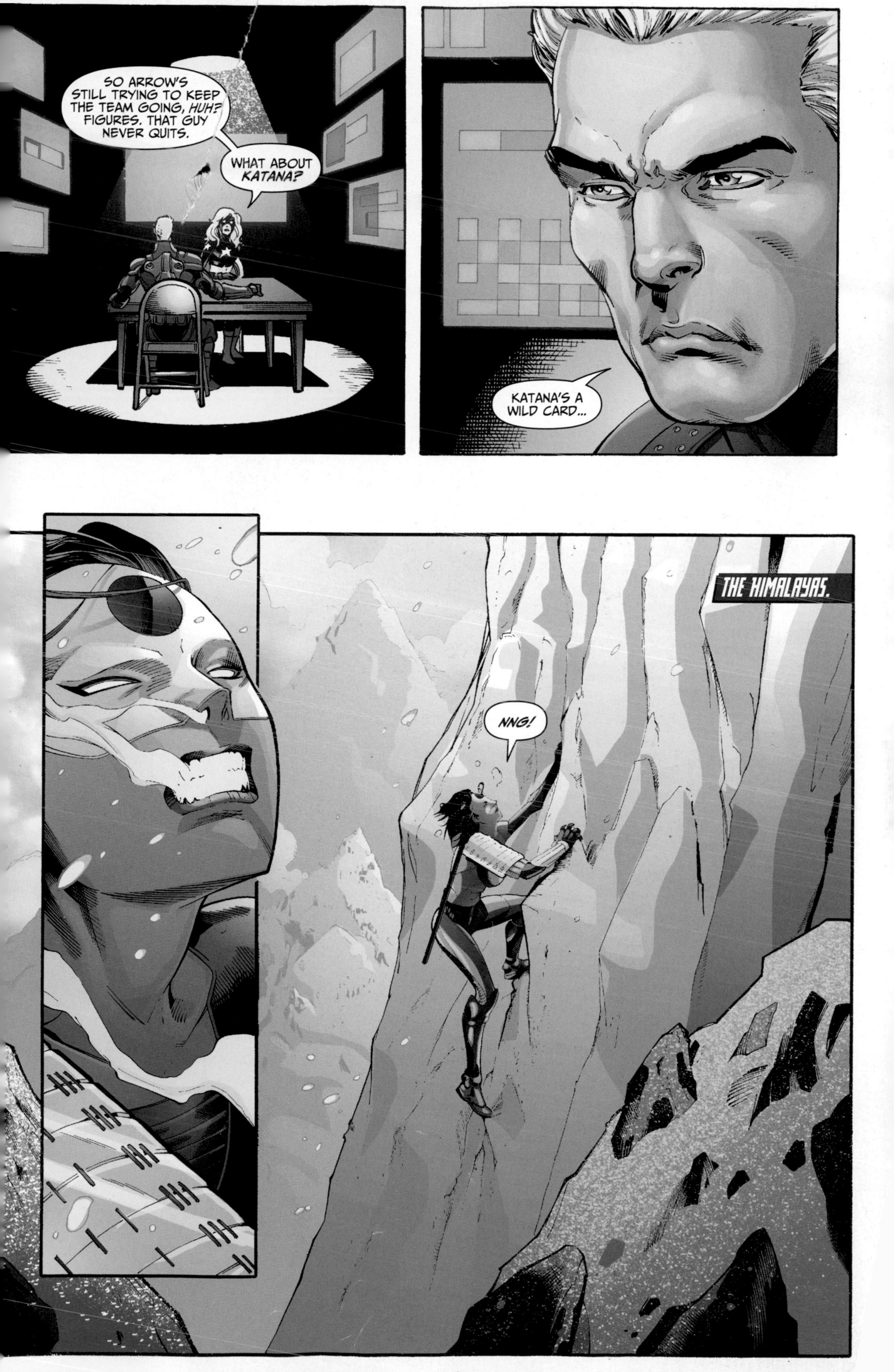
SO ARROW'S STILL TRYING TO KEEP THE TEAM GOING, HUH? FIGURES. THAT GUY NEVER QUITS.
WHAT ABOUT KATANA?
KATANA'S A WILD CARD...
THE HIMALAYAS.
NNG!

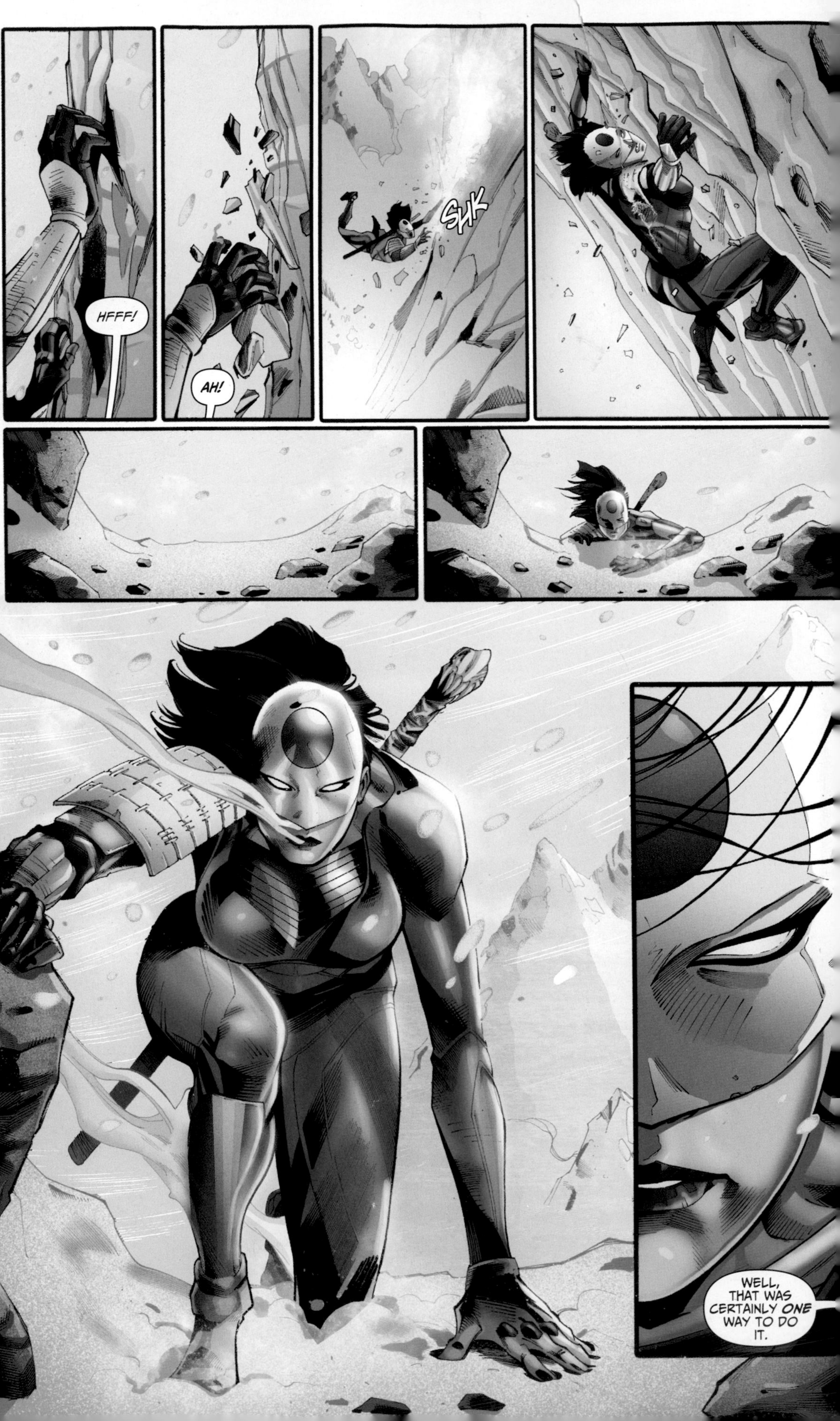
HFFF!
AH!
SHK
WELL, THAT WAS CERTAINLY ONE WAY TO DO IT.

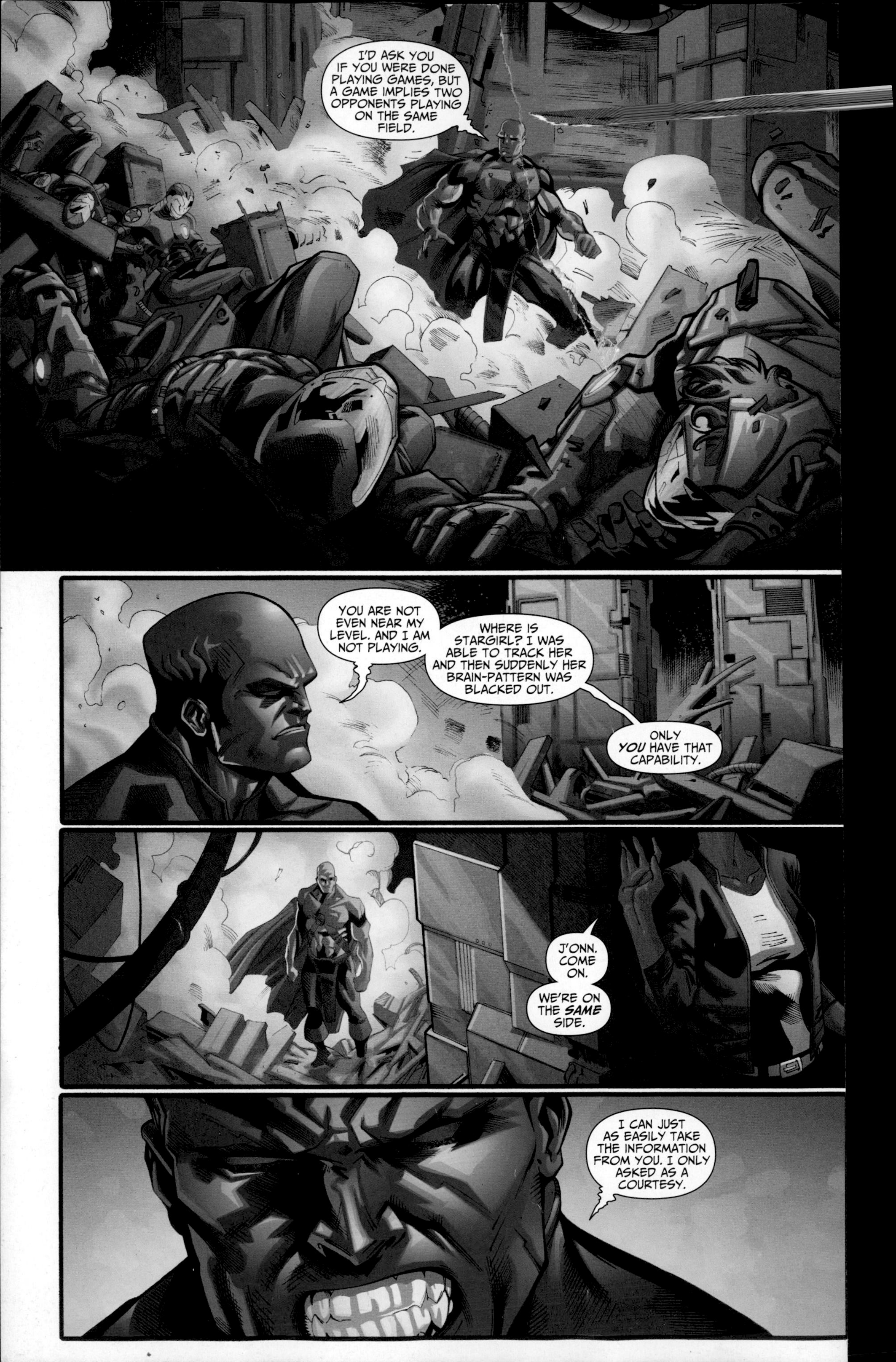
I'D ASK YOU IF YOU WERE DONE PLAYING GAMES, BUT A GAME IMPLIES TWO OPPONENTS PLAYING ON THE SAME FIELD.
YOU ARE NOT EVEN NEAR MY LEVEL. AND I AM NOT PLAYING.
WHERE IS STARGIRL? I WAS ABLE TO TRACK HER AND THEN SUDDENLY HER BRAIN-PATTERN WAS BLACKED OUT.
ONLY *YOU* HAVE THAT CAPABILITY.
J'ONN. COME ON.
WE'RE ON THE *SAME* SIDE.
I CAN JUST AS EASILY TAKE THE INFORMATION FROM YOU. I ONLY ASKED AS A COURTESY.

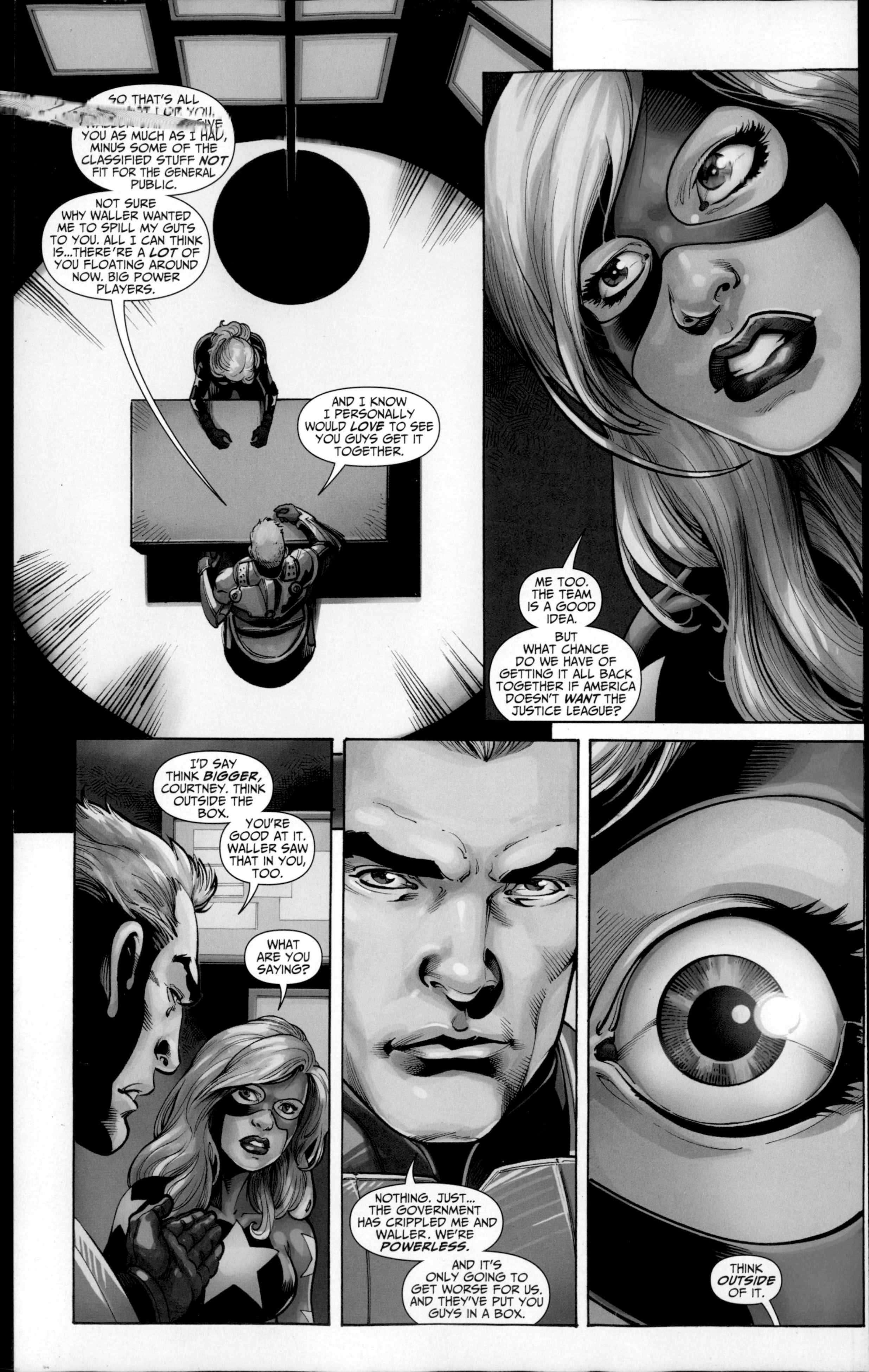
SO THAT'S ALL
YOU AS MUCH AS I HAD, MINUS SOME OF THE CLASSIFIED STUFF NOT FIT FOR THE GENERAL PUBLIC.
NOT SURE WHY WALLER WANTED ME TO SPILL MY GUTS TO YOU. ALL I CAN THINK IS...THERE'RE A LOT OF YOU FLOATING AROUND NOW. BIG POWER PLAYERS.
AND I KNOW I PERSONALLY WOULD LOVE TO SEE YOU GUYS GET IT TOGETHER.
ME TOO. THE TEAM IS A GOOD IDEA.
BUT WHAT CHANCE DO WE HAVE OF GETTING IT ALL BACK TOGETHER IF AMERICA DOESN'T WANT THE JUSTICE LEAGUE?
I'D SAY THINK BIGGER, COURTNEY. THINK OUTSIDE THE BOX.
YOU'RE GOOD AT IT. WALLER SAW THAT IN YOU, TOO.
WHAT ARE YOU SAYING?
NOTHING. JUST... THE GOVERNMENT HAS CRIPPLED ME AND WALLER. WE'RE POWERLESS.
AND IT'S ONLY GOING TO GET WORSE FOR US. AND THEY'VE PUT YOU GUYS IN A BOX.
THINK OUTSIDE OF IT.

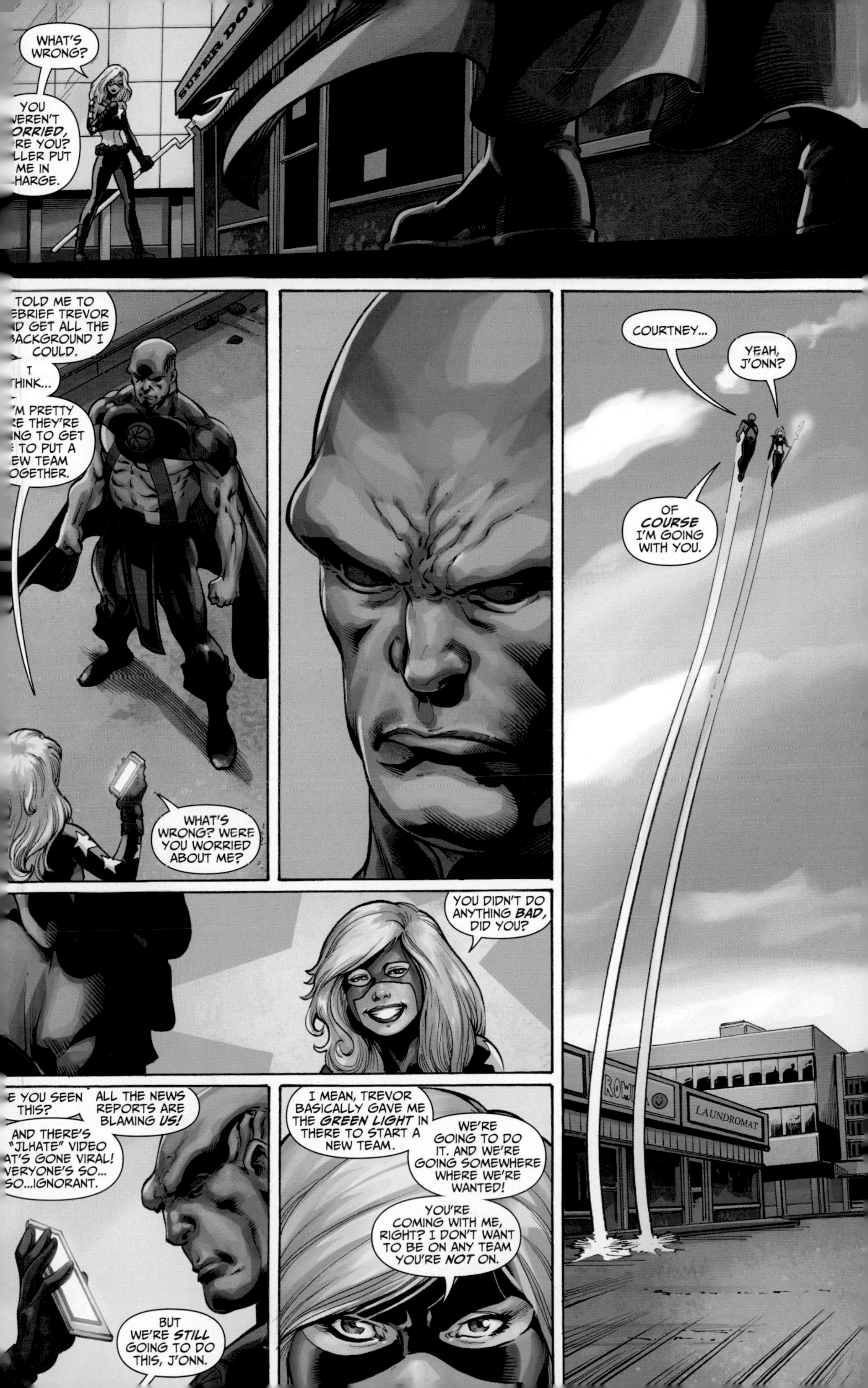

WHAT'S WRONG?
YOU WEREN'T ORRIED, ERE YOU? LLER PUT ME IN HARGE.
TOLD ME TO EBRIEF TREVOR D GET ALL THE BACKGROUND I COULD.
I THINK...
'M PRETTY RE THEY'RE NG TO GET E TO PUT A EW TEAM OGETHER.
WHAT'S WRONG? WERE YOU WORRIED ABOUT ME?
YOU DIDN'T DO ANYTHING BAD, DID YOU?
E YOU SEEN THIS?
ALL THE NEWS REPORTS ARE BLAMING US!
AND THERE'S "JLHATE" VIDEO AT'S GONE VIRAL! VERYONE'S SO... SO...IGNORANT.
BUT WE'RE STILL GOING TO DO THIS, J'ONN.
I MEAN, TREVOR BASICALLY GAVE ME THE GREEN LIGHT IN THERE TO START A NEW TEAM.
WE'RE GOING TO DO IT. AND WE'RE GOING SOMEWHERE WHERE WE'RE WANTED!
YOU'RE COMING WITH ME, RIGHT? I DON'T WANT TO BE ON ANY TEAM YOU'RE NOT ON.
COURTNEY...
YEAH, J'ONN?
OF COURSE I'M GOING WITH YOU.
SUPER DO
LAUNDROMAT

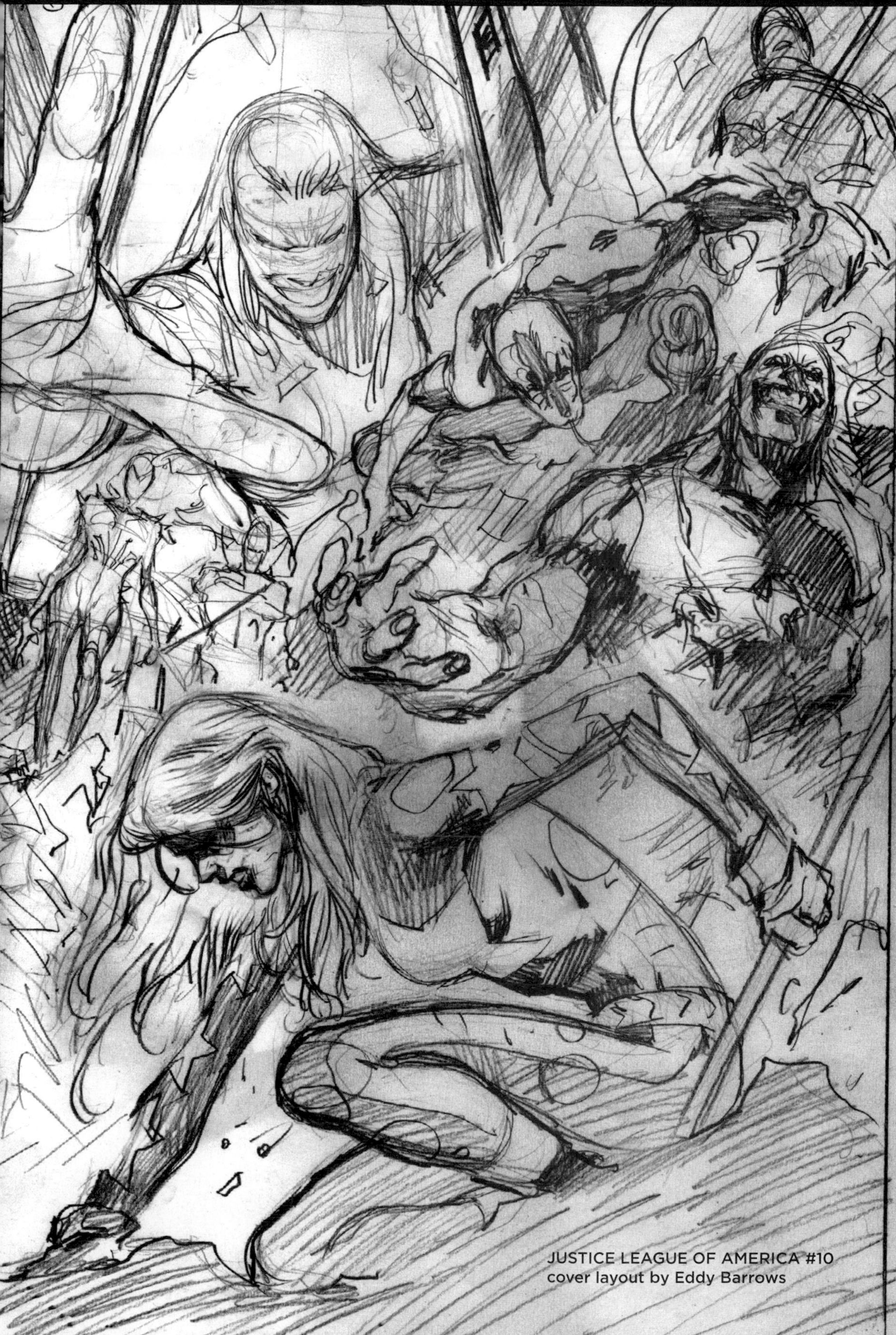

JUSTICE LEAGUE OF AMERICA #10
cover layout by Eddy Barrows

JUSTICE LEAGUE OF AMERICA #8
cover layout by Ken Lashley

JUSTICE LEAGUE OF AMERICA #9
cover layout by Doug Mahnke

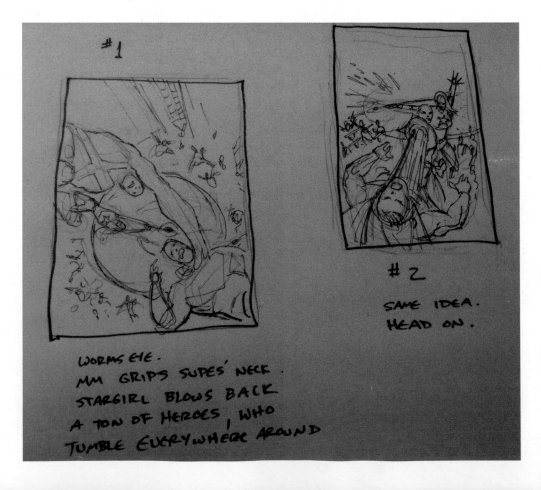

JUSTICE LEAGUE OF AMERICA #11 and #12
cover layouts and pencils by Eddy Barrows

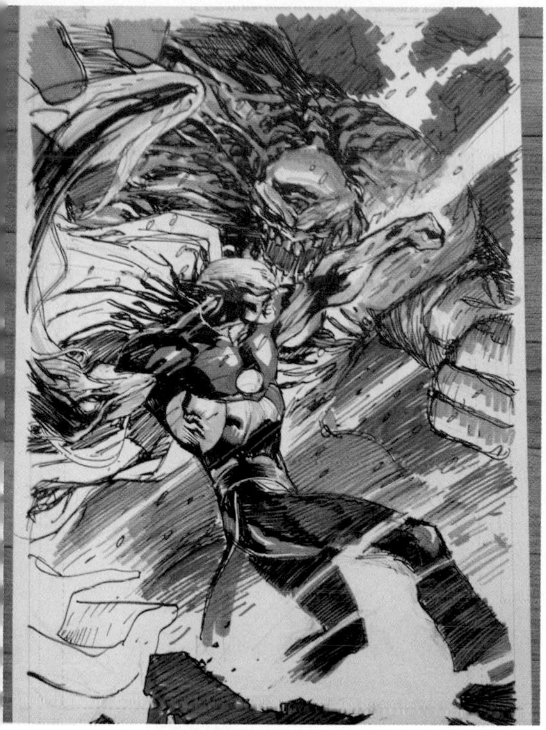

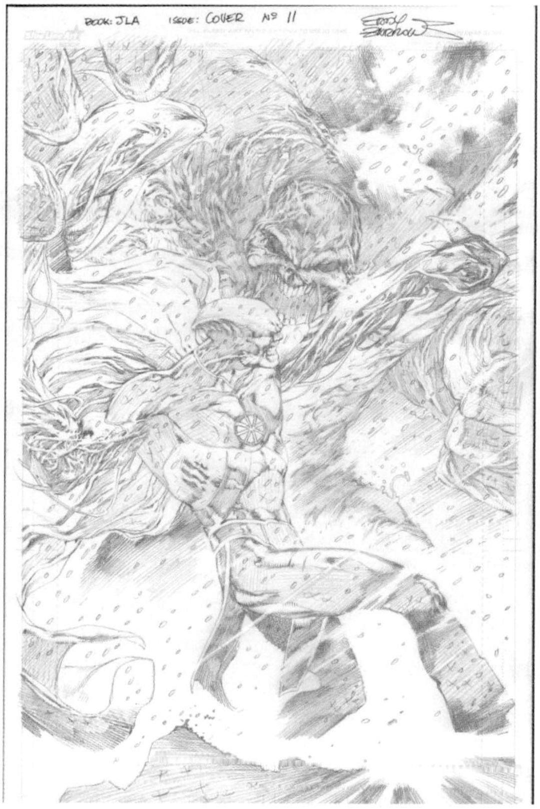
BOOK: JLA ISSUE: COVER Nº 11

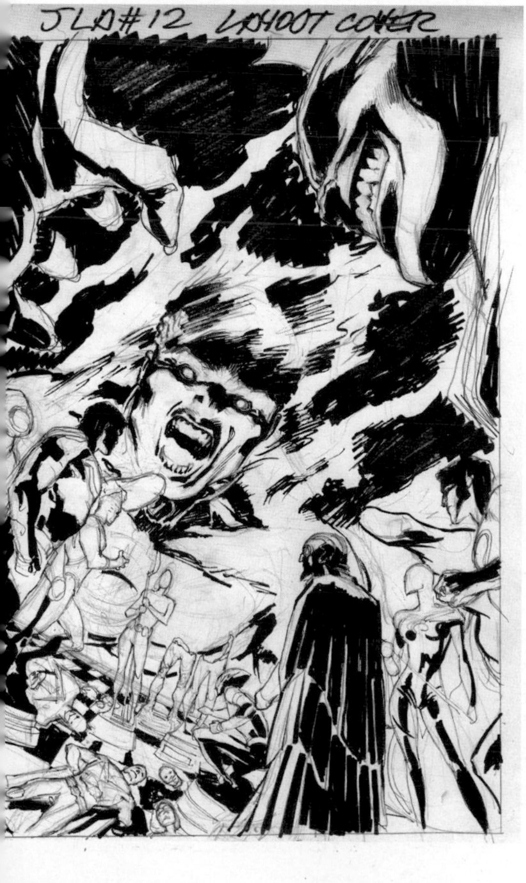
JLA#12 LAYOUT COVER

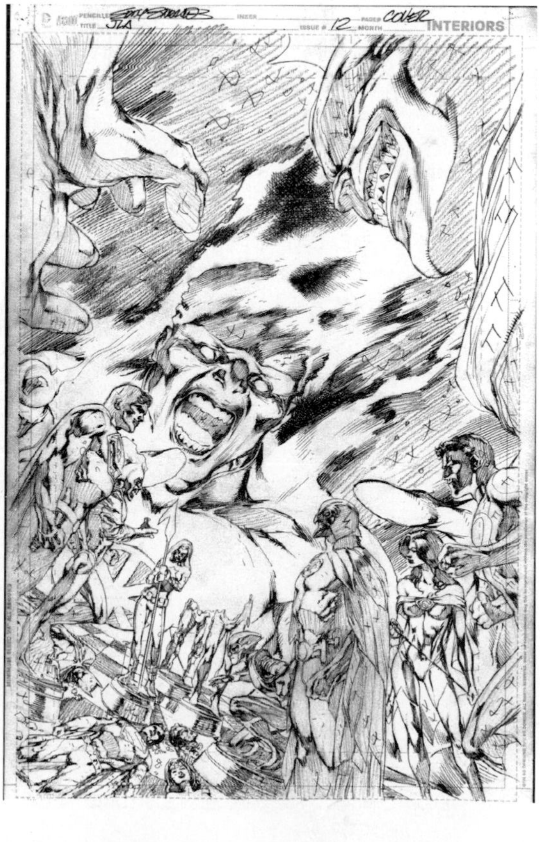
TITLE JLA
ISSUE # 12
COVER
INTERIORS

JUSTICE LEAGUE OF AMERICA #13 and #14
cover layouts and #14 pencils by Eddy Barrows

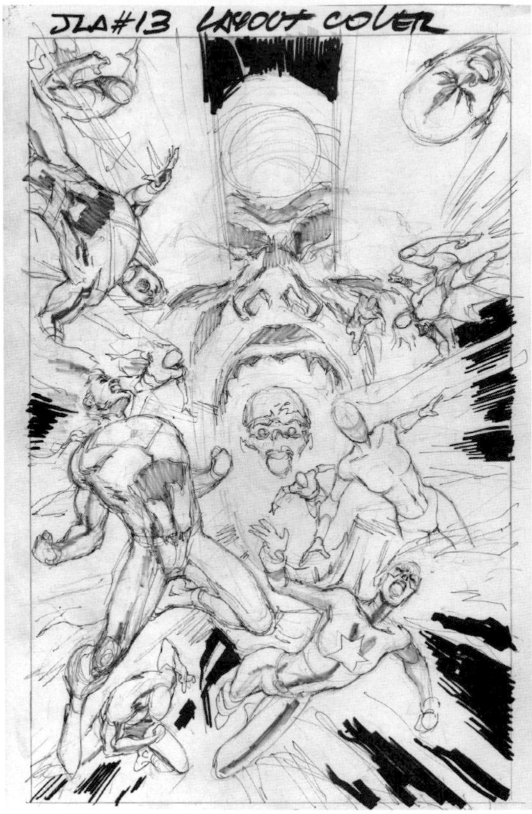
JLA#13 LAYOUT COVER

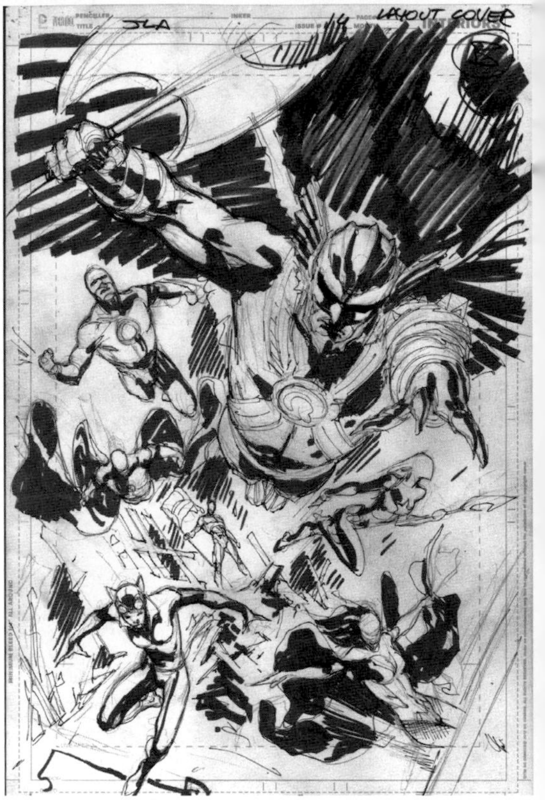
JLA
14
LAYOUT COVER

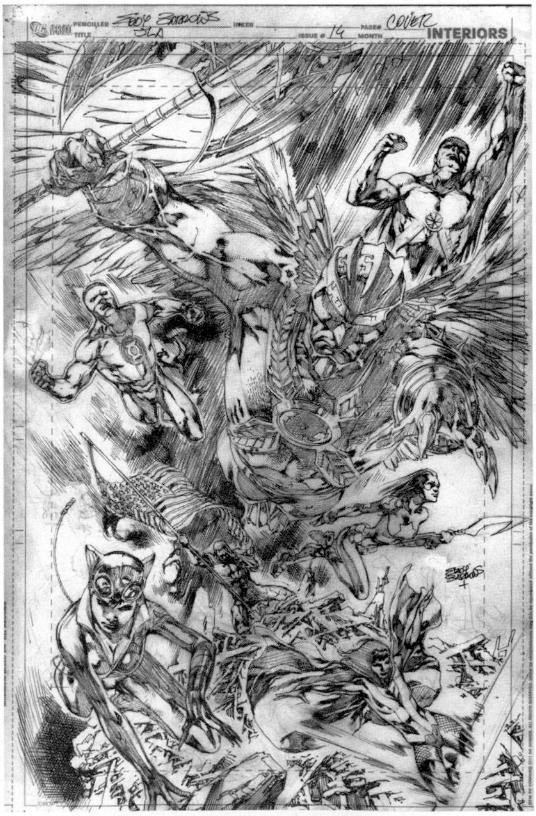
PENCILLER EDDY BARROWS
TITLE JLA
ISSUE # 14
PAGE# COVER
INTERIORS

ternate cover idea for JUSTICE LEAGUE OF AMERICA #14
y Eddy Barrows

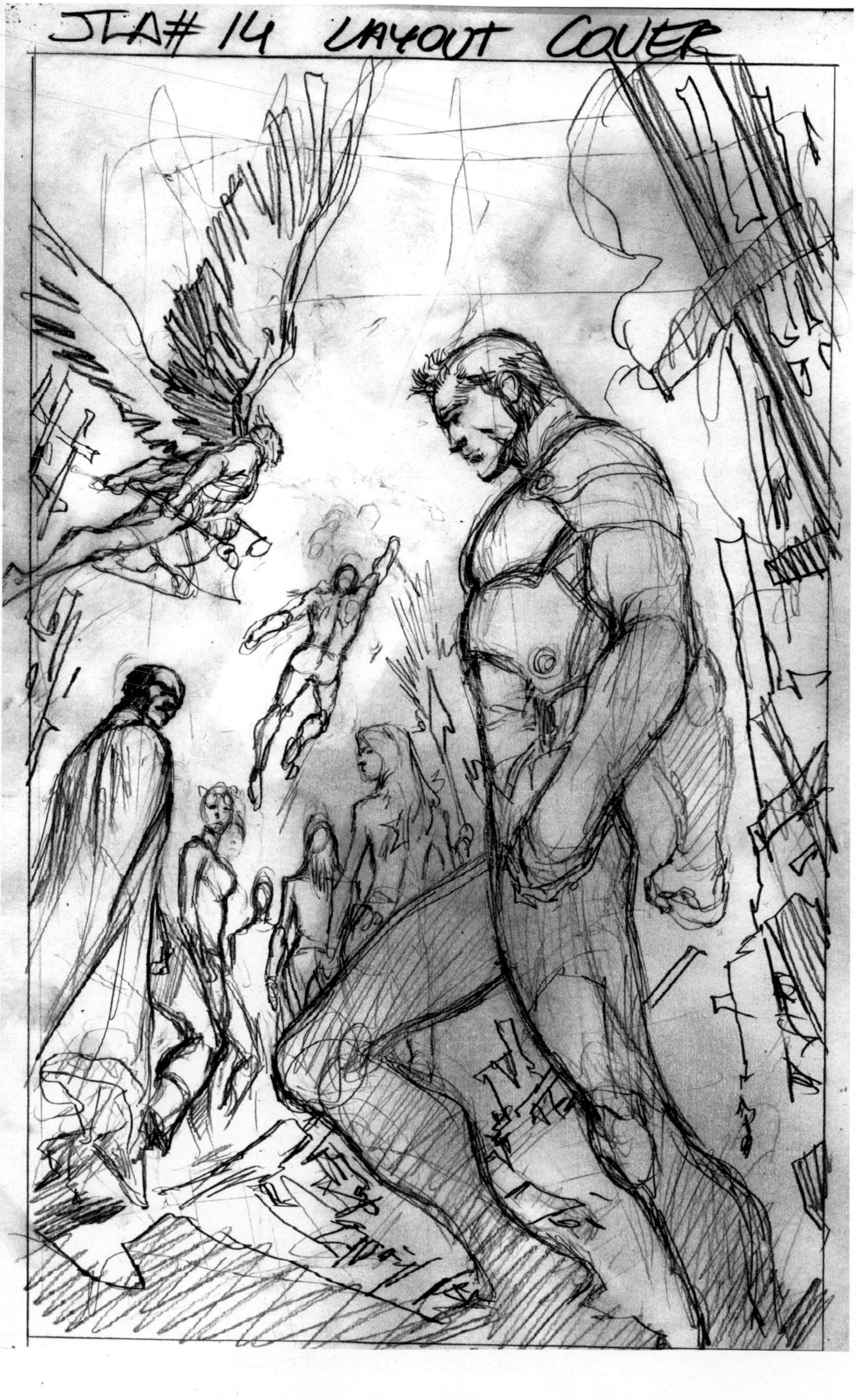
JLA# 14 LAYOUT COVER

**JUSTICE LEAGUE OF AMERICA #8 variant cover layouts
by Guillem March**

**JUSTICE LEAGUE OF AMERICA #10 variant
cover layout and pencils by Dale Eaglesham**

START AT THE BEGINNING!

JUSTICE LEAGUE VOLUME 1: ORIGIN

AQUAMAN VOLUME 1: THE TRENCH

THE SAVAGE HAWKMAN VOLUME 1: DARKNESS RISING

GREEN ARROW VOLUME 1: THE MIDAS TOUCH

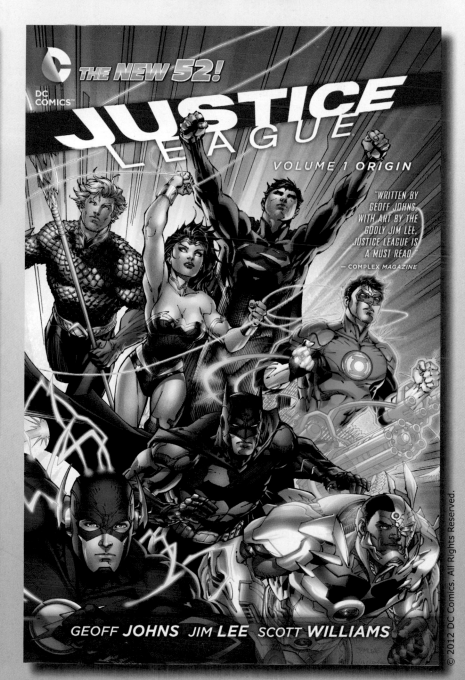

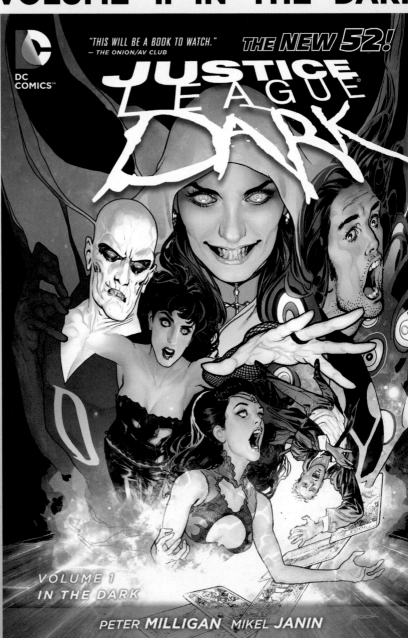

START AT THE BEGINNING

WONDER WOMAN VOLUME 1: BLOOD

WONDER WOMAN
VOL. 2: GUTS

by BRIAN
AZZARELLO and
CLIFF CHIANG

WONDER WOMAN
VOL. 3: IRON

by BRIAN
AZZARELLO and
CLIFF CHIANG

SUPERGIRL VOL. 1:
LAST DAUGHTER OF
KRYPTON

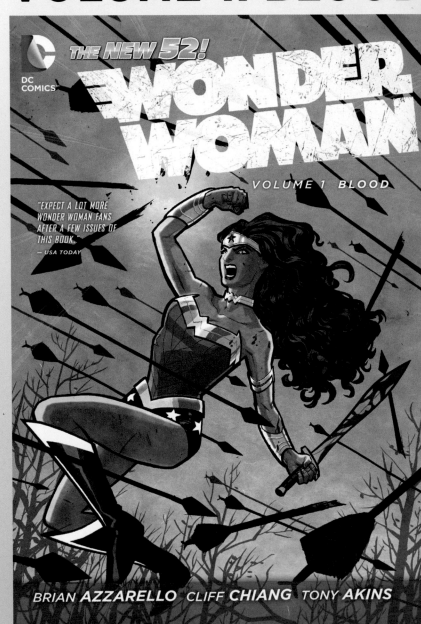